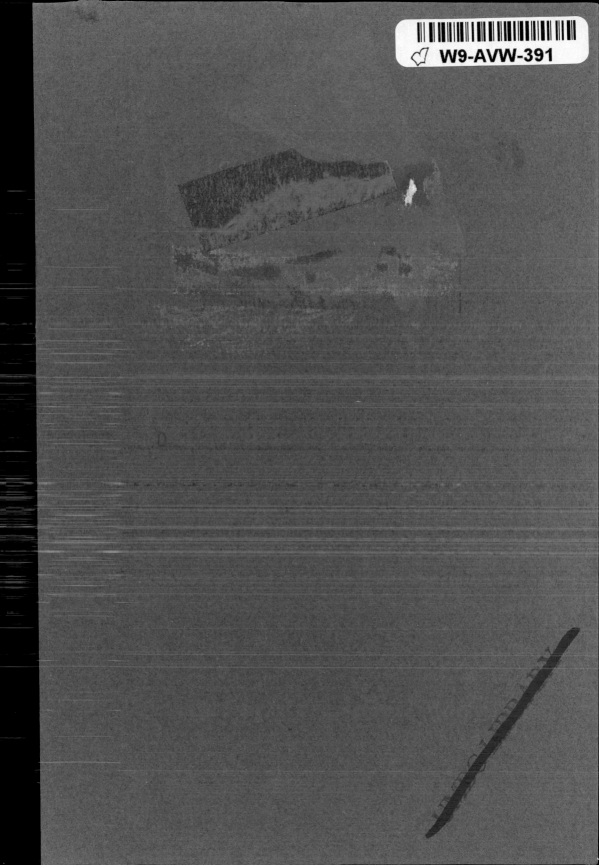

brecht's tradition

brecht's tradition

By Max Spalter

The Johns Hopkins Press,
Baltimore, Maryland

Copyright © 1967
by The Johns Hopkins Press
Baltimore, Maryland 21218

Library of Congress Catalog Card Number 67–12423

Printed in the United States of America

To Dorothy
and to my Father and Mother

table of contents

acknowledgments

I would like to express my gratitude to Professor Eric Bentley for suggesting the basic idea which evolved into the present work, and for extending much valuable advice during the period immediately preceding acceptance of *Brecht's Tradition* for publication.

A debt is owed as well to Professors Ursula Jarvis and Daniel B. Dodson, who read the manuscript carefully in an earlier version and offered cogent critical recommendations. It is relevant to state also that many problems of research and analysis were immeasurably easier to resolve thanks to the training I received in Professor William W. Appletons doctoral seminar on the history of modern European theater.

My one regret is that Professor Walter H. Sokel was unable to advise me on more than the first two chapters. As it is, *Brecht's Tradition* benefited more than I can say from his enlightening comments on the body of drama with which this book is concerned.

introduction

A survey of the accumulating Brecht criticism indicates he was heir to a seemingly infinite variety of traditions. On occasion he has been honored in the same breath with Goethe and Schiller as one of his native land's classic dramatists. His type of epic theater has invited comparison with the Frenchman Claudel's. Brecht's preference for spectators in full command of their critical faculties has called attention to those German romantics who had no qualms about suddenly destroying theatrical illusion in the middle of a performance. If Brecht was not too embarrassed to acknowledge that he, the Communist with a mission to propagate dialectical materialism, was influenced linguistically most by the Bible, he would hardly have minded the observation that, dramaturgically, he was not without debt to medieval religious drama. In a more contemporary context, there is Brecht's relationship to the expressionists, whose stridencies set the tone while he was coming of age. Even naturalism and realism—movements of which Brecht spoke with condescension—very likely affected him more than he realized. The problem of influence becomes more overwhelming when we realize it is restricted neither to Germany nor to Europe: Brecht was greatly impressed with the stylized theater practiced quasi-ritually all through the Orient. One could go on; the point is that there would seem to be scant basis for speaking of any single tradition as Brecht's.

But it has not been sufficiently stressed that from most of the literary streams mentioned as having nourished Brecht's dramatic art, he borrowed formal elements and formal elements only. Comparing his plays with those of writers like Goethe, Schiller, Tieck, Kaiser, and legions of other dramatists to whom Brecht is ostensibly indebted, we are immediately struck by how much Brecht exceeds them in cynicism. Whatever may be said of the others, they are simply not "Brechtian" writers—they do not convey anything like his pitiless debunking attitude, his corrosive antiromanticism, his hardheaded refusal to idealize or glorify, his suspicion of all sentimentalities. No dramatic tradition deserves to be identified with Brecht if it is not composed of writers whose plays refract what one could call a skeptical Brechtian sensibility —which brings us to the reason for this book.

The writers discussed herein—J. M. R. Lenz, C. D. Grabbe, Georg Büchner, Frank Wedekind, and Karl Kraus—share with Brecht not only a variety of common theatrical techniques and a common basic form; they share with him also a common temperament and outlook.

Like Brecht, they demonstrate in vivid episodes that modern society is reducible to patterns of parasitism and victimization; they make us conscious of the degree to which human character implies the stereotyped expression of powerful social, economic, and psychological forces. They suggest at the same time that the world is such a cesspool that it *must* be changed and that the world is such a cesspool that it *cannot* be changed. Like Brecht, they are all incongruous mixtures of moral outrage and cynical perception.

Chroniclers of the drama have not totally ignored this tradition, but too often they damn it with faint praise, content as they are to note merely that Brecht shared with some of the writers in question—particularly Büchner and Wedekind—a proclivity for open drama and episodes of racy realism tinged with poetic feeling. No one has taken the trouble to study closely the various plays of this tradition in order to show in what way they comprise a distinct and well-defined species of theater in which Brecht unmistakably belongs. This work is intended to do just that. If Brecht is the significant dramatist this writer feels him to be, a search for his roots in German drama should yield knowledge relevant not only to Brecht's development as an artist but relevant as well to the broader problem of the evolution of theatrical modernism. This knowledge may yet take on even additional importance; for who knows but that the dramatists under discussion here will in time attract the cultural attention hitherto accorded the dramatic traditions within whose conventions Brecht and his forerunners could not begin to function? Above all, one should never forget that the road to Brecht may be far from ended with Brecht himself. To quote Grabbe in *Napoleon:* "Whenever something ends, you are witnessing a new beginning."

brecht's tradition

j. m. r. lenz

To Gotthold Ephraim Lessing is invariably extended the credit of speaking up for Shakespeare at a critical moment in German literary history, and there is no denying that he championed the English dramatist in an atmosphere of strong neoclassical allegiances. But his quite modern attitude toward drama as an art form free to develop its own internal logic and bound by no a priori body of rules[1] was not so radical as to imply that Aristotle was out of date, or that Shakespeare's episodic development should serve as a dramaturgic alternative to the analytic structure. Lessing viewed Shakespeare as a writer whose plays Aristotle would not have disliked,[2] and this speaks for itself. It meant that the task of discerning what was implied by the differences between Aristotelian and Shakespearian dramaturgy was left to others, a task soon enough undertaken by a number of critics who did not tread with Lessing's caution. Gerstenberg, for example, found the aim of Greek drama to be the excitement of passion, that of Shakespeare the representation of character,[3] while Herder focused awareness on the individualized character of the two types of drama as historical phenomena and maintained that the unique proximity of Shakespeare to nature placed him in an entirely different world from a dramatist like Sophocles.

While it is true that after Lessing the literary apotheosis of Shakespeare became the rule rather than the exception, no German writer seems to have coupled his worship of Shakespeare with as decisive a rejection of neoclassical principles as Jakob Michael Reinhold Lenz.

---

[1] "The only unpardonable fault of a tragic poet is this, that he leaves us cold; if he interests us he may do as he likes with the mechanical rules." Lessing, *Hamburgische Dramaturgie* (1769), trans. E. C. Beasley and Helen Zimmern, *European Theories of the Drama* (New York: Crown Publishers, 1961), p. 259.

[2] "Even to decide the matter by the example of the Ancients, Shakespeare is a much greater tragic author than Corneille; although Corneille knew the Ancients very well, and Shakespeare hardly at all, Corneille comes nearer to them in the externals of technique, and Shakespeare in the essentials." *Literaturbriefe;* quoted in W. H. Bruford's *Theatre, Drama and Audience in Goethe's Germany* (London: Routledge and Paul, 1950), p. 129.

[3] In his emphasis on Shakespeare as a poet of passions, Gerstenberg anticipated Herder. In his emphasis on Shakespeare's characterization, Gerstenberg was himself anticipated by J. E. Schlegel, who as early as 1742 was at pains to distinguish between Aristotelian and Shakespearean dramaturgies. But Schlegel's essay "Vergleichung Shakespears und Andreas Gryphs" seems to have gone unheeded. See Roy Pascal, *Shakespeare in Germany* (Cambridge: The University Press, 1937), pp. 39–47, 55–71.

3

His *Notes to the Theater* (1774) may in some respects be derivative, but it is nonetheless a culturally significant polemic. In the same way that Hugo, Vigny, Hebbel, Zola, and Brecht, among others, were to argue for new aesthetic approaches as concomitants of changed human awareness, so Lenz insisted that his radical concept of episodic theater—influenced powerfully by Shakespeare—was required if drama was to keep pace with thought in general.

Lenz writes as one who is shocked at the quibbling attitudes that prompt some to question Shakespeare's importance. Violation of the three unities poses no problems. In Lenz's view, to postulate three such precepts is as logical as to postulate a hundred. It would still come down to the same thing: "Unity of language, unity of religion, unity of morals. . . . The poet and his public must experience the same unity, but they are under no compulsion to classify it."[4]

As for Aristotle, his rules are dismissed as "poetic horsemanship." His French imitators have shown themselves so eager to follow ancient authority as to make one wonder about their sanity. But it is all in vain. The future belongs not to the play that observes Aristotelian constraints but to the loose episodic play developed by Shakespeare: "Our practice is to have a series of actions which succeed one another like thunderclaps, each scene reinforcing the next and all of them coalescing in the character of the hero."[5]

Lenz's case for Shakespeare and against Aristotle crystallizes in his discussion of the dramatic structures associated with these two figures. For Lenz, a particular dramaturgy is organic to a particular Weltanschauung, and here he anticipates Hegel as well as Hebbel. The Greeks, asserts Lenz, were hardly concerned with man in terms of his concrete experience, his actual aliveness; they were obsessed with his abject dependence on an inscrutable, omnipotent fate. This outlook shows up in plays built around the arbitrary manipulations of a higher force that one is not to question, with the result that the behavior of a Greek tragic hero can never be explained in terms of his intrinsic motives. Such a concept of action Lenz holds to be outmoded; and out of date as well is the hermetic dramatic form that evolved in accommodation of the Greeks' fatalism.

Shakespeare is the quintessential modern because his plays reflect a natural, as distinguished from supernatural, conception of character. His characters are propelled from within; they do not have to be

---

[4] Jakob Michael Reinhold Lenz, "Anmerkungen übers Theater," *Gesammelte Schriften,* ed. Franz Blei (Munich: Georg Mueller Verlag, 1909), I, 238.
[5] *Ibid.*

shifted about by forces from above. Calling Shakespeare's plays *Charakterstücke,* Lenz remarks that in the case of the English dramatist " . . . the hero alone is the key to his fate."[6] In Greek drama, on the other hand, the key is action. In view of this distinction, Lenz finds it quite natural that Shakespeare felt free to employ a sequence of actions, for his principle of unity resides in the very life of his protagonists, not in the tight schemas of artificial plots.

It is this principle of unity that Lenz is determined to establish as the cornerstone of a new drama. In the course of doing so, he collides again and again with his major target, Aristotle. Among other things, he challenges Aristotle's differentiation of the epic and dramatic, and here his reasoning has proved too advanced even for a critic of this century. Thus, one of his biographers asserts that Lenz was unable to distinguish between the epic and dramatic; otherwise, why would he seek to strengthen his case for episodic drama by mentioning the achievements of Dante and Klopstock? The truth of the matter is that Lenz anticipates the modern critic who emphasizes the *dramatic* elements of the *Inferno* as well as he anticipates what the Germans will later call the *Episierung* of modern drama.*

There are other cogent points in Lenz's essay, such as his view that genius penetrates instantaneously to the very essence of reality; that the artist should above all strive to divorce his own personality from the subjectivity of his creations; that the characteristic is preferable to the beautiful; that comedy is distinguished from tragedy by virtue of the fact that comedy is built around happenings, tragedy around individuals; and that French comedy deserves every bit as much contempt as French tragedy. There is also a comparison between Shakespeare's and Voltaire's handling of the Caesar story which confirms by example everything Lenz has been saying.

For our purposes the importance of Lenz's essay lies in his refusal to consider the Aristotelian structure expansive enough to encompass the psychological complexities of human nature and his conviction that Shakespeare's structure shows the way. Like Goethe, who admitted that from the moment he laid eyes on Shakespeare he was hypnotized, Lenz cannot quite take seriously any of the formal rules Shakespeare is supposed to have violated so egregiously. And like Goethe, he goes on to write drama in which Aristotelian prescriptions are thrown to the winds.

But Lenz attempted nothing comparable to *Götz von Berlichingen.*

---

[6] *Ibid.,* p. 254.
* The tendency of modern drama to take on epic elements.

Goethe's contact with Shakespeare had encouraged him to write a German "history." Whatever its merits, the play manifests excesses which make us loath to call it Shakespearian. For here Shakespeare's art is reduced to those of its formal characteristics which the writers of the *Sturm und Drang* took to be its essence—multiplicity of plot and episode, sacrifice of plot to character, vividness of situation, and a general lack of aesthetic inhibition which suited the temperaments of young men up in arms against rationalistic doctrine. For Goethe, Shakespeare may well have been a salutary influence, for soon enough, with the help of Herder, he saw the limitations of the drama of tumult. The damage was done, however; the *Ritter and Räuber* dramas which proliferated upon the burgeoning German stage derived largely from Goethe's *Götz*. And in the case of these dramas, the power which makes even Goethe's sprawling history worth reading was all too often absent. The passage of time has done little to change the view that in theater, as well as in almost every other area of their activity, the writers of the *Sturm und Drang* were sorely lacking in self-discipline.

Lenz, who is appreciated more and more as a dramatist of genius far in advance of his time, can be held up also as an example of what was wrong with the *Sturm und Drang;* this admirer of Shakespeare wrote plays and parts of plays about which it is best to say little. At times he was unabashedly sentimental (*Die beiden Alten*); at times he manipulated his plots wantonly (*Die Freunde machen den Philosophen*); at times he is hardly distinguishable from the many worshipers of countrified simplicity who took their cue from Rousseau (*Die Kleinen*); at times the dramatist who has something to say seems able to do so only by means of the most factitious devices (*The New Menoza*); and at times the dramatist simply disappears and we are left with evidences of frightful pathology.

This is inescapably the feeling conveyed by *The Englishman,* a play in which a young man's obsessive love leads him to cut his throat. The young man is a variant of a type Lenz used often, the individual who is wholly incapable of coping with reality. But there the similarity with works like *The Tutor* and *The Soldiers* ends. For in *The Englishman* the social picture is all but blocked out as Lenz proceeds to invest his protagonist with highly abnormal emotions. Symptomatic of diseased psychology, artlessly pointing to what is plainly an incurable obsession, *The Englishman* is transparently a page from Lenz's unhappy life. It does not surprise us to learn that within two years of finishing it Lenz attempted suicide.

Of German origin, Lenz's family lived in Livonia, in the Baltic provinces, where Lenz was born in 1751. His father's severe religious orientation seems to have been the first strong determinant of Lenz's brooding nature. Goethe and other writers recognized his artistic potential but found him emotionally unstable. Lenz seems to have carried his neuroses into every sphere of social intercourse, harping as he did on his hopes of surpassing Goethe's literary achievements, and becoming a minor scandal thanks to his incurable habit of falling in love with Goethe's women. Much later Goethe would point to Lenz as a writer whose great talent was nullified by flaws of personality, but long before that the sage of Weimar had been alienated by Lenz's explicit treatment of sex in his second major work, *The Soldiers*. In all fairness to Lenz, it must be mentioned that he sometimes forgot he was in competition with Goethe and admitted outright that the latter dominated by sheer genius an age of literary pygmies.

Oddly enough *The Tutor* was attributed for a while to the young Goethe, but only for a while, as Goethe went on to outgrow most of what the *Sturm und Drang* stood for. Lenz, however, moved downhill fast, becoming for his contemporaries less palatable than ever. For the modern reader, his creative life after 1776 is uninteresting. In 1777 his friendship with Goethe was severed for good, his economic situation desperate, and his mind obviously diseased. The rest of his life was a hopeless struggle which ended when he died suddenly on a Moscow street at the age of forty-one.

The two plays which make Lenz more than another eccentric figure of German literary history are *The Tutor* (1774) and *The Soldiers* (1776); by virtue of these works he becomes one of the first German dramatists to succeed in doing something original and influential with the episodic structure of Shakespearian drama. Influenced strongly by the views of Diderot[7] and Mercier,[8] both of whom advocated a theater of social involvement, Lenz sets out to show just those conditions

[7] Denis Diderot (1713–84) is perhaps the man most responsible for the atmosphere which produced a dramatist like Lenz. Diderot advocated a realistic drama of great emotional intensity; the use of gestures and pantomime to communicate stage action; accuracy of psychological delineation; precise representation of milieu; and the replacement of scenic climaxes by a series of visually striking tableaux. These and other elements were to make of the new *drame bourgeois* the modern play, par excellence.
[8] Sebastian Mercier (1740–1814) wrote plays which were bluntly aimed at validating the importance of the middle class. He was just as blunt in his contempt for neoclassical drama. Like Diderot, he argued for emotional realism, and for vivid characterization. Beyond Diderot, he believed comedy and tragedy could be fused. His *Du Théâtre, ou nouvel essai sur l'art dramatique* (1773), in which he argued for an enlargement of art so as to bring it

in his society which deserve exposure. By the time he gets through he has created a new kind of play, one which would later prove to be the beginning of a new tradition stretching from this hapless eighteenth-century figure to Bertolt Brecht.

The Tutor or Advantages of a Private Education reveals by its title that Lenz went along with Diderot, who urged dramatists to stress at every opportunity what their characters did for a living. But there is irony here of the kind Diderot never hinted at in his prescriptions for sentimental drama. Lenz's title is a joke, for not a single advantage of private education is brought out in the play itself. Such irony will prove to be symptomatic; Lenz was always torn between the resigned detachment of the cynic who sees through everything and the social passion of the reformer who must convince himself that the evil around him is correctible; he was never so fervent a special pleader that he could not discern the comic overtones of any human situation.

The organization of *The Tutor* bears out Lenz's conviction that dramatists can work as freely as composers of epics. The play has close to three dozen scenes, as well as three separable plots, and it is sometimes quite unclear how all the actions in progress interrelate, so arbitrarily does Lenz seem to shift around. The first six scenes, however, raise no special problems. We meet in the opening scene a jobless intellectual named Läuffer, and in succeeding scenes we meet the family into which he is taken as private tutor. This family consists of a Major, his wife and two children—a boy whom Läuffer finds it difficult to teach anything at all, and a young woman named Gustchen whose delicate nature the tutor is specifically ordered to take into consideration. Beyond such unpromising working conditions, it soon becomes clear that the simplest social exchange between the tutor and his employers partakes of unpleasantness. The Major and his wife blandly expect Läuffer to work for next to nothing, and they exploit every opportunity to cut his wage. To add insult to injury, they impress upon the tutor that no amount of learning can make up for his tainted class origin. Here, as elsewhere, Lenz underscores the extent to which personal relationships are social relationships and the degree to which social relationships rest on naked power.

An exhibitionist at heart, Läuffer cannot resist dramatizing his state

---

close to everyday life, was translated into German by Heinrich Leopold Wagner (1776) and became a favorite of Lenz as well as of other *Stürmer und Dränger.*

of mind to the one person who does not armor herself with class consciousness. Gustchen may be too naïve to fathom why the tutor claims so stridently the world is against him, but she does what she can to be friendly. When her boy friend Fritz goes off to the university, the relationship intensifies. Its subsequent course deals a shocking blow to the Major, who had noticed for some time that his daughter was not well, but who had never imagined she would disgrace the family by taking as her lover a low born type like Läuffer:

MAJOR'S WIFE: Help, somebody! It's all over! The family! The family!

PRIVY COUNCILOR: God forbid, sister! What are you up to? You'll put your husband into a fit!

MAJOR'S WIFE: Let him go into a fit—the family—infamous—oh, I can't go on. (*She falls on a chair.*)[9]

The infamy which the Major's Wife cannot bring herself to mention sends both Läuffer and Gustchen out of the house before the Major can get to them. It leads to all sorts of complications which Lenz resolves by having Gustchen return to the fold after a year of fugitive misery, and by having the tutor reach the bizarre conclusion that he lives in a world where unfortunates like him are better off castrated. For the decision to emasculate himself, he is eulogized by an eccentric schoolmaster named Wenzeslaus at whose place Läuffer obtained refuge during his flight from the Major's homicidal wrath. But Wenzeslaus soon realizes how foolish he had been to commend Läuffer upon his grand "spiritual" gesture, for the latter turns right around and marries a country girl who is quite aware of his condition. It does not stop her in the least; in fact, she views a sterile husband as a distinct blessing—how better to insure that there will be no additional mouths to feed.

Lenz presents all of this, plus much more,[10] in five acts composed

[9] Lenz, *Gesammelte Schriften,* I, 368.

[10] Specifically, two subplots which succeed only in distracting the reader. One deals with Fritz's university life and makes much of a student named Pätus, whose economic problems and social immaturities may well remind some of Lenz's own difficulties. Pätus is presented to us in a boarding house setting which allows Lenz to exhibit realities of German society not on display in an aristocratic home. Another subplot deals with the attempt at seduction of a musician's daughter by an amoral aristocrat named Vos Seiffenblase (sic), an attempt foiled by Fritz's father, the Councilor.

of thirty-five scenes of varying length. His treatment of these scenes makes them appear least of all as links in a chain of complications, so consistently does he subordinate action to character exposure. To this extent, at least, he lives up to what he said about the importance of character in his *Notes to the Theater*. His concern with motivation is discernible from the synopses of typical scenes: thus, one episode is nothing more than a bringing to light of Läuffer's pathological sensitivity; another is essentially an exposure of the Major's irascibility and greed; and still another informs us that even the callous Major has his sentimentalities. In most of his scenes Lenz puts his characters into normal enough situations and then has them act and speak in such a way as to reveal the confluence of social and psychic forces which drives them on. Never are we unaware of a character's social status, and never are we permitted to forget for more than a moment that a character has something typical about him that is bound to come out no matter what the circumstances. Another way of putting this is to say that Lenz exhibits his characters with a view to demonstrating those traits which are most characteristic of their behavior as human beings suffering the stresses of a highly class-structured society.

As much as Lenz subordinates action to character, none of his characters ever gets close enough to us to elicit our identification. One reason for this distance is no doubt Lenz's tendency to drop one thread of action as casually as he picks up another. Another is that he goes out of his way to delineate character in such a way as to stress what is laughable about it. A conspicuous example of this is the play's most preposterous scene, in which Läuffer realizes that his self-multilation has by no means ended his chances with the opposite sex:

LISE: Why impossible, Sir? How impossible if I want to and he wants to, and my father wants it too? You see, my father always said to me, that if I was to marry an intellectual—

WENZESLAUS: But—can't you get it through your thick skull— he can't do anything! God forgive me, but you must listen!

LÄUFFER: Maybe the young lady has no such expectations. Lise, I'll never be able to sleep with you.

LISE: Well, at least he can stay up with me, even if we only spend the day together, laugh together, and kiss hands once in a while—For by God! I like this man! God knows, I do like him!

LÄUFFER: You see, Mr. Wenzeslaus! It is only love she's after. Must a happy marriage cater to animal lust?

WENZESLAUS: Oh, come now—Connubium sine prole est quasi dies sine sole. . . . Be ye fruitful and multiply, that's God's word. Where there is marriage, there must children be too.

LISE: No, Mr. Schoolmaster, I swear to you, in my life I can do without children. Children, no less! As if I needed them. My father has ducks and chickens, and that's enough to feed day after day; to add children. . . .

LÄUFFER: (*kissing her*): Lise, you are a goddess![11]

Neither Lise nor Läuffer nor Wenzeslaus can escape our laughter here. Lise actually believes that a eunuch must be a spiritual man, and in her eyes the perfect marriage is the sexless marriage. Läuffer underrates Lise's sexuality to the point of believing she will never make any biological demands on him which he cannot satisfy. And Wenzeslaus adds to the comedy by trying to cover up his natural masculine outrage at what is going on in religious phraseology. When we recall that the *Stürmer und Dränger* believed above all in vital living, we can gauge the ironies at which Lenz was aiming.

Lenz, says Gundolf, was possessed of "monomanic clarity."[12] The phrase certainly applies to his treatment of character. He is forever making clear that a few basic forces determine all behavior. These forces are made evident by the content of a highly explicit type of dialogue as well as by the manner in which content is set off by linguistic and gestural style. Characters literally betray themselves with almost every word they utter, every motion they make or are compelled to make; and it is not long before we identify with them stereotyped reaction patterns of a kind which Brecht was later to associate with his characters. The very first monologue of the play, by the tutor Läuffer, will bear this out:

LÄUFFER: My father says: I am not suited to be his assistant. In my opinion, the fault lies in his purse; he's not willing to pay anything. I am supposed to be too young for the priesthood, also too well built, too much the world traveler, and, of course, the Privy Councilor has

[11] Lenz, *Gesammelte Schriften,* I, 414.
[12] Friedrich Gundolf, *Shakespeare und der deutsche Geist* (Berlin: Georg Müller Verlag, 1920), pp. 254–55.

no room for me in the state school. So be it! For pedants of his type
the devil himself would not be learned enough. Just six months would
have sufficed for me to catch up on what I knew when I got out of
school, but then, of course, I would possess too much education for
a preceptor—but who am I to question the wise Privy Councilor? He's
always calling me Monsieur Läuffer, and when we talk about Leipzig,
he asks about Händel's pastry garden or Richter's coffee house—I
really don't know, is he trying to be comic—he can be serious enough
when he converses with the assistant headmaster. I guess in his eyes
I lack maturity—even now he approaches with the Major; I dread him
worse than the devil. Something in the man's face I find wholly unbear-
able. (*He passes the* PRIVY COUNCILOR *and the* MAJOR *with obsequious
bows.*)[13]

Läuffer's grievance is that society has no place for him and excludes
him unjustly from positions he is qualified to fill. Even his own father
is in on the conspiracy to keep him down. Along comes a man, the
Councilor, and he too is in on the plot. It is easy enough to see
what Lenz is getting at here—the portrayal of a character who is
as passive as he is hostile and suspicious, who, to salve his frustrated
ego, has no qualms about attributing all his ills to a relentlessly hostile
world. This is conveyed as much by what Läuffer says as by how
he says it. The measured tones in which he enumerates his enemies,
the compulsive way in which he catalogs the insensitivities of others
to his quality, the almost dispassionate mechanical manner in which
he simply goes on and on—such stylistic features serve merely to
extinguish the very case he is at pains to make. The over-all impression
is of a man who does not mind vegetating as long as he can convince
himself it is all someone else's fault. Those who cannot see through
Läuffer's words will surely be enlightened by the gestures with which
he departs the scene. He bows and scrapes to the very people who
play villain in his private fantasy.

Läuffer invites contempt mixed with pity for his weaknesses. His
employers, for their part, invite simple contempt. The Major's Wife
exposes her character from the moment we meet her in the process
of hiring Läuffer as the family tutor. She wants his services as cheaply
as possible: his scholastic attainments excite no interest. Important
is his ability to dress well and strike acceptable social attitudes. A
measure of the Major's Wife's snobbbishness is that she asks for
Läuffer's name only as an afterthought. Her moment of glory finally

[13] Lenz, *Gesammelte Schriften*, I, 330.

comes when she discovers the new tutor speaks French, confident as she is that with a few Gallic locutions she proves herself a woman of the world. But all masks slip off a few moments later when she sends Läuffer out of the room for daring to speak freely in the company of his social superiors; and as he leaves she bemoans not having gotten something better for her money.

It takes even less to inflame the Major. Läuffer soon finds out that not only must he be careful not to give offense by how he speaks but he must also be most careful about how he sits on a chair:

Stay put, Mr. Läuffer, stay put. Just a few words with you, that's why I kicked out the young gentleman. Look, it's all right for you to remain seated, perfectly all right; but sit fully *fully!* For Christ's sake, you'll break the chair in two sitting on the edge. . . . What's the chair for anyway? To sit on! With all your traveling you don't know even that? Now just listen to me: I look upon you as a nice polite fellow, a God-fearing man quite willing to follow orders; otherwise, I never would do what I am doing for you. I promised you one hundred and forty ducats annually: which makes three—wait—three times one forty; how much does that make?[14]

For the most trivial of reasons the Major drops his civilized pose and lets Läuffer have it. He will explode in this fashion all through the play. Though it is small consolation to Läuffer, the Major can be just as unpleasant with members of his own class; in fact, he goes so far as to threaten his own wife and son with violence. If his wife strikes us as a puppet tied to the string of social convention, the Major appears the puppet of something far deeper: he is one of those types who, unable to cope with their aggressions, disperse them upon the nearest human target. For that matter, all of Lenz's characters are either social or instinctual marionettes. Läuffer, for example, exudes social servility while seething with hostility and sexual conflict. Gustchen is almost ruined by her sex drive which sends her into Läuffer's arms. The Major, as we have observed, maintains his social pose at best tenuously, and his wife is a *poseuse* of the first order. Away from this aristocratic milieu, the picture is no brighter. The schoolmaster Wenzeslaus, for example, is only too plainly a mental case, so much is he driven by inner forces that come out in his speech.

Wenzeslaus may be a minor character, but the method employed

[14] *Ibid.*, p. 336.

to make us aware of his disturbed mentality (so that he strikes us
as being every bit as comic as he is mixed up) is highly pertinent
to Lenz's portraiture in general. Lenz makes no attempt to tone down
those caricatural elements which stimulate laughter; at the same time
he manages to catch what is quite unamusing about the very thing
he is caricaturing. Thus we laugh at the predictability of Wenzeslaus'
eccentric mental processes, but we realize simultaneously there is nothing funny about a mentality so diseased:

But . . . but . . . but . . . (*tears the toothpick out of his mouth*) just
what is it we have here? Is it possible? A man of your stature should
be so little concerned with what is good and bad for his body? Toothpicks
are dangerous; as a matter of fact, it is sheer suicide playing with
a toothpick, sheer suicide, the very destruction of Jerusalem, that's what
toothpicking does to your teeth. All right, it happens, something happens
to get stuck in your teeth (*takes water and rinses his mouth out*):
that's the way to go about it, that's exactly the way to go about it;
why, it does honor to God and neighbor to do it that way. Lose your
teeth, and you wind up an old leash dog who can't keep his jaws straight;
lose your teeth and your toothless mouth will fail to give birth to words:
you'll have just your mouth and nose to rattle with. The conclusion
follows: neither beast nor man will have the power to make you out.

It is odd that so many critics tracing influences on Büchner's vivid
dialogue will mention Shakespeare and Goethe but not Lenz. Even
this small excerpt should indicate how guilty they have been of the
sin of omission. Wenzeslaus, like the hapless Woyzeck, communicates
his mental state by the very rhythms of his speech and by linguistic
idiosyncrasies. Wenzeslaus, like Woyzeck, has a need to repeat himself;
like Woyzeck, he has so much to say at times that he falters over a
single word; and though he is hardly as incoherent as Woyzeck, he
too can discern in some innocent object a world of threats and anxieties. One may note here that neither Lenz nor Büchner availed
himself of the rhetorical approach basic to classical drama. Both
rejected symmetrical verse and cadenced utterance for the dissonances
which characterize everyday speech, and to this end their diction excludes little on the grounds of decorum. Inasmuch as Lenz's dialogue
is bound to be grotesque when the mental forces shaping speech act
erratically, his eccentric characters make the most vivid impression.
This is something which at least one critic finds aesthetically de-

plorable without realizing it follows quite logically from Lenz's basic approach.

As far back as Hebbel, a conflict between psychology and sociology in *The Tutor* attracted attention. Quite simply, what bothers critics is that Lenz is obviously writing a play in which his characters stand for certain values; at the same time he negates social allegory by virtue of his characters' peculiar motivations. A good example of this is Wenzeslaus. It has been pointed out that much of the philosophy of the *Sturm und Drang* comes out in his speeches; those in search of a character in *The Tutor* who stands for the Rousseauistic integrity Lenz and his contemporaries admired have not been averse to pointing in his direction. But it is surely strange that Lenz should have chosen a character as eccentric as Wenzeslaus to act as spokesman. By and large, Wenzeslaus seems suspect as the representative of anything but his own peculiar mentality, and if Lenz intended differently, something must have gone wrong.

The same difficulty seems to apply to Läuffer. Unquestionably his circumstances are bound up with what was generally wrong with the social structure of his day. But when all is said and done, Läuffer's fate is of little relevance to the tendentious play Lenz may have had in mind. Läuffer is not so much a social victim as a victim of himself: no change in external conditions would have much effect on the life style of such a man. The view that he embodies genuine human value smothered by social injustice is borne out neither by his opening speech, with its paranoiac overtones, nor by any subsequent action up to his emasculation and marriage. He never manifests any qualities to soften the portrait of a repellent weakling, anxious as he is to twist himself into the most reassuring servile postures for those who treat him like dirt. When he expatiates on the number of dancing teachers in his past and announces with pride that in Leipzig he took in every ball, he comes through as a sad parody of his aristocratic masters. Either he glows with happiness at some morsel thrown his way by the upper class, or he bristles with discontent at their undisguised negations of his importance. That he should allow himself to become involved in an affair with the daughter of the very people at whose every word he jumps only confirms one's impression of a spineless rationalizer shuttling between self-destructive impulses.

His castration comes as a distinct shock and may appear highly out of character to those who feel Lenz has given us throughout the play a tutor who can react in no such decisive fashion. Does not self-mutilation presuppose a certain unsqueamish boldness which one would hardly imagine within Läuffer's capabilities? Actually, there is nothing odd or illogical here in terms of the psychopathology of character Lenz has been indicating all along. By castrating himself, an individual torn by deep conflict is trying to make sure that he will never again be at the mercy of what he cannot consciously control. Läuffer confirms the psychological mechanism by which he has always lived, directing against himself fierce aggressions which he dare not express to his tormentors. His action is quintessentially passive: it is designed not only to avert any clash with forces in the real world of social power, but it ensures quiescence in the one area where even the most innocuous man may act in spite of himself. The power Lenz imputes here to instinct is very much in line with modern attitudes. Lenz conceived of instinct as an explosive force posing a constant threat not only to personal sanity but to the very structure of society. In one of his less important plays, *The New Menoza,* he has a character argue for brothels on the grounds that sexual love is "fire." The image is apt, for Lenz demonstrates in both of his major plays that human sexuality is dangerous to ignite and impossible to control once started.

Only when we recognize the bedrock of pessimistic psychology beneath the social texture of Lenz's best plays do we appreciate his modernism. Aware as he is of the demonic springs of human behavior, he avoids the falsified psychologies which date so many eighteenth-century plays. In Lenz's important plays, characters do not come to a sudden awareness of untapped spiritual resources, are not momentously transformed into greater souls, and do not eventually glimpse the light that ennobles. Nor are characters in these plays prone to generalize on their circumstances in sentimental outbursts which today strike us as absurdly unreal. In Lenz's major plays, characters who are mixed up to start with remain so until they wind up quite ingloriously. Nothing in the *action* of these plays suggests the meliorist psychology so rampant at the time. As a matter of fact, Lenz is at the opposite pole, suggesting by his presentation of character that he is skeptical of man's ability to learn from experience.

This aspect of Lenz's plays has been overlooked by those intent upon stressing his place in the vanguard of class-conscious writers. Critics emphasize Lenz's importance as a social critic and note that whenever the German theater became an instrument of social criticism, Lenz proved a good model. Cases in point are the Büchner of *Woyzeck* as well as the naturalists and Bertolt Brecht. But it is a simplification to view Lenz primarily as a class-conscious opponent of the aristocracy. Even to the extent that he does work social criticism into his plays, it is by no means partisan. His target is not merely the aristocracy, much as he realized that class was frustrating those social groups which had their hopes raised most by the diffusion of rationalism. Lenz was quite aware that in a world of constant interaction the nature of the victimizer is only half the story; and his realization that the aristocracy was callous and stupid is matched by his realization that the middle class was passive and cowardly.

In *The Tutor* Läuffer typifies this class most vividly. Enough has been said about him to indicate that in his portrayal Lenz intended nothing complimentary. One may just add that in the course of being introduced to the Major's Wife he cannot restrain an impulse to fawningly kiss this superficial woman's hand, transfixing in an almost obscene image of action everything about him and his class that is repellent. Lenz has frequent recourse to such effective visual summaries.

However, the scene in which Lenz goes into most detail on his feelings about the middle class presents a discussion between Läuffer's father, who is a pastor, and the Councilor. Though the apparent dramatic motivation here is Pastor Läuffer's desire to arouse the Councilor over the shabby treatment his son is receiving from his aristocratic employers, the scene is actually pure commentary and anticipates the programmatic conclusion of *The Soldiers*. For a while Lenz forces the action into the background and shifts our attention to the larger significances of what is going on.

The Councilor is not moved in the least by the revelation that Läuffer's salary is a mere fraction of what he had originally been promised. His view is that any man so lacking in backbone as to work at tutoring for the aristocracy deserves no better. Pastor Läuffer's argument that "one must live" falls on deaf ears, while the Councilor argues forcefully that nothing compensates for the surrender of basic human rights. And tutors of the aristocracy surrender just those rights; they are not even free to perform their bodily functions naturally but must always strike artificial poses pleasing to their exploiters. The Councilor deplores the fact that young men with the capacity to make meaningful contributions to their society are content to serve as pets for the aristocracy.

Pastor Läuffer finds this unconvincing. He is concerned with the hard facts of a society in which one has no choice but to get along.

He points out that nothing in that society is untainted, and even public education, which the Councilor champions, is notably deficient in quality. But the Councilor will not be put off. He insists that if things are not the way they should be, it is the fault of those who are not dynamic enough to change them. Only when the middle class makes the aristocracy realize that it *must* change, only then will German society cease to stagnate.

The texture of German society simply reflects bourgeois tolerance of the status quo. But Lenz hardly spares the aristocracy by pointing a finger at the class it suppresses. It is precisely because the aristocracy is such a horror that the middle class must not be what it is. The frightening character of the aristocracy comes out in the caricatured representatives of that class which Lenz gives us. It comes out as well in a crisp exchange of dialogue between the Major and his brother, the Councilor, quite early in the play. Here we are informed in no uncertain terms that the German aristocracy of the time was determined to employ the intelligentsia on its own terms only. The Councilor asks his brother a legitimate enough question: What is the new tutor supposed to teach? The Major's reply speaks for itself:

Well, he should—whatever I— well, his job is to provide my son with intellectual and social—say, what are you after anyway with your questions? I'll make up my mind in due time, and the tutor will know just what I want.[15]

In succeeding scenes the Major and his wife reveal only too clearly what constitutes in their eyes the purpose of private education. But even at this point the indictment is quite explicit: "You wish, in other words, to be the tutor of your tutor. . . ."[16]

Walter Höllerer has remarked that in *The Soldiers* Lenz opened the way for a new relationship between dramatist and audience by combining elements of programmatic commentary with the loose structure of the open play.[17] Actually, Lenz starts doing this in *The Tutor*, chiefly by way of the Councilor, who, in spite of some participation

<hr />

[15] *Ibid.*, p. 331.
[16] *Ibid.*
[17] Walter Höllerer, "Die Soldaten," *Das deutsche Drama vom Barock bis zur Gegenwart*, ed. Benno von Wiese, I (2nd ed.; Düsseldorf: A. Bagel Verlag, 1958), 144–45.

in the action, is actually the unimplicated bystander—perceptive enough to see what is going on and free enough to express himself. That Lenz should work this way is hardly surprising when we realize he is trying above all to communicate to his audience an awareness of the social forces behind the action depicted. It is for this reason, after all, that he gives us distortions and exaggerations of character as well as vivid dialogue rich with suggestions of gesture. The explicit formulations of the Councilor merely take Lenz's art one step further on the road to maximal clarity. He does not believe for a moment that a dramatist is bound by inhibitory Aristotelian conventions. He rejects neoclassic formalism if only on the ground of its placing form ahead of the substance of what a dramatist wishes to say.

Nowhere is Lenz quite so unpredictable as at the close of his major plays. At first glance his endings seem made to order for those who would like to dismiss him as either too disturbed to know what he is doing or sorely lacking in a sense of proportion. But the castration of Läuffer, which Brecht was later to find quite symbolic, may, like the anticonventional ending of *The Soldiers,* stem from an attitude which we shall later find at work in the drama of those who followed up Lenz's innovations, namely, a contempt for middle-class psychology so powerful that it must be discharged in images of shock value. Lenz's ending of *The Tutor* could hardly be more blatantly designed to assault bourgeois sensibilities, for he makes castration the prelude to a marriage and illegitimacy the product of easily forgivable human weakness. One can well see Lenz initiating a tradition in which one purposely departs from standards of conventional taste in order to manifest derision of the Philistine mentality.

This aggressive rejection of conventionality in life is paralleled by Lenz's rejection of conventionality in the theater. He rejects not only the more traditional concepts of tragedy and comedy, based on their mutual exclusiveness, but he rejects as well the homage to tradition implied by Diderot's conceptions of intermediate dramatic forms. Diderot had never presumed it possible to unify the intensities of tragedy and comedy per se but had favored attenuated blendings of a new type. Lenz, however, felt that tragedy and comedy could coexist within the same play.

Whether Lenz achieved what one may call tragicomic integration is a subject in and of itself. One might say Läuffer is tragic because his blighting environment destroys whatever is intrinsically of value in his personality; he is comic as well because of his total ineffectuality.

But beyond this issue it is important to recognize that in Lenz we can discern already that peculiar awareness of life which hovers uneasily between uproarious derision and existential anguish, an awareness of life as at best a very bad joke at man's expense. Such tragicomic perception underlies Lenz's thinking on the mess German society became thanks to aristocratic parasitism and middle-class venality. Like Büchner, he seems to realize that at bottom life is by its very nature grotesque.

It has been said that by violating the Aristotelian unities Lenz was able to work into *The Tutor* aspects of milieu which only an open structure can accommodate. While true, this is hardly the key to what is original about Lenz's dramaturgy. In fact, Lenz violated the Aristotelian unities with an abandon which is scarcely commendable. His abrupt transitions from the aristocratic environment of the Major's home to shabby environments of student life are highly distracting, and Lenz is definitely open to the criticism that he did not yet know how to keep an episodic play from becoming chaotic.

Lenz's originality lies, rather, in his use of the episodic structure as a vehicle for a set of specific attitudes, which he conveys not merely by what he puts into his scenes but by the order in which he arranges those scenes. Content and form interact to make a compelling indictment: episode after episode repeats essentially the same basic picture of a society which is economically and socially unviable, whose members are either strong and sadistic or weak and masochistic, and whose classes cannot begin to relate to one another humanely. Very much like Brecht, Lenz practices what may well be called *episodic reinforcement*. Whatever action fleshes out a scene, it will manifest either subtly or explicitly the operation of certain constants, especially the hunger of have-nots for what life has so far denied them. Lenz's plays are constructed of episodes designed to get across the truth that concrete human need can be evaded but never transcended. No conception of *idealistic* freedom is seen to have any relevance to the way things really are. For Lenz, as for Brecht, the *real* world is the world where one struggles for what one usually does not get because those who have it struggle just as hard to keep others down.

Lenz and Brecht share not only common attitudes toward social forces; they share as well an ambivalence that will be seen to run through the entire Lenz-Brecht tradition, in one form or another. Both manifest a cynicism which would seem to preclude the social passion which undeniably motivated their writing. In essence, they strike us as too resigned to believe anything could be done about the hopeless amoral swamps they depict and, conversely, as men of too much social conscience to be all that cynical. Their plays take on a disturbing quality, hard to pin down, for they seem to have been written, weirdly enough, by idealistic cynics. Brustein said of Brecht that "he seems constitutionally incapable of creating a positive idea without somehow undermining it." One could say the same about Lenz. For in *The Tutor* he demonstrates a world that is simply beyond help, even if on the last page he still attempts to prove that his main worry has been the dangers of private education. The reformer in Lenz may want to convince himself that the tragedy of Läuffer and others like him is avoidable: the cynical realist knows better.

A similar dissociation is at work in *The Soldiers* (1776). Once again Lenz is ostensibly writing as social reformer, and once again the social cure he puts forth seems hardly adequate for the disease. The cure is simply to train a corps of sexually compliant women who will accompany that male army which every state needs for its security, and by satisfying the erotic needs of the military, keep soldiers from preying sexually on the civilian populations with which they are thrown in contact. Those who find Lenz somewhat disturbed to start with have held up *The Soldiers* as a case in point. But in an age of sexual radicalism which pretends not to be shockable on such matters, the critical question in regard to Lenz's proposal is merely whether or not it is worked persuasively into his play. Far too many prudish commentators have used *The Soldiers* to ventilate their own prejudices on a touchy subject.

In this play the main character is once again someone who is educated painfully on the importance of class distinctions. Marie Wesener is the daughter of a jeweler whose prudent mercantile instincts tell him Marie can do no better than to marry a draper named Stolzius; but Marie is very much alive to other possibilities, especially Baron Desportes. She goes out with this aristocrat often—until her father, too, catches sparks of social ambition. The protestations of her rejected bourgeois boy friend fail to change her course for she takes literally Desportes's declaration that his love transcends class considerations. But soon enough Marie realizes she has made the wrong choice; Desportes deserts her upon deciding another affair has ended.

The fact that after enough stress individuals will unconsciously crave an even greater measure of suffering seems to have obsessed Lenz in good plays as well as bad. Her lover's desertion has just such an effect on Marie. She plummets into deep depression, but she cannot admit to herself that what is over is over for good, with the result that she ends up begging for bread in the streets she has haunted in search of Desportes. Though Lenz attaches to *The Soldiers* the kind of lachrymose family reunion that was commonplace with Diderot and other practitioners of sentimental bourgeois theater, he does not conclude matters as lightly as in *The Tutor*. Marie survives, but her lovers do not: Stolzius poisons Desportes and then dies by his own hand.

In the final scene of the play this unfortunate sequence of events is discussed by the Countess La Roche (for a while Marie's protectress) and Colonel Graf von Spannheim, who, like Desportes, represents both the army and nobility. The Colonel cannot get over one of his men having been involved in so seamy a course of events and he blames it all on sheer villainous fate. The Countess does not agree; she ascribes it to the fact that soldiers cannot marry. Spannheim seems to realize she is right, but what can possibly be done? After all, did not Homer himself point out that good marriages make bad soldiers?—The Countess remarks that she has always looked upon the soldiery as a monster to whom an occasional innocent woman must be fed to insure public safety. It is then that the Colonel makes the proposal which has provoked so much comment.

A common view is that the proposal is of no relevance to the play. This seems too strong, for Lenz goes out of his way to indicate that soldiers deprived of legitimate sexual outlets will find satisfaction some other way, will in fact become that much more sex-preoccupied by virtue of the unnatural restraints imposed on them. An officer remarks that the situation is getting out of hand—everywhere soldiers are caressing women.

Actually, what makes the Colonel's proposal suspect as an answer to the problems posed by *The Soldiers* brings us back to that clash of attitudes shared by Lenz and Brecht. Here again the social reformer offers inappropriate solutions; Lenz attempts to equate the darker forces of his world with unenlightened social practice. Last time his recipe was public education; this time it is public sex. But Lenz testifies to no such meliorist convictions when he has an old woman sing a ballad of despair while the stage resounds with the laughter of Desportes and Marie from another room:

When girls are young, they are like dice
Thrown out upon a table
Little Roesel from Hennegau
Will soon be on God's table

Why smile you so, my loving child
Your cross is only waiting
Until the word is out that Roesel
Will soon a man be taking

Oh, little girl, how much it hurts
To see the sparkle in your eye
When I cannot help but see as well
How often you will cry.[18]

A close analysis of this ballad is hardly required. Lenz is using song as commentary, and his intention is to let us know that the happy mood of the moment is actually quite deceptive, is in fact quite ironic, in view of what Marie will soon have to bear. Unlike the dramatist whose patterns of suspense require him to make momentary surfaces as impenetrable to the audience as they are to the characters on stage, Lenz deliberately strips from the action before us any element of fictional reassurance. He does not hesitate to neutralize the dominant mood of a scene by hinting at what is to come. One could well see here a remote anticipation of Brecht's concept of *Verfremdung*.

Lenz was at pains to link the tragedy of Marie Wesener's betrayal to the enforced celibacy of the garrison from which Desportes emerged, but he could not achieve the connection, if only because of his own psychological acuity. No more than Läuffer does Marie strike us as a mere victim of circumstance. Her affair with Desportes could have been avoided quite easily; in fact, it was not avoided only because of the social ambition of this vain and very average girl, who refused to heed the cautionary advice of her father and to respect her obligations to Stolzius.

Marie Wesener comes through very much like a moth around a flame, so obsessed is she with the desire to rise socially. In spite of her girlish charm, she is basically a selfish, egoistic creature with an eye for the main chance. She is perhaps Lenz's most successful uneccentric character, and the dialogue he has given her illumines the forces behind action with a subtle precision he was never to surpass. To a great extent this dialogue is equivalent to a series of masks

[18] Lenz, *Gesammelte Schriften*, I, 57–58.

suited to the social strategy of the moment. Thus, in the first scene of the play, where Marie can easily be herself inasmuch as no one but her sister Charlotte is present, she shows herself to be sensitive and volatile; she bursts out crying when Charlotte insists on pursuing a conversation about Stolzius. When we next see her she is talking to Desportes, and here she conveys an impression of incontestable humility: "My mother has told me time and again that I am not yet grown up; I am at the age when one is neither beautiful nor ugly."[19]

When Wesener steps into the room, Desportes requests permission to take Marie to the theater. For a moment Marie loses her poise, so badly does she want to go. Wesener is against the idea, but that does not stop Marie, who quickly arranges a rendezvous with the Baron behind her father's back. As soon as Desportes leaves she tries to rationalize her maneuver by suggesting to Wesener that the aristocrat has good qualities. It is not long before she lets her whole family know what she is up to, giving away some of her tactics in bursts of uncontrollable emotion, releasing others with the exquisitely feigned innocence of the born schemer. The whole point is that she realizes her course of action places her up against extremely powerful social forces. Her origin is much too low to gain for her an easy acceptance into Desportes's circles. At the same time, she must contend with those social inhibitions which make her behavior incomprehensible to her own class. In part the conflict is external, placing her in outright opposition to the rest of her family. But it is almost as much an inner conflict, and this comes out at the end of the first act when Marie is finally all alone:

MARIE (*kissing her father's hand*): Good night, Pappuschka!—(*When he is gone, she sighs heavily and steps to the window while undressing.*) My heart is so heavy I'm certain thunder is coming. Suppose it should strike— (*She looks up, pressing her hands upon her exposed breast.*) God! What evil could I be guilty of? Stolzius—I do still love you—but if I can improve my luck—and Papa himself so advises me (*closing the curtains*)—well then if thunder strikes, let it; I would be only too happy to die. (*She puts out the light.*)[20]

Just as Marie's dialogue reflects tensions which in turn reflect upon certain social realities, so old Wesener's dialogue operates as a kind

[19] *Ibid.*, III, 35.
[20] *Ibid.*, p. 46.

of social psychograph. This is most apparent when he has to face someone of higher status:

WESENER: Well, look here now! Herr Baron, I am your loyal servant; to what do we owe the honor (*embracing him*)?

DESPORTES: I shall only be here a few weeks, visiting with some relatives from Brussels recently arrived.

WESENER: Forgive me for not having been home to receive you. My little Marie must surely have tried your patience. May I ask about your worthy parents—they've gotten the snuffboxes, I'm sure. . . . [21]

The studious avoidance of informality, the overpolite phrasings, the attempt to communicate nothing so much as respect (which amounts to reverence)—all these features of Wesener's speech are instantaneously evoked by the appearance of an aristocrat like Desportes. Lenz makes the very syntax of Wesener's speech socially significant and succeeds in delineating the merchant in terms of values which he never questions. Dialogue thus becomes highly illustrative and helps to build the frame of reference for a full understanding of the play's social implications. To put it quite simply, the nature of dialogue clarifies the psychology of the speaker and the nature of the society in which he functions.

This applies to Desportes as well. Of all the dialogues in the play, his strikes the ear as most artificial. A sample will make this quite clear:

DESPORTES: I false? Can you believe such a thing of me, divine Mademoiselle? Is it false to have stolen away from my regiment, and, when I get back to it, to run the risk of prison for not having stayed with my family—is it false to have done this only for the bliss of seeing you, most perfect one?[22]

Desportes, like Wesener, is highly conscious of the effect he is creating. What he says sounds forced and insincere, but to the inexperienced Marie it might strike just the right note of outraged nobility.

[21] *Ibid.*, p. 35.
[22] *Ibid.*, p. 34.

What exposes him more laughably, however, is the poem he dedicates to Marie:

You highest object of my purest drives
I do adore you with eternal love
Who with each morn that blossoms new
Doth guarantee a love most radiant and true.[23]

Lenz seems to have been convinced that any affectation of personality will come out in speech. His tendency in *The Soldiers* to make speech pregnant with idiosyncrasies was certainly observed by Büchner, and *Woyzeck* owes much to Lenz. There is one piece of dialogue (by a minor character) that we can be quite certain Büchner pondered over:

PIRZEL (*who has meanwhile seated himself now gets up hastily*):
As I had the honor and pleasure to tell you, Herr Pastor! It is all because people don't do any thinking. Thinking, yes thinking about what makes a human being—that is what I am talking about. (*He seizes his hand.*) If you will observe, that is your hand, but what is it? Skin, bone, earth (*taps him on his pulse*); there, there, there is where it stays fixed, that is only the scabbard, there is where the sword stays fixed, in the blood, in the blood. . . . [24]

This excerpt foreshadows not only the pompous Philistinism of the Captain and Doctor who torment Woyzeck but also the circular mental processes of Woyzeck himself, who must cling to the resonances of words by ritualistic repetition. Lenz uses dialogue not only for the purpose of making us feel the social pressures of his characters; he has an ear as well for their metaphysical anxieties.

Lenz utilized gesture in *The Tutor* to underline traits of character in such a way that long after we have read the play we remember the scraping postures of Läuffer, the frenetic gesticulations of Wenzeslaus, and the physical aggressiveness of the Major. In *The Soldiers* he uses gesture as well, but not so much to vivify satiric thrusts as to delineate psychic tensions. Thus, at the sudden appearance of

[23] *Ibid.,* p. 45.
[24] *Ibid.,* pp. 48–49.

Desportes, Marie's attempt to stick into her pocket a letter from Stolzius, and her breaking into tears at the implications of the letter, define more precisely than anything she says the contradictory emotions she experiences in throwing over the draper for the aristocrat. These physical reactions expose the clash within Marie between her enormous fear of playing a losing game and the intoxicating social ambition which makes it impossible for her to stop playing that game.

She is again caught off guard a few scenes later. Here it is best to give the original stage directions and dialogue:

Marie's room

(*She sits upon her bed, has a pin in her hand and, lost in revery, stares at it intently. Her father comes in; she jumps up and tries to conceal the pin.*)

MARIE: Ach the Lord Jesus—

WESENER: No, let's not play the child. (*Walks up and down several times and then sits down next to her.*) Listen, Marieel! You know I'm good to you, so be honest with me, it will be to your benefit. Tell me, has the Baron said anything to you about love?[25]

The similarity of Marie's actions to those of Büchner's Marie at a critical moment of surprise should be noted here. There seems to be little doubt Büchner realized how much of the powerful forces motivating character Lenz was able to convey through nonverbal theater.

In *The Tutor* the psychology of Lenz's characters was at bottom quite simple, a simplicity made to order for caricatural portraiture. In *The Soldiers* Lenz is still pinpointing with unmistakable clarity the forces which manipulate his characters, but here the shading is subtler, the distortion less self-evident, the action more faithful to the psychopathology of everyday life. Behavior is still a matter of putting on the appropriate social mask, but the masks are less obvious. Yet, the black-and-white exposure of the earlier play is at times here as well, especially in the scene where Desportes, in a monologue that is ingenuously informational, presents himself as totally without principles as far as his relationship to Marie is concerned. Lenz is still intent on stressing that beneath the varied surfaces of human behavior one finds a bedrock of reprehensible emotion.

[25] *Ibid.*, p. 44.

As in *The Tutor,* the bourgeoisie is viewed as thirsting for some taste of the status and power monopolized by the aristocracy. And the aristocracy once again is pictured as a class whose representatives all too easily come to assume that those socially below them exist only for their sport. Lenz does not give expression in this play to anything like the call for radical action in *The Tutor.* In fact, he seems to have come to the rueful realization that such action is hardly likely on the part of a class every bit as obsessed with the superficies of status as the aristocracy. If he preaches any course of bourgeois action at all in *The Soldiers,* it is that of social segregation. Thus the enlightened Countess de la Roche tells a broken Marie that her mistake was to overlook the insuperable barriers which separate the aristocracy from the bourgeoisie, barriers which will be minimized only by those who do not know how the real world operates to penalize the socially ambitious.

Concrete depiction of milieu serves to reinforce this sense of absolute class division. Whether in the merchant's home, or in the midst of a gathering of soldiers who do not know what to do with themselves, Lenz creates his scene with meticulous concern for authenticity. In the Wesener home, for example, we are made aware by any number of small details that this family must scratch for a mercantile living. At the same moment that Desportes and Marie are arranging their rendezvous, old Wesener enters with a large box of brooches: "As you can see, here we have them at all prices—these at one hundred thaler, these at fifty, and these at one hundred and fifty, as you wish."[26]

As for the soldiers, Lenz's attempt to delineate the way they actually live, in a sexless limbo which affords them no real outlet for their energies, makes him once again subordinate plot development to observation of social behavior. One scene, for example, gives a mere conversation about the moral value of theatrical entertainment on the part of some officers who, we sense, work themselves up over the issue simply because there is really nothing else to get worked up about. The boredom of the officers reaches the point that they turn their ingenuity to devising a prank for one of their more unpopular members, and Lenz does not hesitate once again to depict this in a seemingly unnecessary scene. For Lenz, of course, there is no irrelevance in anything which helps us to understand why men behave as they do; plot progression is of less importance than the illumination of an atmosphere with characteristic details which tell their own story.

[26] Ibid., p. 37.

It should not go unnoticed that what Stolzius goes through with Marie is quite close to what Büchner's Woyzeck goes through with his Marie. Stolzius, like Woyzeck, loses the capacity to function when Marie betrays him. Stolzius, like Woyzeck, discovers through the sheer gratuitous nastiness of an unimplicated gossiper that the woman who means so much to him is up to something. Like Woyzeck, Stolzius suffers in silence while listening to the small talk of those to whom his emotional crisis means nothing. And like Woyzeck, he lets loose most emotionally when talking to himself, enjoying no peace of mind until he has committed murder. Both men are totally alone, no matter how completely life surrounds them.

As far as basic attitudes are concerned, Lenz and Büchner have much in common. Though Lenz may be more of a patient realist than Büchner, he is as aware as the latter that the larger forces directing human lives operate with an irrational sadism all their own. What happens to Marie, for example, may in part be blamed on an acutely class-conscious society and the traits of a particular personality; but when all is said and done, Marie still strikes us as the victim of more powerful forces which are not reducible to psychic and societal causations. Even the Countess de la Roche, with her total commitment to the social code which Marie has violated, hints at this in a speech which suggests how powerfully Lenz was aware that human beings are tormented simply for having human inclinations: "I wonder whether I can in good conscience deprive the girl of her romance. What charm does life hold, if we are not seized by our imaginations. Eating, drinking, hopeless preoccupations devoid of self-created satisfactions—these only make for a drawn-out death. . . ."[27]

To students of expressionism the accelerated manner in which Lenz strings his scenes together in the fourth act of *The Soldiers* has always been of special formal interest. But it should not be overlooked that Lenz switches scenes as rapidly as he does primarily because it is the most economical manner of communicating basic information on his plot and of reinforcing the ironies he has been creating all along. Scene after scene is reduced to a bare minimum of action. In succession we witness Desportes in an Armentieres prison, extremely worried about being exposed to his family by a distraught Marie; Old Wesener close to hysteria upon learning his daughter has run away from home; Stolzius discovering the same thing and joining the search; and, ironically enough, Desportes's rifleman relishing the easy conquest awaiting

[27] *Ibid.*, p. 81.

him in the girl his superior has jilted. Lenz makes it perfectly clear that Marie is on the point of utter self-destruction and that it is entirely out of her hands whether or not that destruction is averted. The bleak atmosphere of these episodes is sustained through glimpses of Marie plodding along on the road to Armentieres, by now crazed from hunger and frustration, and of Stolzius shivering in the rain outside the apothecary where he hopes to obtain poison.

All this misery goes unnoticed by Desportes. He wants only to forget that he ever laid eyes on Marie and he is not above viewing himself as the injured party. Marie, he tells himself, was "a whore from the start," and if she was nice to him, it was for cold, material reasons. In fact, if someone was to blame for his going into debt, it was that same whore, doubtless out to separate him from his last penny. With every line, Desportes twists reality to his own ends, going so far as to convince himself that by donating Marie to his rifleman he manifests real nobility. Nothing after this points up with as much directness the saddening incongruity at the heart of *The Soldiers*—the naïveté of a young woman in pursuit of a better life and the callousness of an aristocrat who would not hesitate to destroy her for his comfort.

In the final analysis Marie and Läuffer are indeed cut from the same cloth. Both are foolhardy enough to disregard the unwritten code whereby their aspiration level is to be dictated by their place on the social scale. Acting on impulse rather than social convention, they unleash forces far too strong for any individual to cope with. Marie, however, comes through far less laughably than Läuffer, and there is in general less comedy in *The Soldiers,* which Lenz called a *Schauspiel*. It is sheer anguish, the insurmountable frustrations of people for whom there is literally no second chance, that preoccupies Lenz in this play, to the point that he comes close to investing almost every scene with tragic resonances.

What has been said about the illustrative function of individual scenes in *The Tutor* applies as well to the later play. The action of a scene is by implication a bitter comment on the nature of a society in which such action is possible. Whether Marie is struggling for social status, or Wesener is aghast at her presumptions, or Desportes is trying to seduce her, the basic emphasis remains the same. Once again Lenz is not concerned with the passions and strategies of individuals for their own sake: he wishes to pinpoint decisive social and economic forces.

In this connection, *The Soldiers* constitutes an advance in technique, but nothing in the play is a radical departure from the form and content of *The Tutor*. In the later play, characterization is a more careful blending of dialogue and gesture; dialogue itself proves more revealing of the interrelationship between social posture and social pressures; scenes are more dynamically concatenated; the plot is more absorbing and unified; and society is depicted in far greater detail and with far more concern for documentary realism. But with all of these qualitative differences, the two plays are variants of a type. Lenz is saying the same thing, passing the same judgment, namely, that the ostensibly civilized life of his society camouflages a shocking core of parasitism and victimization. In both plays, individuals come to grief because they have been naïve enough to believe they have a right to enjoy life, or, more precisely, to enjoy it as much as those in power. In both plays, Lenz leaves his action diffuse enough to encompass as much social observation as he would like to insert. In both plays, he comments on the action in a variety of ways, going so far as to devote an entire scene to the explication of forces behind the action. In both plays, the unities are abandoned—all of which brings us to a most important area of our study, the way in which the episodic structure allows Lenz to communicate what he wishes to say more effectively than if he had employed the unified Aristotelian organization. Or, in what ways would he have been hampered by observing those unities of time, place, and action which he violates so blatantly? If Lenz is indeed the initiator of a significant theatrical form, then the above question must bear pertinently on the nature of his influence.

Aside from action, the number of unities Aristotle considered necessary is still arguable, but the fact remains that in the course of time his name became associated with the unities of time, place, and action, as well as the unity of tone which precludes the mixture of tragic and comic emotions. It is this concept of theater which Lenz rejected so violently—for various reasons.

He rejected unity of time, for example, because he wished to put upon the stage not merely the final phase of a development whose origins antedate the commencement of the play; his aim was to show the entire development of a situation, even if its initial phase took place months or years before the crisis. For Lenz, the last phase is merely the residuum of everything which has led up to it; hence it does not deserve to monopolize the substance of a serious play.

Thus, in both major plays Lenz does not restrict himself to the day or week in which things finally come to a head but starts his action at that point where the characters in question are about to make those decisions which will in the end prove their undoing.

Since Lenz was intent on demonstrating the crucial relationship of social forces to his characters' vicissitudes, he may well have thought along the lines of Brecht, who wanted his plays to show not the inevitability of tragic consequences but their avoidability. Such an untragic point of view can only be conveyed by showing those events prior to the moment of crisis which point up the causal factors responsible for the crisis. And, indeed, those events may go far into the past. Thus, Läuffer's decision to become a servile tutor of aristocrats, and Marie's decision to throw over the draper Stolzius for the aristocrat Desportes are both in essence social decisions, and they are decisions which precede by great intervals the bitter harvest they reap. It is this relatively slow process whereby social decisions are transmuted into personal catastrophes that Lenz makes the core of his plays.

The Aristotelian suspense play validates in most momentous fashion the idea that life proceeds with inexorable logic toward climactic moments. The action commences quite close to these moments and approaches them by rapid accumulations of intensity. Life comes through as having a preternatural, compacted excitement simply because time and space are contracted in the interests of an overpowering unity of impression. Exposition exists only to usher in complication, and complication intensifies until it explodes into climax and recognition.

The world this kind of Aristotelian suspense plays suggests is not Lenz's. For him the most decisive turns of life may well be the least dramatic. He seems to have brooded upon the apparent innocence of our most fatal moments. At any rate, his best plays are ironic in a way that might have proved very difficult had he employed the tight Aristotelian form. Unlike Sophocles', Lenz's irony is not plot centered; it pervades every aspect of his dramaturgy. Such irony is implicit in the assiduous efforts of his essentially helpless characters to fabricate a world in which they have some importance—an irony which juxtaposes the vitality of their bustlings with the futility of their actions, an irony at play in the pompous rationalizations of Läuffer, the social simulations of Marie Wesener, and the bourgeois pontifications of her father. All of this Lenz observes with such ironic detachment that he makes it impossible for his audience to take his serious reform proposals at face value.

Episodic structuring helps Lenz to illustrate the repetitious nature of experience. As pointed out above, neither the psychology of his characters nor the situations into which they get themselves are subject to much change in the course of the play. The more things change, the more they are the same. Läuffer is always the impotent victim at the receiving end of someone else's aggressions; Marie is always the hypersensitive creature buffeted by emotions she cannot discipline. Nothing substantive is really decided in these plays. In fact, it is very likely that the action ends at another beginning, there being little to suggest that the past patterns of these characters will never recur. Again, the Aristotelian play tends to suggest the exact opposite, for things are resolved once and for all at the conclusion of the play.

Lenz disregards unity of place and action in a way that has proved irritably distracting. It sometimes seems that his erratic shifts from one locale to the next are in conformity with the general disposition of the *Stürmer und Dränger* to thumb their noses at Aristotle in the name of Shakespeare. Some of this censure is no doubt valid, but it is important to realize that unity of place, like unity of time, would hardly have facilitated the synthesis of social observation and dramatic action Lenz was out to make. As it is, his plays give us a variety of social types and a diversity of social relationships simply by shifting to locales where these types and relationships are normal. Examples of this from *The Tutor* are the landlady of the boarding house scenes, Wenzeslaus in the forest, the musician in the university town; from *The Soldiers* they are the Jew in his pawnshop, the Countess de la Roche at her home; the officers in their quarters. In each case, a character who is not crucial to the action of the play is presented to us in the surroundings where he or she ordinarily functions, with the result that a far richer social picture emerges because of the casualness with which Lenz violates unity of place.

As for unity of tone, Lenz would have rejected it above all for its falsity. Why exclude from serious drama vast areas of human experience simply because they imply emotional connotations not sanctioned by an ancient doctrine? In this case Lenz rejects Aristotle for the very reason he enjoyed Shakespeare's plays, which he found full of irresistible, pulsing life.

Lenz, himself, seems to have done a great deal of thinking on the relationship between general cultural conditions and the nature of drama. Conceiving of the distinction between comedy and tragedy as primarily social and not psychological, he insisted comedy could reach a far greater audience, that tragedy attracted only a serious-minded minority. Lenz translated the fact that comedy was more popular into an aesthetic determinant: Inasmuch as comedy can reach the ordinary man, comedy should play an important cultural role by helping to create a greater audience for the tragic artist. And inasmuch as comedy is so intelligible to the average man, there is every reason to invest it with the seriousness one associates with tragedy. We are very close here to Brecht's aesthetics.

In conclusion, Lenz differs from his contemporaries far more than most casual literary historians are prone to reveal. No writer of his day matches him in pessimism, resignation, and irony. No one manifests his powerfully concrete social awareness which makes urgent the kind of problems easily attenuated into conversational abstractions. At the same time, this sense of urgency never prompted Lenz to sum up all that was wrong with his society in the indictment of a single villainous class. Just as he rejected the histrionic hero who is almost stock with the *Sturm und Drang,* so he rejected the histrionic class villain of the kind Lessing and Schiller did not hesitate to utilize.

Lenz exhibits the moral squalor of the aristocracy as well as the moral cowardice of the bourgeoisie. But his interests do not end here; his basic concern seems to have been that of the *Sturm und Drang* in general: the interrelationship of social organization and human instincts. It would not be wrong to say Lenz anticipates the Wedekind who dramatized the powerful destructive essence of the sexual impulse. It is no accident that in both major plays, individuals come to grief because of that impulse and that in *The Soldiers* the need for sex is viewed so threateningly. Lenz implies that all men have powerful instinctual needs, and to attribute to any class or individual an absence of such needs is to sin against reality.

Lenz begins in German drama a tradition in which the animality of man is not softened by optimism or idealism, a tradition which faces squarely up to stark facts without sentimental coatings. This tradition will emphasize again and again that European society is sick to the core, confirming forcefully the judgment of a character in *The New Menoza* that Europeans leaving their continent should be quarantined, so morally diseased is their nature.

Toward the last quarter of the eighteenth century the appearance of drama with some of the stylistic features present in *The Tutor* and *The Soldiers* might strike some as inevitable. After all, the Shakespearian episodic structure was being held up in German culture as the dramatic form of the future; the reign of Aristotelianism seemed to have ended for good; Diderot and Mercier had effectively made a case for drama which would concern itself with the realities of the average man; and last, but not least, the social situation in Germany had become so blatantly inequitable that a dramatist was bound to arise who would choose this society as his target.

Still, Lenz's emergence is surprising, more so than the fact that in the plays of contemporaries like Schiller there are overtones of his vision. Most remarkable about his work is the fact that in it several contemporary approaches to theater coalesce. Lenz appeared at a time when it was only natural to think of combining the social awareness of a Diderot and Mercier with the formal structure of Shakespeare, in order to rival Shakespeare's depth of characterization against a social background highly relevant to contemporary experience. But Lenz's peculiar achievement was that he synthesized the views of Diderot and Mercier and the aesthetics implied by Shakespeare into an entirely new species of play.

Lenz pioneers a tradition in which a realistic treatment of social conditions goes hand in hand with a highly subjective outlook. This tradition, from Lenz to Brecht, will put on stage the kind of ordinary life and prosaic environment which it was beneath the dignity of classical and idealistic dramatists to give more than their passing atten- tion. The dramatists of the Lenz-Brecht tradition, like those naturalists who took Zola's word for what the focus of drama should be, identify the sordid and brutish with the true nature of reality, and, like the Zolaesque Naturalists, they identify human psychology with the opera- tion of basic instinctual forces. Stylistically, however, Lenz and com- pany are a far cry from "objective" naturalism, if only because they resort to a number of techniques which make quite clear that their point of departure was sheer outrage. They make no secret of the fact that the society in which they live leaves them viscerally antago- nistic. And if not their society, then life itself.

Their approach is above all functional. Character, dialogue, episode, scenery, gesture—almost anything that goes into the making of a play is used to demonstrate vividly how unsavory a place is the world implied by the play's action. Character is portrayed ironically, action is developed didactically, dialogue is employed illustratively, and the totality of the play's action implies very much the same value judgments as its dramaturgic elements.

This kind of drama, which focuses at all times on what is behind the action, as well as on the patterns which the action will invariably assume, is hardly made for heroics. Lenz's characters could not possibly rise to idealistic heights because they merely crystallize in a peculiar way what is in general true of their society. Heroics imply a measure of independence and individuality which these characters lack, not only because of the way they are made, but also because of the way the play they are in is made. The play is structured to deny them heroic autonomy: it is structured to show the horrible nature of the forces which control them, to make of these characters egregious examples of what is sadly inevitable, given certain conditions.

One need go no further than Lenz to sum up the distinctive character of the drama that was to be written from Büchner to Brecht. Its structure is episodic, its variety of episodes apparently combined in an aimless enough fashion. Staple attributes of the well-made play are not much in evidence; and critics will be as annoyed by the absence of suspense and climax in Lenz as they have been by such omissions in Büchner and Brecht. In general there are few exciting confrontations in the drama here under discussion; one confronts only one's own helplessness. Formally, these unorthodox plays violate what are supposedly elementary rules of playwriting; their authors blandly employ character as a vehicle for special pleading and they have no compunctions about straight recourse to melodrama. By what right do they call themselves realists? No less disconcerting are the attitudes behind this drama—an unsettling blend of comic perception and tragic feeling, of fierce moral outrage punctuated by ice-cold cynicism, or, put another way, of unabashed nihilism grounded in the kind of apocalyptic despair that is available only to confirmed moral idealists. In a seemingly perverse refusal to define themselves, these writers inveigh against a world crying out for change and then go on to suggest that their moralizing will not make a bit of difference.

Lenz, himself, would very likely have rationalized the structure of his two major plays by pointing out that it is ideal for a drama of naturalistic character study. This would bring his practice into conformity with the views he had expressed in his *Notes to the Theater* on the relative merits of Aristotle's and Shakespeare's aesthetics. The odds are that he would not have argued for episodic structuring by pinpointing those elements which strike us as most original today. But the kind of play he wrote is not distinguished primarily for what it tells us about human character. It is distinguished above all for what it tells us about human character as a symptom—a symptom not only of what is wrong with the nature of a particular society but of what is irrevocably wrong with the very nature of the human situation.

chapter two:

christian dietrich grabbe

The enthusiasm for Shakespeare that was generated during the *Sturm und Drang* remained strong through the opening decades of the nineteenth century and was, if anything, reinforced by August Wilhelm Schlegel's fresh revaluations. Schlegel emphasized over and over that Shakespeare was not the freakish genius which the eighteenth century had so often made him out to be. He stressed also that Shakespeare was unsurpassed in knowledge of human nature and in imaginative power; more important, he asserted that all of Shakespeare's art was highly deliberate. Such eulogy by a leading critic could not help but intensify the prevalent idolization of Shakespeare in Germany; and, in retrospect, it seems inevitable that someone should have gone on record against the apotheosis of a writer who was not even a native son.

That someone turned out to be, paradoxically enough, a German dramatist whose work was obviously influenced by Shakespeare and who at one time had found Goethe and Schiller "thin soup" in comparison with the English writer. But in his *Concerning the Shakespeare Madness* (1827), Christian Dietrich Grabbe writes as one who finds nothing praiseworthy in the German regard for Shakespeare; in Grabbe's opinion the Germans take to Shakespeare only because a collective inferiority complex prompts them to prefer anything that is not homemade; and German critics in particular take to the English dramatist because they do not understand him.[1] As for German stage productions of Shakespeare, they prove little since they are all too often sentimentalized perversions; *King Lear,* for example, is staged as another *Père de famille,* and a partiality to bourgeois drama becomes a partiality to Shakespeare.

This state of affairs Grabbe cannot tolerate, and in his essay he proceeds to attack it from several angles. He tries to show that Shakespeare's reputation is meretricious, not only because of the way it has developed, but also because of Shakespeare's aesthetic failings, which Grabbe finds egregious enough to make him say: "Shakespeare does not deserve to be identified with the most exemplary form of tragedy."

Oddly enough, Grabbe finds Shakespeare lacking the very gifts which Lenz and other *Stürmer und Dränger* had found so admirably present on every page of his work. Above all, Grabbe finds an insuffi-

[1] Grabbe's main targets are Schlegel and Tieck.

ciency of deep feeling which leads to such mistakes as the unnecessary and unmotivated death of Cordelia. Shakespeare is censurable as well in the area of characterization, for how else could he have given us a Julius Caesar who is in essence no more than a self-important coiner of phrases? The indictment of Shakespeare is quite elaborate, and, to be fair to Grabbe, he does raise issues which could be profitably discussed today. Of most immediate relevance, however, is his assertion that Shakespeare's dramaturgy is inferior to that of Schiller.

But what I demand of a poet, in the event he represents history dramatically, is that his treatment be dramatic and concentric in such a way as to make manifest the idea of history. Schiller strove for this, guided by healthy German common sense; none of his history plays is lacking in dramatic focus or concentric idea. Shakespeare may be more objective than Schiller, but his historical dramas are still nothing more than poetically embellished chronicles. In the majority of his plays there is discernible no focal point, no catastrophe, no poetic goal. . . .[2]

To view this comment as a reflection of Grabbe's dramatic philosophy is to invite confusion. For Grabbe went on to write plays which remind us very little of Schiller and very much of Shakespeare, especially of Shakespeare's histories. *Concerning the Shakespeare Madness* remains, in the final analysis, a document less valuable for its cultural substance than for the light it sheds on the psychology of a very strange man, a man who admits that there has never been anyone quite like Shakespeare but who belittles Shakespeare every chance he gets; who ascribes great value to the literary taste of the average German but finds that same taste offensively spurious; who gives the distinct impression of writing as much out of chauvinistic emotionalism[3] as out of aesthetic discernment—all in all, a weird mixture of contradictions.

Grabbe's plays intensify this impression. Like Lenz, he speaks with two voices which would seem to be mutually exclusive but which

[2] *Grabbes Werke* (Leipzig: Bibliographisches Institut, 1910), ed. Albin Franz and Paul Zaunert, I, 401.
[3] A sample of Grabbe's xenophobic approach to drama: "We have no need for any English theater, can have no such theater, least of all do we want a Shakespearian theater. It is German drama that we want . . . Shakespeare's work is full of English idiosyncrasies as well as national prejudices." *Ibid.,* p. 415.

interact oddly. A corrosive cynicism which spares nothing is joined to a powerful sense of pathos. Again like Lenz, Grabbe has a very strong need to be concretely realistic about the very things which inspire his strongest enthusiam. But what links Grabbe most importantly to Lenz is his use of the episodic structure. He, too, employs this structure as an element of illustrative realism. Episodic development allows him to pinpoint whatever social and historical forces control the action of the play and, by implication, human action in general. Once again a dramatist confronts a world of hard facts in a manner which isolates him decisively from the dominant theatrical movements of his period. Though there may be value in noting those qualities which relate Lenz and Grabbe to the Romantics, there is no value in trying to make them quasi-Romantics; they are simply another breed.

In Grabbe's first play, *Theodore, Duke of Gothland* (1827), the structure is not episodic; it is, in fact, very much that of the typical classical-idealistic play written in verse a generation earlier. But it deserves attention, if only because it proves again that the youthful emotions of a dramatist clarify all later attitudes. *Gothland* has been called a pile of filth, and it is easy enough to see why; it is not quite so easy to discern that the emotions Grabbe puts into his first play will be less apparent in his more mature work but nonetheless decisively present.

There are five changes of scene in the final act of *Gothland,* enough to prompt one to say that Grabbe was not made for the Aristotelian unities; it is just as obvious that he was not made for Aristotelian decorum or for Aristotelian imitation in general. Certainly Grabbe diverges most patently from Aristotle in his treatment of *Gothland's* plot (which is really no more than an excuse for Grabbe to get things off his chest). As early as this, one can sense that for him each scene is a separate temptation to get down to fundamentals, that he is only secondarily concerned with developing a suspenseful continuum. The action does not advance to a climactic development but to a state of indifference on the part of a world-weary protagonist.

Gothland is an idealistic young nobleman who is tricked into committing a senseless murder by a human fiend named Berdoa, the first of Grabbe's energetic nihilists. When Gothland learns that he has been an instrument of evil, he goes to pieces; his philosophy has no room for a world in which good intentions introduce the worst of consequences. Having taken in idealism with his mother's milk,

he sees no alternative but to invert those ethical values which he
has always lived by religiously and to become as destructive as the
processes apparently dictating impersonal nature. The fury of his conversion to inhumanity is unlike anything the German theater had ever
seen, and that includes the stridencies of the *Sturm und Drang*:

That which is created is created
Only to decay
For that alone is the body's smallest nerve
Responsive to most monstrous pain
For that alone do we have fragile limbs
For that alone are we stark naked born!
To guarantee that our seduction be complete
We have stupidity galore, and
Immortality as well—for the punishments of hell!
—That which is created is created
Only to decay!
The so-called vault of heaven
Circles like an executioner's wheel;
Day and night, sun and moon
And stars are
Twisted thereupon like unfortunate delinquents
Who get their final stroke
By being torn and ground to pieces.[4]

Such nihilistic feeling is sounded throughout a play in which plot
never gets in the way of diatribe. Again and again characters explode
into frenzied ejaculations which Grabbe seems to relish for their own
sake,[5] just as he relishes gruesome descriptions of sadistic and can-
nibalistic activity. Plainly the intent is to demonstrate that man is
as vicious as life is meaningless. By no means is Grabbe willing to
allow even this meaninglessness to become a stimulus to existential
value, for he goes out of his way not only to deride the good faith
which keeps the passionate idealist going but to deride as well the
despair of the idealist who has lost that faith. Thus, beside the an-

[4] *Grabbes Werke*, I, 116.
[5] If aggression is the psychological essence of nihilism, then Grabbe would
seem to deserve the dubious honor August Closs bestows on Büchner as
perhaps "the most uncompromising German nihilist of the nineteenth century."
See *Medusa's Mirror, Studies in German Literature* (London: Cresset Press,
1957), p. 157.

guished reflections of Gothland, he places the crisp deflating commentary of Berdoa, to whom the sight of human suffering is a tonic:

GOTHLAND: Woe! Woe! How everything has changed! How much the sight of nature woke up but yesterday my sickly heart! And how the sun did smile!

BERDOA: Oh, the fool! Nature
Is every bit as magnificent as she ever was!
It's only his spirit that's changed since yesterday![6]

This Shakespearian technique of distancing an attitude by ironic annotation allows Grabbe to keep attention focused on the general picture of life his play implies. It is a picture that could not be more revolting, and a measure of Grabbe's determination to make it so is that he deliberately associates those values which make life worth living for most of humanity with viscerally repellent details. The sight of a young man in love for the first time provokes Berdoa to assert the incompatibility of the erotic emotion with bad breath and to observe that divine women invariably turn out to have hair full of lice and noses full of mucus. And the cynicism never lets up; small wonder that by the end of the play a career of treachery and murder has so dehumanized Gothland that his own imminent death fails to move him. How can one possibly get worked up about the fate of something so noxious as a living creature which survives by cancerously feeding on its own kind? It is hard to share the view that Grabbe's first play is really a constructive attempt to teach the dangers of misplaced idealism; it is much easier to understand why upon Gothland has been bestowed the dubious honor of constituting the first out-and-out nihilistic play. Thus viewed, Gothland need occasion little speculation as to Grabbe's tendency therein to shift back and forth between lyrical pathos and brutal sensualism. Both postures have the same obvious cause—seething frustration at a world which leaves Grabbe agonized when it is not merely making him bitter. The note of repelled alienation sounded here would re-echo in all of his succeeding works.

Gothland gives us the emotional mechanisms of Grabbe's art; Marius and Sulla reveals intellectual processes which anticipate his most mature

[6] Grabbes Werke, I, 117.

work. It is a play Grabbe left unfinished, though he outlined with great explicitness what he intended the omitted dramatizations to cover. For the first time he employs the episodic structure in order to convey panoramically what happened in a crucial period of history. The fact that his approach was dictated by a desire to stress impersonal factors as much as personal qualities may be assumed from such assertions as: "Above all, a poet is obligated to decipher the true spirit of history."[7] Becoming more specific with regard to *Marius and Sulla*, Grabbe informs us that his play is to make obvious history's need for the strong leader.[8]

In this latter aim Grabbe does not succeed, and the reason may well be laid to his epic technique. Individual episodes tend to lack focus; they are provocative enough for the observation of life in general that Grabbe works into them but not for their relevance to his central theme. This is borne out by the first scene of the play, the tone of which may well remind some of Brecht, and in which a fisherman cannot help agreeing with his wife's remark that small people like themselves exist only to be stepped on by big people.[9] Grabbe wastes no time striking cynical chords. Like Brecht, he is aware that the major events of history are not in the least glamorous from the bottom up.

By episodic development Grabbe takes us from one military camp to the next, to the Roman Senate, to the field of battle, and into the public streets. Early scenes make us aware that the two men whose struggle will determine the fate of Rome are not cut from the same cloth. Marius is a world-weary, brooding exile with a grudge against the times, Sulla a decisive tactician who wastes no time on philosophy. In his notes Grabbe makes it plain that Sulla is his man, but he resists making him the object of emotional identification. In scene after scene we learn that humanitarian considerations simply do not exist for Sulla, the savior of Rome; and Grabbe even goes so far as to make Sulla the focus for the demonic sadism which provoked horror in *Gothland*. Only here the sadism provokes cold, cynical laugh-

[7] *Grabbes Werke*, II, 487.
[8] "With greater and greater clarity is the truth brought to light that the Roman world lacked any earthly or religious foundation, and that if this world were not to fall apart totally, it would be only through the intervention of a despot. For that reason, men like Marius and Sulla had to appear and to become what they became." *Grabbes Werke*, II, 465.
[9] "We have a small being, and when anyone takes an interest in us, it is only to oppress us; we can do little but jump aside when great men fall." *Grabbes Werke*, II, 408.

ter. Thus, to the plea of a woman that he spare her children, Sulla can only ask quizzically: "Why?"

Grabbe sees such cruelty as normal because of the forces directed at Rome. One kind of peril is posed by wily foreigners ready to act at the proper moment; others are purely internal, and Grabbe illuminates them by showing the Roman Senate in action and by showing how utterly infantile is the psychology of the crowd that fills Rome's streets. Here Grabbe cannot resist voicing his own contempt for common life, and he does it through the mouth of the tribune Saturninus who declares that the mob is street filth and regrets only that he must use such garbage as his instrument. Most of all, he would enjoy drowning the masses in the Tiber.

Saturninus is the kind of character Grabbe would have had difficulty putting into *Marius and Sulla* had its structure been less open; he is of no real importance to the play's plot and certainly does not advance its action. But the episodes in which he appears provide insight into the general moral decay of Roman politics, and in this regard an instigator of Saturninus' proportions is by no means out of place. Actually, he anticipates the character Jouve, who, in *Napoleon,* will occupy a similar role, that of the detached, sarcastic observer whose allegiance to any authority is motivated by the sheerest opportunism, and who takes for granted that all human beings are hypocritical swine. He may also be said to symbolize the brute animal instinct that so obsessed Grabbe, the sinister irrepressible force of nature which is purely destructive of any value we may wish to cling to. Aside from this, it is important to realize that by giving us characters like Saturninus Grabbe is actually exploiting the freedom of epic structure in order to comment freely on the action of his play; through Saturninus he reminds us that the forces which shape events are wholly irrational. Certainly Saturninus' behavior fits in with the general action of *Marius and Sulla* since he illustrates perfectly the necessity for a cynical Weltanschauung such as permeates the whole of this drama.

Grabbe does his utmost to substantiate by a succession of morbidities that the Christian ethos is of no relevance to the nature of the historical process. Each of the twenty-two episodes of *Marius and Sulla* depicts a world where only force and cunning matter and where the success of public policy invariably depends upon who kills first. One begins to wonder whether it is possible to conceive of ancient life in less humanistic terms, so obsessed was Grabbe with the ferocities of rule and conquest. At times his content is nothing short of lurid—e.g., an enemy of Rome taking his daily ration of poison homeopathically; another foreigner shuddering at the prospect of Sulla's scourging him and receiving his cries of agony with the same relish evoked in children by captive insects; Roman soldiers at a loss to see what is wrong with burning infants alive—they will refrain from doing only that which is punishable by instant decapitation. As in his first play, Grabbe goes about shocking his readers into an awareness he felt most of mankind was only too anxious to repress, that history is in essence a continuum of murder.

The climax of horror comes with the return to Rome of its two most powerful men. Marius gets there first, and his state of mind is such that nothing makes him happier than the blood-spattered corpse of an old opponent.[10] Prodded by Saturninus, Marius' inhuman rage-mounts to fearful proportions until, at the moment of his most ecstatic triumph, lightning strikes: Sulla is on the way![11]

An explicit outline by Grabbe of his undramatized scenes reveals that Sulla returns to Rome convinced that henceforth he must be without a speck of mercy in order to set things right, that he must steel himself to be bigger than conscience itself.[12] For Grabbe, great-ness is often the residue of inhumanity. Sulla is able to make the transition to the demonic, says Grabbe, because of his sense of humor, and the scene in which he laughs off a woman's anguish at the im-minent death of her family supposedly illustrates this trait.

In shifting back to Marius, whose impotence is as pronounced as Sulla's dynamism, Grabbe touches on something of concern to him in almost every important work—the relationship between time, as an autonomous force, and the extraordinary man's capacity for action. "Time itself is my affliction," laments Marius, who feels he would

[10] Grabbe actually adds here a bizarre touch by having Marius regret that he was not the statue onto which sprayed the blood of his old enemy Merula. For those who would like insight into Grabbe's method of visualizing the past, this scene is recommended. *Grabbes Werke,* II, p. 466.

[11] *Ibid.* How Marius hears of Sulla's impending invasion is again indicative of the histrionic approach to theater which Grabbe would later take pains to counteract. " 'Sulla,' repeats Marius with involuntary sudden fear, and like an echo in mountainous forest does 'Sulla! Sulla!' resound through a nation of bystanders. The name alone seems possessed of something shattering. As in the rest of the play, it serves to make up for Sulla's absence."

[12] His decision is clear and complete: he will cleanse the time of its abuses, and do so without inhibition. He will subdue with terror, so that something better can raise its head. No matter what he will do, pangs of conscience hold no fear for him—for that he is too much a law unto himself." *Ibid.,* p. 471. Grabbe's *Führer* mystique was never plainer.

have stamped his character upon any age in which no Sulla blocked the way. Grabbe was to become quite fascinated with the manner in which critical junctures of history invited and negated heroic action at the same time. That Marius was a figure wholly capable of titanic enterprise—and that he should not be dismissed as a mere fancier of greatness—is warranted by Grabbe's comment on Marius' following: "He who has such a following must indeed be great in power."

Meanwhile, Sulla is busy proving that Rome can be saved if treated like a diseased organism afflicted with gangrene. Only profuse bleeding can remove the poison at the source; to spare life is tantamount to allowing the infected part to expand beyond the cure. And so we get, mostly in outline, the picture of a mass of frightened human beings cowering before a man of action who is quite merciless, to whom their screams are indeed no more moving than the buzzings of flies. Only for a moment does humanity surge up in Sulla at the sight of exterminated life, but he immediately recovers his aplomb and goes on with his methodical killing, which Grabbe fully approves.

At any rate, Sulla proves strong enough to dispose of Marius as well as other enemies of Roman stability, and to make sure no one gets the wrong impression, he tells a fable about a farmer who finally rids himself of all the insects troubling him by throwing his clothes into fire. Only Saturninus seems to miss the moral. Sulla has him quickly executed and then makes a very surprising move; at the moment of triumphant celebration, he gives up his powerful leadership and steps down from the stage of history. Hoping that the Romans can live up to his teachings the way he will now live from the very substance of himself, he declares that he will use his laurel wreath to season his soup.

One has to pause over this final image. The idea that the laurel wreath, symbolic of the highest attainments to which a Roman could aspire, is, in the final analysis, at best good for the kitchen spice shelf—this cynicism is Grabbe in a nutshell. From the beginning, he could see no reason why what is built up should not in turn be gleefully demolished. Obsessed with the belief that disintegration and decay are nature's favorite processes, he pictures this world only as a vale of corpse-making. Even the value of great men was suspect, for necessary as they might be to the course of history at one moment, so superfluous they might be a moment later. Sulla is the first in a line of extraordinary men who pass from the stage of history as quickly as they come.

But if *Marius and Sulla* ends on a cynical footnote, this hardly makes up for a great deal of extremely naïve matter in the body of the play. The later Grabbe would realize that no hero functions in a historical vacuum, that no action is divorced from a multiplicity of other actions. The early Grabbe, in contrast, seems to suggest that while the hero rides high, he is a supreme, autonomous force constituting the one and only key to historical developments; the spirit of the age speaks with his imperious voice. *Marius and Sulla* is permeated with a respect for heroism which Grabbe was soon to qualify by the knowledge that heroes are all too mortal and in no sense divorced from the complexities of the time in which they live. Only in Marius—and in the Sulla of the final scene—does Grabbe approximate that latter attitude.

Grabbe's notes leave little doubt that the many separate episodes of *Marius and Sulla* were intended to depict persuasively the chaotic mess which once-great Rome had become. But the illustration pattern leaves much to be desired; individual episodes sacrifice historical insight for immediate dramatic effect; far too often Grabbe tries to devise interludes of horror so as to demolish with a vengeance any idyllic notions one might have about the distant past; one's reaction to the play is clouded by misgivings about a writer prone to relish evocations of carnage. The play's panoramic content encompasses the leading factions of Roman politics as well as the host of external powers threatening Rome, but the context of these forces is largely missing. Rather, historical complexity gives way to the simplification that events are born only in the matrix of lurid violence. Quite plainly, a good deal of this is history melodramatized by a writer fascinated with personalities devoid of conscience. Not to be dismissed, however, in Grabbe's first episodic play are adumbrations of maturer work. As later, he dramatizes history to show how it precludes by its terrible nature any belief in transcendental value. Some of his scenes, though sensationalistic, are quite effective in getting across an utterly cynical vision of history as a barbarous process; and one must say that if there is sickness here, there is also imaginative brilliance. Most important, in *Marius and Sulla* Grabbe breaks radically with the classical-idealistic tradition; this time his hero is not an overemotional idealist, but a realist so cold and hard as to repel civilized taste. The change of hero is in fine accord with the report we have of Grabbe as a man intent on throttling within himself an uncontrollable emotional element.

The two Hohenstaufen dramas which Grabbe completed in 1828,

as well as *Don Juan and Faust* (1829) and *Jest, Satire, Irony, and Deeper Meaning* (1827), are by no means of secondary importance; but they do not give us that fusion of historical awareness and episodic form which links the Grabbe of *Marius and Sulla* to his best work. Still, in the intervening plays, Grabbe's basic attitudes are conspicuously in evidence; in *Kaiser Friedrich Barbarossa* and *Kaiser Heinrich the VI* he attempts to indicate that leaders are particles of forces which radiate far beyond their immediate selves; in these plays he is concerned with stressing the impersonal nature of what would strike many as essentially personal struggles. "The *I* serves as exponent whereby an age renders judgment upon itself." So Wiese phrases Grabbe's belief that the individual merely executes historical necessity; and historical necessity, as Grabbe sees it, works itself invariably into patterns of authoritarianism, militarism, and nationalism, the same traits now linked automatically to the peculiar course of German history. Though Grabbe himself was eager for military service and sang the glories of battle in more than one play, he was not unaware that this is only half the story: the lamentations of war's victims always constitute a realistic footnote to jingoistic speeches.

The Hohenstaufen dramas are flooded with rhetoric and are not devoid of comic-strip heroics, but it would again be unfair to overlook those moments which afford glimpses of Grabbe's final vision. All sorts of romantic fantasies are deflated by hard facts. Heinrich VI, for example, falls dead at the very moment he asserts his aim to mount the sky above and to extend his hegemony to the vast dark continent of Africa. Barbarossa's grandiose plans lead him straight to oblivion; and Heinrich the Lion is only too anxious to find sanctuary in the grave from eighty years of what he calls "bloodpounding." The extent to which royal pomp is simply one big lie is brought out also in a scene far from court. It takes place in a field and gives a casual conversation between a master and slave. The slave, awed by the power of Heinrich VI, voices anxieties about the new regime to be imposed by the Kaiser. His master tells him not to worry—long after the Kaiser has vanished from the earth, the sheep will still be herded in and out with regularity.[13] The world goes on in spite of its leaders, who are far less important than the fear inspired by them would suggest; one should be awed only by time's ceaseless continuity.

Grabbe's last phase begins with *Napoleon* (1831). Once and for

[13] "THE SLAVE: 'How terrible is the Kaiser.' THE MASTER: 'He'll die—Our crops will always grow back.—Drive out the sheep!'" *Ibid.*, p. 310.

all he leaves behind the classical rhetoric which makes parts of his Hohenstaufen so unreadable today; and he settles upon the episodic structure. From now on, language as well as form will serve to give his dramas a strikingly modern tone and make him, along with Büchner, an anticipator of Brechtian theater in particular and twentieth-century realistic drama in general.

A year before he wrote *Napoleon* Grabbe remarked that Napoleon was smaller than the Revolution from which he emerged. This would seem to invite the idea that Grabbe's play was not intended as an out-and-out heroization of Napoleon, and critics have understandably taken pains to note the Emperor's shortcomings. Some have gone so far as to sum up Napoleon exclusively by what he lacks, to assert that Grabbe has given us a misguided egoist pathetically out of touch with reality. There may be a danger here of trivializing Grabbe's best historical play on the basis of secondary evidence; for a reading of the play without preconceptions makes clear that Grabbe extended to Napoleon a level of respect no other character in the play approximates; and even in defeat at Waterloo, he remains a fateful presence. Still, he achieves little; his fate is merely to be another visionary whose gifts history was in no mood to appropriate. As with Marius, time itself is his affliction—as well as something in the nature of man which is at odds with greatness. In *Napoleon* and *Hannibal* Grabbe hopes to show, above all, that the heroic will personified by exceptional natures is bound to be stultified by the quality of human life in general, that same human life which begins to deteriorate the moment it is deprived of the powerful leader; the relationship between history and hero turns out to be a paradox which Grabbe can see no way of getting around.

Napoleon begins in a kind of whirl. All sorts of people, of a variety of social and political allegiances, collect under the arcades of the Palais Royal and make the stage resound with a crossfire of comment. There are those who remember the Revolution with nostalgia; those who hate the Revolution as much as they despise Napoleon; those who live for his return; and those who have become part of the latest power structure and desire no more changes. Grabbe is trying to depict simultaneously two worlds—the world of yesterday, which centered around the brief efflorescence of the French Revolution and is now flickering out, and the new world in the process of developing, whose distinguishing marks seem to be displacement and disillusion. More than anything else, Grabbe impresses upon us in this first scene the reality of a historical period coming to an end, and the mark it has left on those unfortunate enough to survive it.

An ex-soldier named Vitry cries out to his companion Chassecoeur: "Cheer up, Chassecoeur, the world is still with us—I hear her right now—up there on the second floor the noise is something awful."[14] It turns out that the noise and excitement stem from an argument of gamblers, and this will prove to be quite characteristic, for Grabbe is concerned with pointing out that the trivial can always be depended on to follow the momentous. The Revolution is dead, but gamblers continue to gamble.

The belief that the present exists to make the past trivial comes through in the dialogue of two barkers. One is announcing for a picture gallery in which portraits of the high and mighty are on display; the other advertises a peep show: "—The whole world can be seen right here, as she rolls and breathes." Grabbe makes a Brechtian point indeed when he has the two veterans look in vain for any picture of the torment of battle as they experienced it—an ironic comment on the divorce of art from life, in general, and from unpleasant life, specifically.

At any rate the general mood is an unhappy one, so much so in fact that one cannot help feeling the time is ripe for something, be it the return of Napoleon or a retrenchment of the present regime. Not that either alternative would make much difference in the long run; for as Vitry declares: "The waves of fate carry some aloft and hurl others to the bottom." Grabbe comes close here to the same conception of history's fickle impersonality that the young Büchner expressed in his letters.

Grabbe ends his scene most ironically, although the full implication of his device will not be apparent until much later. A Savoyard youth sings the following song:

> La marmotte, la marmotte
> Avec si, avec là etc. etc.

The youth has on him a marmot and a set of bagpipes, and his simple tune underlines the absurdity of the general commotion.

---

[14] *Grabbes Werke*, III, 155.

Grabbe's depiction of this commotion may strike some as artlessly reportorial; but this is to miss self-concealing art of a first order. Grabbe is a master at grouping clusters of individuals whose comments suggest the temper of a people. To visualize this first scene in directorial terms is to realize the exciting possibilities offered by its juxtapositions; repeatedly Grabbe exploits them to make pointed cynicism the dominant chord of an exchange of dialogue. A police officer tells the menagerie barker that he is insulting the King and his princess, to which the barker replies that this is hardly possible in view of the fact that he is exhibiting apes only. The menagerie barker's announcements coincide with the announcements of the gallery barker, and the implication is again that Louis XVIII and his entourage are at best interesting examples of animal life fit for a zoo. At a point when the mob is worked up over the possibility that Napoleon may have returned, the peep-show barker can only express concern for the damage done to his equipment. Grabbe always has time for such cynical footnotes; with rare exceptions he can allow no scene to go by without trying to rip something down. Thus, the appearance of the King in the gallery of the Tuileries provokes from two citizens a volley of derisive comments; and well justified their sarcasm seems to be once the King opens his mouth to display a very prosaic mind. All of this is set to a chorus of soulless sycophancy on the part of opportunistic emigrés.

Three scenes pass before we get our first glimpse of Napoleon. We quickly realize he is bound to be an improvement on what is now in charge of France. The only strong will in evidence resides in the Duchess of Angoulême, and she is reaction personified. Valid indeed seems one of Napoleon's first remarks, that when he was in action the world lived on deeds; now it subsists on memories. He goes on to voice his conviction that fate watched over his cradle and will do similar service at his grave. In a pensive mood at the beach of Elba, he wonders whether the mob is really worth it all. Only upon being convinced that stupidity rules France does he find reason to return. There is not enough here to allow a rounded judgment of the man, but it is quite clear that Grabbe has endowed Napoleon with a dimension of sensibility which sets him apart from every other character of the play.

If Napoleon's appearance puts us momentarily in a mood receptive of heroic value, Grabbe quickly makes certain that we snap out of it—so replete with cynical generalization is his second act. A young woman compares rulers to plants: new ones shoot up every year. Another woman reminds the veteran Vitry of a pledge of love; he replies that the women of his past have made about as much impression on him as the uncounted small change that has passed through his fingers. To swear eternal love has always been a joke to him.

In the streets of Paris, citizens continue to ventilate their disenchantments while the boy with the marmot keeps singing. Some kind of upheaval is bound to come, if only because the cries of the gutter will never be heard by France's present rulers, who remain unaware of the potent symbol Napoleon has become for the multitude. Ironically, while the mob seethes, the king hunts; the impending invasion must compete with sport as a topic of royal conversation. Napoleon's stature can only benefit from the self-deceptions in which his enemies are enmeshed; for them the exile at Elba is simply not worth trying to figure out because history gives no second chances to upstarts. Much more tough-minded is the appraisal of liberals who realize nothing can stop Napoleon's re-emergence, that they will soon enough have to cope with his disinclination to share power with anyone. But even they are at a loss when it comes to Napoleon's charisma; in the end this magnetic figure may choose to apply to the liberals the same hard rules they have applied to their own defeated enemies. For the liberals have no romantic notions about their rise as a political force; they are fully aware that the history of liberalism will, in the long run, be as much etched in blood as any ideology that lives by the sword.

In *Marius and Sulla* Grabbe had given evidence of his contempt for mob psychology. In the third act of *Napoleon* this contempt is driven home as never before. Once again a street-corner demagogue lights the match which fires a crowd of malcontents to act out the beastly fantasies of its momentary dictator. What words can paraphrase these:

JOUVE: Chop off that traitor of a tailor's fingers and stick them into your mouth as cigars of the nation!

MANY SUBURBANITES: . . . Over here with those fingers! Ach, he has only ten![15]

To say that Jouve is an opportunist is accurate but not sufficient. The object of his manipulations seems to be nothing less than the power to destroy at will. He may well symbolize absolute human

[15] *Ibid.*, p. 222.

alienation, but we miss much if we fail to realize he incarnates Grabbe's belief that the fund of human aggression is as irreducible as the push of history is irreversible. Nothing is sacred to this aggression; everything exists only to be rent asunder. Like Büchner, Grabbe discerns in human nature a horrifying demonism, a destructiveness so innate it will always make progress a refinement of the art of murder.

It is not accidental that Grabbe gives us back to back a scene in which Jouve expresses his desire to stretch Napoleon's neck and the scene of Napoleon's return. Grabbe is intent upon impressing on us that the glory of the Emperor's return is only half the story; the other half lies in the unpredictable area of human instinct. While Napoleon triumphs, Jouve seethes.

Napoleon himself is a strange mixture. He appears snobbishly anti-democratic when he expresses contempt for the crowd below his window; an intelligent student of history, he declares that as potent historical forces, prayers and Jesuits are gone forever; a brilliant student of politics, he indicates that written guarantees are not worth the paper they take up if they mean nothing to the average citizen. At the same time, Grabbe implies on Napoleon's part an element of irresponsible belligerence. The Emperor realizes that his step-daughter has come up with an insight when she says he fights not for causes but simply for the sake of fighting.

Repeating the pattern which bridged his first two acts, Grabbe switches from a picture of Napoleon to a scene of generalized cynicism. The first scene of Act IV is very important: it shows us a supposedly great moment of history from the point of view of the total cynic. Grabbe hands the commentator's role back to Jouve, and he is at his vitriolic best, finding nothing to get enthusiastic about in Napoleon's ceremonious legislative enactments. When a woman declares that this is indeed a great moment, Jouve remarks that there are no great moments, only noisy ones. When the woman describes Napoleon's appearance as earnest and majestic, Jouve asserts this is nothing but a pose for public consumption, something worked out in conference with the actor Talma. After all, life *is* comedy.

It is hard not to hear Grabbe's own voice here, especially when the woman's remark that the Revolution is over prompts Jouve to declare that all endings imply new beginnings. This deliberate attempt to view things as unsentimentally as possible prompts Grabbe to subject the various parts of the royal announcement to Jouve's sarcastic annotations. As far as he is concerned, it is all old stuff with a new label.

Jouve rises to invidious heights indeed when to the woman's statement that Napoleon is a great man he adds that Napoleon knew how to raise himself on "our backs."

Jouve is not the only cynic Grabbe uses as a mouthpiece. As everyone rises to take the oath demanded by the occasion, the boy with the marmot sings his customary song. It is Jouve who takes him to task for trivializing a great moment: "The additions to the French nation's Charter are being sworn to here." To which the boy replies, "Nothing more than that?"

For the psychoanalyst who relates nihilism to inner aggression, Jouve is made to order. On the sanctity of oaths he has this to say: "Scaffolds and street lamps are far more effective." Only brute force works in a world without value. In truth, even those who seem to care about things really do not, and this is surely the point of the woman's preoccupation with an ostentatiously dressed maid-servant at the very moment when she should be participating in the general oath.

The last word of the scene is Jouve's, and if naked hostility can rise to heights through sheer force, it does so here:

THE LADY: The Kaiser is withdrawing. What enthralling music from the troops!

JOUVE: Madam, your arm?

THE LADY: With pleasure, my lord.

JOUVE (*to himself*): The perfidious coquette!— Perhaps, in the unplumbed depths of the earth there lurk black legions of hell who, upon breaking through to light, will extinguish once and for all this shameful tinsel? Or perhaps the day will come when comets with fire-red tails the size of mountains—but how could either the depths of the earth or the reaches of the stars get worked up over a miserable corruption-drunk swarm like this collection. (*Aloud.*) Let us go, madam.

One would be hard put to find in all of drama a scene in which nihilistic emotion is expressed so forcefully. Grabbe gives voice to a cynicism which consumes whatever comes into view, to a relativism which reduces all historical phenomena to a matter of mere appearances. As Jouve says, "It will soon be difficult to tell stage princesses apart from the real thing."

Grabbe admitted that nothing thrilled him as much as war. He proceeds to depict the fighting which finally ended Napoleon's career,[16] and one can sense his enthusiasm for the opportunities war affords to manliness. But, as always, his longing for heroism does not blind him to what is really going on at Waterloo. He shows the armies lined up to be composed of men in whom the forces that would explode in our own time are already at work, specifically, nationalism and racism. The German soldier waiting to fight Napoleon is resentful that his country does not yet have a place in the sun, and he is not without a scapegoat. A Jew by the name of Ephraim learns quickly that neither his German citizenship nor military status means anything to those who will not let him forget his ethnic origin. This Jew gets his head blown off fighting not the French but a fellow German soldier. Whatever Grabbe's motivation for writing such a scene, he cannot be accused of falsifying German social realities.

Napoleon becomes memorable once more with the post-mortem speech of its leading figure, who surveys ruefully the wreckage of all he stands for. Napoleon realizes too well that with his defeat no end to tyranny will come; the world will remain the parasitic place it is. Appearances will change, but that is all; the mass of mankind will not be free. Mediocrity will rule until the day when the vacuum will once more be filled with power. In the most memorable speech Grabbe gave Napoleon, one senses both a cynical conception of man's potential and a mystical conception of history's need for the great leader. Unsuccessful as Grabbe is in his efforts to bring the panorama of Waterloo to the stage, he is successful in making Waterloo symbolize the moment our age really began.

In spite of its title, *Napoleon* is not a heroic play; and in spite of the way Grabbe avoids making Napoleon a conventional hero, it is easy to fall into the error of expecting conventional characterization. "What, after all, does Napoleon stand for?" one critic has asked. Does he return as tyrant or liberator? Actually, Grabbe is trying to demolish the idea of a single Napoleon; such a Napoleon would indeed be the wax-works dummy Grabbe has been accused of fashioning. There are as many Napoleons as there are occasions for their appearance. There is the man of action who can manage affairs of state with brilliant dispatch; the cynical pessimist who knows he does

---

[16] Grabbe very likely learned a great deal about the art of treating war in episodic drama from *Richard III* and *Henry V*. Like Shakespeare, he shifts panoramically from one enemy camp to the next in order to show us what is on the minds of both military leaders and ordinary soldiers.

not call all the shots; the egoist hungry for greatness; the ultimate realist who thinks from facts only; the democrat; the snob; the philosopher—might it not be reasonable to assume that Grabbe attributed to human personality the same patchwork construction he saw in everything else? If history is a maddening flux, would not the great man, who is in some unique relationship to this flux, have to be uniquely plastic? Just as Grabbe pictures the spirit of a nation as a spectrum of intellectual and emotional reactions, so he pictures the personality of a great leader as a spectrum of adaptations and postures. Grabbe was well aware that in the modern world adaptation would be barely distinguishable from pose.

The importance of *Napoleon* was not recognized until recently. It certainly did not make enough of an impression on Marcuse to change his opinion of Grabbe as a dramatist of scenes who gives intensity without substance. Grabbe has been taken to task for crude, studied effects in his mob scenes. Nieten's view was that Grabbe wrote a dissociated play which begins as milieu drama and ends on the battlefield, with the unfortunate result that his central thesis gets lost. Nieten also joined the chorus of those who found the battle scenes theatrically unfeasible. Above all he felt that if Grabbe intended the logic of events themselves to be the hero of *Napoleon,* he failed, for this does not come through. Other critics have given the play short shrift in the manner of Eloesser, who feels it is not enough for a dramatist to bring us into the street.

Surely the emergence of Brecht has something to do with the revaluation of Grabbe by Höllerer, Jahn, and Martini, among others. Looking backward, it is hard not to single out *Napoleon* as one of the most significant episodic plays of the nineteenth century. Like Brecht, Grabbe uses the episodic structure to say something about the nature of the modern world, and like Brecht, he makes the episodic structure a perfect mold for his own peculiar way of seeing things. There is so much in *Napoleon* that is worth noting that one can hardly sympathize with the view that the work fails because it lacks an over-all integrating idea.

Grabbe's point is that history is literally a brutal farce; that beneath the trappings of progress it is always the same old world; that man is at the mercy of demonic forces; that each of us is an incorrigible egoist; that people do not talk to but *at* each other; that pure instinct is eternally waiting to explode into primitive behavior; that the modern age will have to cope with the dynamics of mass action; and, most prophetically, that the modern age will be characterized by the interplay of so many forces as to make life nightmarishly chaotic.

Implications of this vision, which one only melodramatizes by calling "dark," are frequent enough in all of literature. But it is rare to find a dramatist who will resist diminishing its horrible essence as strongly as Grabbe did. Büchner comes to mind, but there is a world of difference between him and Grabbe, a difference of emotional temperature which will make Grabbe unpalatable long after Büchner has become an established classic.

Napoleon recalls Shakespeare, the *Sturm and Drang*, and Grabbe's first historical play, but it fully deserves the recognition given it as a truly original work. Like Lenz, Grabbe enriches his drama with implication by such techniques as episodic reinforcement, scenic juxtapositions, and generalized commentary. Unlike Lenz, he knows exactly what he is doing and does not try to make *Napoleon* say something at odds with the dominant effect. Napoleon's final observations only serve to reinforce the pessimism and cynicism which pervade the entire play.

The way Grabbe links up his scenes in *Napoleon* produces an overwhelming panoramic effect. From moment to moment we jump to the various power centers of France, and the swift transitions of atmosphere create an almost kaleidoscopic effect, Grabbe stopping only long enough for us to get the feel of another place, another pocket of ambition or discontent, another seat of forces. Aristotle is left behind, first of all, because Grabbe feels history is made not in one single place but whenever men are ready to go into action, or wherever they are content to do nothing.

Much more radically than Lenz, Grabbe splits the action of his play into units which are independent of a dominating plot line. Anticipating Büchner, he makes the scene in front of us hang together by its own intrinsic dynamism and by its presentation of action that is immediately significant. The *Guckkastentechnik* is refined in the direction of maximum exposure, and the exposure is achieved in scenes which are not designed to milk suspense from what would seem to be potentially a very suspenseful situation. Instead of making Napoleon's impending arrival an omnipresent key to action, Grabbe handles most scenes in a way which suggests Napoleon's importance without overdramatizing it. Essentially each episode is a slice of life which tells us what the French were thinking at a crucial period of their history, or, to be more precise, what the French were feeling, even though Grabbe may well have gone out of his way at times to indicate the glorious emotions they were *not* feeling in the least.

Scenes commence with jarring abruptness and conclude quite desultorily as Grabbe makes the very linear outlines of his actions communicate dissonance. Like Büchner, he combines scenes whose implications complement one another in order to avoid distortion by omission. Napoleon speaks for Grabbe when he suggests that the view from his chair does not take in all that is going on. Invariably, Grabbe pulls us out into the street to remind us that the rhetorical postures of "important" men mean very little by themselves.

In the street scenes we do not get one action so much as a multiplicity of actions—Grabbe proceeding to create a mosaic of dialogues. To the front of the stage comes whichever little group Grabbe wishes us to see in action, and in a matter of moments the group dissolves back into the crowd. Some idea of the effect Grabbe hoped to create with these scenes may be gauged by his quite simple stage directions:

(Beneath the arcades of the Palais Royal. Huge crowds surging about in confusion, among them citizens, officers, soldiers, charlatans, youthful chimney sweeps, and others. Those who speak remain in the foreground.)

Lenz's use of language to suggest gesture was integral to his approach to theater. Grabbe, too, employs language in this fashion. In the street scenes, especially, it is difficult not to visualize the expressions and postures which spoken words suggest. The most obvious examples would be the lines assigned to the two barkers in the first scene of the play; no director would have any trouble discerning that Grabbe imagined them grossly exaggerating with their faces and bodies the boisterous attitudes they are so hucksterishly trying to project. Just as gesturally suggestive is Chassecoeur's brief reminiscence of the crossing of the Bersina:

Bersina! Ice and the shudders of death!—I was there too—this must be seen! *(He goes to a window of the peep show.)* My God, how wretched! Vitry, take a look![17]

---

[17] *Grabbes Werke,* III, 158.

Many more examples could be listed. The fact is that Grabbe, like Lenz, wants theater to make an immediate impression, not to come alive principally through developments of plot punctuated by climactic speeches. Though Grabbe is often taken to be antitheatrical, he is not really. His handling of some of the most minor action of *Napoleon* shows him to be very much aware of the interactions possible between audience and actors on a level independent of literary contexts.

The Hohenstaufen suffered from the forced quality of dialogue which was often versified quite mechanically. This artificiality is gone in *Napoleon*. Here Grabbe writes some of the most striking dramatic prose in the history of German theater. Like Brecht, he sheds the linguistic habits which, perhaps more than any other factor, explain the resistance of the modern reader to much of classical drama. Like Brecht, he seems to have been nourished by the strong phrasings of the Lutheran Bible, which stimulated him to make his own compromise between the language of everyday life and stage language. As it is, Grabbe's dialogue may often catch something of the careless and telegraphic quality of ordinary speech under pressure, but it is not naturalistic. Like Lenz's dialogue, it is designed to convey inner agitation when there is such agitation and in general to come through with a vividness and directness which bespeaks a minimum of literary stylization. But it is stylized nonetheless to reinforce Grabbe's general view that history is a maelstrom of quickly passing events occurring in anything but a related, logical fashion. Choppy dialogue indicates each person is spinning around on his own treadmill, that human speech is far more an outlet for aggression than communication. Following the lead of the *Sturm und Drang*, Grabbe frequently reduces a portion of dialogue to one or two exclamations which it takes the speaker no more than a moment to get out. It may not be inaccurate to say that Grabbe's characters spit out their dialogue:

A GENDARME: Peep-show man, get out of here—you're making a tumult—

THE BARKER: I praise the King.

THE GENDARME: Then you need blacken no one else—get!

PEOPLE: Wonderful! Long live the police!

AN OLD OFFICER: Chassecoeur![18]

---

[18] *Ibid.*, p. 160.

Grabbe's dialogue is not always swift or adrenalized, but it is always crisp and concise, and when a character gives utterance to the kind of pithy observations or memorable aphorisms which are sprinkled throughout the play, it seems entirely natural. In fact, after a while we begin to expect striking words or phrases, so casually does Grabbe have recourse to vivid expressions. Napoleon, for example, refers to Austria as a worm which jerked convulsively in his hand; a marquis refers to the French people as proliferated cattle, and Vitry refers to two emigrants in a burst of disparaging metaphor which is worth repeating:

Both those emigrés! What coattails, what cheek pouches, what obsolete French faces and ideas, what specters from the good, old, and very ridiculous days![19]

Another aspect of Grabbe's dialogue has not received enough attention. Perhaps Büchner learned something about dialogue not only from Lenz but from Grabbe as well. Certainly the following extract suggests Grabbe may have dipped into the edition of Lenz which Tieck brought out:

SUBURBANITES AND OTHERS: Ha! Blood! Blood! Look, look, look, there it flows, there it flames—brain, brain, there it spurts, there it smokes—how magnificent! How sweet![20]

The use of repetitious, incantatory prose to expose the horrible blood-lust of men who delight in killing—this is bound to bring to mind Lenz's technique of using such prose to expose mental eccentricities. Grabbe's lack of illusion regarding man's inner potentialities has never been more evident. And this is a writer who felt close to Schiller!

Every once in a while *Napoleon* is punctuated by a song. There is the song of the boy with the marmot, the song of the people of St. Antoine, the song of Napoleon upon his return to his room

[19] *Ibid.*, p. 165.
[20] *Ibid.*, p. 221.

in the Tuileries, the song of a major and rifleman before battle, the song of a regiment approaching combat, etc. Sometimes one feels Grabbe employs song in order to vary the pace of the play, to give his audience much-needed relief from his adrenalized dialogue; but principally his songs imply a comment on the artificiality of human speech. One is left with the impression that all of speech is so much noise, that in song man is in closer relationship to the undercurrents of his own nature. Aside from this, Grabbe invests song with the kind of sinister overtones perceptible in both of Büchner's tragic plays; large blocks of cacophonous or meaningless dialogue enclose bits of melodic verse that serve to give a frightening hint of life's demonic nature.

Grabbe wished above all to depict a chaotically misrelated world in which nothing happens to validate anything else. Events merely happen, and one lies if one groups them together in any pattern which confirms our need for a reassuring logical sequence. Certainly the rules propounded by Aristotle cannot be taken seriously by a dramatist with Grabbe's violent distaste for preconceived epistemologies. Seeing life as bits rather than a whole, he pours into *Napoleon* whatever helps him to communicate a fragmented vision of existence. The loose episodism of this drama makes room for both the vulgarities of the rabble and the dignifications of the high and mighty; the visionary rhetoric of Napoleon and the commercial barkings of the showman; the pomposities of the royal and the simplicities of the low born; the poetic recitations at court and the songs sung in the gutter. One could easily go on to show what a quantity of disparate detail fills *Napoleon.*

In an early play Grabbe had made the point that the very things which we take with the utmost seriousness are truly the most laughable. In *Napoleon* he makes that point in a variety of ways, most unforgettably with the character who is very likely the most minor character of the play. The boy with the marmot has almost nothing to say; he merely shows up a couple of times in the play to sing the same old song. But it should not escape notice that the youth sings his song first under the kingship (I,1;II,2), next during the anarchical transition between the kingship and empire (II,2), and then at the oath-taking ceremonies presided over by Napoleon. In each case the unconcerned singing of the boy breaks strangely into an atmosphere charged with human activity to suggest that no matter how man may organize his life it will always be quite meaningless.

Like Lenz and Büchner, Grabbe does not hesitate to resort to caricature at the same time that he attempts to give an honest picture of a particular social atmosphere. The nobility appears grotesque indeed when we see its members preoccupied with proprieties of dress and decorum and anxious at a time of national crisis about nothing so much as considerations of status. It seems that this class can feel anguish only at the thought that the times may make it possible for an ordinary man to come into social contact with one of them: "Ach, the good old days—the smart, elegant salons of that time—now teeming with common cattle."

If we take comments such as this one and place them beside far more intelligent ones made by less ridiculous characters, we come to realize that *Napoleon* is not at all to be summed up as a nihilistic play with overtones of hero worship. A play may say much more than is suggested by its dominant implication. It is too easy to overlook that Grabbe does make distinctions and judgments in the course of *Napoleon* which link him not only to the nihilistic Brecht but to the socially conscious Brecht as well. For again and again Grabbe makes it clear that he is sickened by the self-assurance of aristocrats who see things only in terms of their petty self-interests; he points out that behind patriotic postures and chauvinistic glorifications there is a reality of suffering which only those who suffer will remember; and he makes us conscious of how much sham and self delusion is implied by our acceptance of things as they are. Like Brecht, Grabbe makes us feel that life is bitter hell for most people unlucky enough not to have a slice of the pie.

Brecht was to champion a drama of conditions. Grabbe lays claim to no reformist zeal; in fact he had little but contempt for those who took to heart the worsening political situation of his own day. But Grabbe, like Brecht, knows how easy it is for what is happening upon the stage to shift our minds away from ugly facts. Repeatedly, he has characters give voice to emotions which define how utterly painful the facts of the French Revolution and its aftermath must have been to those who lived through them. Long after we have forgotten the power machinations which run through *Napoleon,* we remember the powerful reactions of ordinary people to great events. Sometimes the reaction is as cryptic as it is fierce, and sometimes it is quite elaborate, as in the case of the Old Milliner, who bristles at the fact that only she knows how much history her "decayed, old" table symbolizes:

THE OLD MILLINER: Respect it, man! This table is classic—on this spot fell first the spark which ignited the world. Here I sat on the twelfth of July of the year seventeen hundred eighty-nine, in the afternoon about half past three; it was sunny and, still young and gay, I sold a bride from St. Marceau a few little things. We joked about the price and thought of nothing but the wedding day. Then in came a man with wild flowing locks, fiery eyes, heart-shattering voice—it was Camille Desmoulins—tears were in his eyes, he pulled out of his pocket two pistols and shouted: "Necker is dismissed, another Bartholomew's night is upon us, take arms and choose cockades, so that we can recognize one another." And since then, he, as well as the mighty Danton and terrible Robespierre, have gone to the guillotine; since then, the Kaiser has shone upon the earth with such radiance that one had to shield one's eyes, and he, too, has vanished like a will-o'-the-wisp; three of my sons have been taken by battle—much, much blood and countless sighs the Revolution has cost me, but it has only become that much dearer to me for all that—and it was at this table that I read the most important newspapers!—Yes, that is my last and only pleasure![21]

   This speech embodies principles of dramaturgy evident throughout *Napoleon*. Perhaps most obvious is that the old woman is only an excuse for Grabbe to make a point that he could not seem to make often enough—that exciting events soon work themselves into depressing aftermaths. The subordination of character to comment is one way Grabbe makes *Napoleon* resonate with cynical despair. Almost every character at some point of the action speaks the dramatist's bitter insights; only the truly stupid fail to see how horrible things really are. For Grabbe, to be intelligent is to be realistic, and to be realistic is to be cynical with a vengeance.

   Grabbe's aim to put things in vividly concrete terms, to avoid above all the abstract, bloodless renderings of history which for him constituted the perversion of history—this too can be glimpsed in the old woman's speech. Her narration is replete with concrete description, from the trivial commercial transaction in which she was engaged at the start of the Revolution, to the vivid picture she gives of the excited Camille Desmouslins, to the blood and sighs that the Revolution has exacted from her. Grabbe reminds us with remarkable conciseness of Robespierre's Reign of Terror and reminds us as well of the continuous carnage which the Revolution commenced; not only the high and mighty were swept into oblivion, but the low and anonymous had their families exterminated and their lives despoiled.

[21] *Ibid.*, pp. 166–67.

Although *Napoleon* is ostensibly about the hundred days before the Emperor's end, it is as much a play about the French Revolution. As in the Milliner's lines, Grabbe infuses much of the dialogue with the regrets, reminiscences, disappointed hopes and hostilities which that cataclysmic event inspired in every variety of Frenchman. It is to Grabbe's credit that he gets across to his reader that no matter what complications the Napoleonic interlude is in for, the events of 1789 will continue to exert an irresistible, pervasive influence. In this case the acute historian proved more insistent than the passionate cynic.

By the time the final episode of *Napoleon* has unfolded, it is quite clear that for Grabbe concreteness does not imply simplicity, at any rate not the kind of simplicity which would allow us to reduce Napoleon's downfall to a specific material cause; for Grabbe takes pains to invest *Napoleon* with an overriding sense of fatalism, to suggest that it is laughably simplistic to say, for example, "Napoleon lost because of the Battle of Waterloo," or "Napoleon lost because he could not come to terms with a new age." Napoleon lost, Grabbe suggests, for the same reason he once won, for the same reason a bright star is dead by the time we see it, for the same reason any force in the universe builds up powerfully prior to its inevitable dissipation. The commotion of crowds surging through Paris, the formulation of policy by royalty in chamber, the ceremonious enactment of weighty legislation—these, Grabbe suggests, constitute a mere smoke screen behind which some inscrutable force operates by its own unstoppable momentum. There is little doubt that what fascinates Grabbe is the vast mechanism of history, which makes use of a great man for a while and then consigns him to the scrapheap. Grabbe's achievement is that he does not make Napoleon's fate ultimately a function of tangible factors; he sees all tangible factors themselves under the sway of inexorable dark forces which play with human and territorial destinies. If history favors anything, it is the conglomerate mass, never the highly individuated hero.

In *Napoleon* Grabbe anticipates Brecht by virtue of the relationship he sets up between drama and audience. Emotional identification between spectator and character there is almost nil, if for no other reason than Grabbe's abrupt changes of scene; but even if the scenes were sustained longer, there would be little identification with characters who generally come through as marionettes tied to a single emotional string. Perhaps it is right to attribute the stereotypy of characterization in *Napoleon* to Grabbe's imitation of puppet theater. At any rate, when Grabbe is not deliberately grotesque and caricatural, he is usually cool enough for us to sense objectively what is going on. The result is that we experience *Napoleon* very much the way we experience a Brecht play, conscious as we are that everything happening in front of us illustrates a certain attitude toward life in general, that the dramatist takes greater pains to share his cynical perception than to communicate a moving experience, that he wants us to see through what he sees through.

In *Hannibal* (1834) Grabbe remains fatalistic, but with a difference. Here the episodic structure is once more adopted, and the play is divided into sections rather than acts, each one with a legend which identifies broadly the subject to be dramatized, e.g., I. *Hannibal ante Portas;* III. *Departure from Italy;* V. *King Prusias.* By the time we finish *Hannibal* we have once again seen a great man shunted aside by the forces which determine history, but much more than in *Napoleon* do we experience a sense of avoidability. For in *Hannibal,* Grabbe, like Brecht, goes out of his way to pinpoint the fact that society's day-to-day life centers around preoccupations with making money. Again like Brecht, Grabbe indicates that a society where money is king cannot survive. Hannibal is less the victim of history than of commercial greed.

The acquisitive impulse dictates the behavior of Carthage's citizens to the point of sheer madness. Threatened by Rome, they have only one man who can save them from brutal extinction. But Hannibal is of less concern to them than the next expected caravan. They have lost the capacity to respond to any cause that does not promise immediate enrichment. Too late, they snap out of their greedy pursuits; too late, they decide to stop trading and start fighting; they are plowed under by Rome, which makes sure that Hannibal does not survive his people.

A scene-by-scene analysis of *Hannibal* would show Grabbe working very much the way he did in *Napoleon*. Almost every scene is quite brief, and the action of one scene may unroll in a place removed by an ocean from the place of the previous or following scene. As in *Napoleon,* the effect is panoramic as we go from Carthage to Rome, from Rome to Capua, as we observe Hannibal planning his latest move, the Roman Senate debating, and the citizens of Carthage increasing their commercial wealth. Again Grabbe gives us the life of a society in motion, makes a vivid transcription of the texture of what goes on in the streets. Episodes constantly reinforce the point that ancient religious and military codes were designed to make the senseless taking of life a prime virtue. It seems that Grabbe wrote *Hannibal* to prove once more that he, unlike most of us, is not afraid to face up to the real truth of man's gruesome history.

The most noteworthy change revealed by *Hannibal* is in Grabbe's language. Lenz may well have affected Grabbe's final style at certain points, but the concise bitterness put into Hannibal's mouth is *sui generis*. Hannibal's speech is pregnant with incisive cynicism and mental toughness, with a hardness of heart Grabbe attributed to no other leader. He sums up his metaphysics with the statement "We can't fall out of the world—that's for sure. We're in it once and for all." Although he gives way momentarily to emotion at having to depart from Italy, he is never sentimentalized by Grabbe, who shows him to be in his way every bit as vicious as his enemies. An example of this would be the beginning of that same section where he softens at his last glimpses of the land he could not win:

HANNIBAL: Crucify the guides immediately!
BRASIDAS: They've only made a mistake, taking Casilinum for Casinum.
HANNIBAL: Makes no difference! Crucify![22]

Hannibal is literally a chamber of horrors. Babies are flung into fire, soldiers are crucified, one victim is suffocated in a box, and the stink of death is everywhere. It is only natural for Hannibal to manifest this in his speech: "That would now make for a tight, thick-as-stone cerement, drenched by the sun's blood. And now the sun sets as well, and all grows as dark as the grave."[23]

That vision of the world which Brecht was to face up to in his early work is very much the vision at the heart of *Hannibal*. Like Brecht, Grabbe puts into almost every episode material that illustrates how truly impossible the average human situation is. At all times he makes us aware that the vast majority of people who ever lived, lived only to be oppressed. Obsessed as he was with greatness, he could not overlook the implications of smallness; obsessed as he might be with striking postures, he could not hide from himself the truth that pain is pain no matter what appearances might suggest. When a character in *Napoleon* declares no art is worth a damn which cannot

[22] *Ibid.*, II, 353.
[23] *Ibid.*

reproduce agony, he is anticipating the observation of the Carthaginian who orders some Roman messengers crucified. He implies that even if they do not so much as utter a cry of pain or move a tormented muscle at their execution, it will hurt all the same. The fact that nothing can argue away the suffering life brings is underscored in all of Grabbe's work, and it is given memorable expression when a character in *Hannibal* orders the temples destroyed. To those who balk at desecrating holy objects, he replies that the gods seem perfectly able to tolerate damage done to their worshipers.

There is no climax to *Hannibal;* at best the final scene is an ironic footnote. Carthage is wiped out, and Hannibal must seek refuge with a king named Prusias, who is the very antithesis of the man who needs his help. Prusias is impossibly mannered; his sense of decorum is so overdeveloped that he banishes from his presence for twenty years an official who has sneezed publicly. This ridiculous fop, who lives in his own make-believe world, presumes to criticize Hannibal's battle tactics, but it takes very little to make him hand Hannibal over to his Roman pursuers. Prusias cannot help exploiting to the hilt the death of the great Carthaginian. All his life his aesthetic fantasies have clamored for the chance to play funeral with a great man. He covers Hannibal's corpse with his coat, making sure that the garment is wrinkle free. His subjects burst into applause, and in this ridiculous setting Hannibal fades from view. Unlike Napoleon, he does not have the last word. In none of the enormous number of episodes which comprise Grabbe's drama does he crystallize as effectively his conviction that life favors what is fake and mediocre and exposes greatness only to besmirch it.

Hannibal has an exotic atmosphere such as Grabbe aimed at in no other work. But its theme is hardly exotic. It may well be that Grabbe wrote here a play that is only too modern. For what destroys Hannibal? In a word, the profit motive. Grabbe hated the increasing commercialization of his day, and in *Hannibal* he states the issue quite bluntly: either the commercial spirit or the heroic spirit—you can't have both. When we realize that for Grabbe the heroic spirit is synonymous with the totalitarian spirit, we can break his dichotomy down to capitalism versus autocracy. The final choice is between scum and Führer. Is it any wonder Grabbe has so long been a prophet without honor in Germany?

As interesting as *Hannibal* is for the tragic overtones with which Grabbe invests the futile quest of the great leader in a banal world, the play is less relevant to modern epic technique than *Napoleon*. Going back to the world of *Marius and Sulla,* Grabbe once more occupies himself with those customs and habits of ancient life which lend themselves to sensationalistic presentation. If anything, the illustration pattern is too obvious, as Grabbe fills scenes with unsavory details to make his point that Carthage is a moneyed cesspool. As in Wedekind's final plays, a note of self-pity is unmistakable. There is more sadness than cynicism here.

Up to his death Grabbe employed epic technique. In his final play, *The Hermann Battle* (1838), he uses episodic freedom to write in dramatic form a veritable epic of the first union of ancient German tribes. There is always a deliberate homeliness in Grabbe's depiction of the lower elements, but this technique is most pronounced in this last play. For Grabbe wished to portray a people with no national spirit but with lots of appetite for salami and wine. Much more than in any other historical drama, Grabbe depicts here the concrete aspects of historical developments, and this includes the rainy climate, the perilous terrain, all the geographical and climatic factors which affected the day-to-day life of the Teutons. He even catalogs the foods carried in knapsacks. Aside from this, there is emphasis on local custom, idiosyncrasies of language, and folk habit to a degree which makes the life of these forest-dwellers come alive with a remarkable vividness, which makes us feel with our senses what it must have been like to live in a jungle of rocks and trees, with oppressive moisture, unseasonal colds, dense thickets, and threatening hillocks. In a way, Grabbe gives us the archetypal jungle.

Grabbe does not romanticize the ancient Germans. In scene after scene he shows them to be the deficient human material which their leader Hermann realizes they are too late. They are barbaric to the core, stupidly shortsighted, and every word they speak reveals their savage nature. Their language has a rough guttural quality, a gruff abruptness, a harsh, clipped rhythm which seems the ultimate in linguistic dehumanization. Not that one has to listen to them talk to know their nature; they give themselves away by their delight in the impromptu execution, and their leader has to restrain them from ripping out the tongues of their prisoners.

The Hermann Battle may not strike us as relevant to modern epic theater. But surely what comes out here is *emotionally* relevant to what came out in all of Grabbe's earlier work. Eric Bentley has commented on the attraction which Brecht's work holds for individuals with strong aggressions.[24] It is this writer's contention that Grabbe speaks most persuasively to the same kind of individual. In *The Hermann Battle* the psychic pressures which one finds present in everything Grabbe wrote come out most uninhibitedly. Significantly, Grabbe chooses as the locale of his last play a dark hermetic place where the civilized superego is yet to be born. Here aggression is the very spirit of life and dictates almost every word or action. Here Grabbe can present more bluntly than ever his view of man as mere beast.

In his last play Grabbe is once more out to paint a picture of a particular time in such a way that he cannot be accused of sentimentalizing anything or of making anything abstract. Once again he is deliberately harsh and choppy and caustic at every opportunity. The general run of man is, as usual, presented as scum. Here again a leader is fighting a losing battle, even if his side does enjoy an occasional victory. *The Hermann Battle* says little that is new, but what it does say, it says with a ferocity that may well be available only to those driven by pathological aggressions. More than any other, this play makes pertinent the reputation of Grabbe's psychopathology, his violent anti-Semitism, his belief in nothing but the rightness of his contempt for common mankind.

Any evaluation of Grabbe's importance must include the fact that his episodic plays imply by their structure and content an answer to the question "What is history?" Grabbe's answer is that history is definitely not a transcendental moral pattern building up to some kind of higher synthesis or integration. The Schillerian approach made no impression on Grabbe, whose history plays illustrate by their form that nothing leads up to anything new, that history crystallizes discontinuously; closest to the truth of history would be that transcription which conveyed by its rhythms and interruptions the very nature of that discontinuity. This Grabbe achieves with his episodic structure. Episodism is more than a dramatic device; it is, as in Büchner's *Danton's Death,* the theatrical manifestation of a metaphysical attitude. It was Grabbe's genius to make what happens within his scenes in *Napoleon* reinforce the attitude implied by their chaotic alternation. The shifting groups that traverse his stage are as cut off from one another as the larger events which subsume them. For Grabbe, history is incoherent and man inconsequential.

With Grabbe, episodic theater strikes a completely new tone. Lenz,

---

[24] *Seven Plays by Bertolt Brecht,* ed. Eric Bentley (New York: Grove Press, 1961), p. xv.

for all his sophistications, did not try what Grabbe felt he was doing, creating an entire world upon the stage. In Lenz's plays aggression sometimes breaks through quite strikingly, as in the case of the Major, but in general Lenz restrains himself from striking sparks in the night. With Grabbe, this restraint is gone; the open structure is exploited for all the violent and ironic effects it can carry, for all the vivid life that can be squeezed into it, for all the incongruous actions it can encompass. Such a proliferation of actions as Grabbe gives us makes Lenz seem a modest theatrical rebel indeed.

But the link between Lenz and Grabbe is secure enough. Like Lenz, Grabbe uses the episodic structure not only to fit in relevant social material which a tighter structure would exclude but also to expose persuasively the hypocrisy and parasitism which rule society. Like Lenz, Grabbe shifts around with an eye open for grotesquery, and scene after scene adds to the impression of a world energized by base motivation. Character is as fixed in Grabbe as it was in Lenz, even if Lenz by and large restricts himself to the world of the bourgeoisie and aristocracy while Grabbe moves through every sector of society.

Both Grabbe and Lenz give us patterns rather than plots, repetition and reinforcement rather than progression and development, illustration and demonstration rather than action. Both rely heavily on irony; both are alive, as Büchner shall be, to those dissonances which life never resolves. One major difference between Lenz and Grabbe is that Grabbe makes less of an attempt to convince himself that life is not an absolute horror. When we remember that Schopenhauer came out with *The World as Will and Idea* less than a decade before Grabbe gave us *Gothland,* and that Büchner was tormented by the fatalism of history at about the same time Grabbe put this fatalism into *Napoleon,* we may well feel justified in saying that the change from Lenz to Grabbe reflects the darkening landscape of intellectual Europe.

The history of modern European realism in theater can be attacked from different angles. One can take the path that leads from France to Norway and back to France before reaching the Germany of the late nineteenth century. This is the conventional route, and it is by no means totally irrelevant to any modern realistic dramatist. But when one comes to Grabbe's realism, this tradition seems so incongruous that one is tempted not to view him as a realist at all. The picture would be far less confused if we realized that Grabbe, like Brecht, belongs to that tradition of theatrical realism which never lost sight of its *raison d'être*. Here realism as an attitude to life implies burning opposition to classicism and romanticism and for that matter to any idealized conception of life, any ism whereby ugly facts are sweetened into palatable illusions. Here the realist does not feel it incumbent on him to make believe that he, as a cynical observer of life, is somehow detached from the photographs he is taking. The inhibitions which characterize most realistic art are rejected with a vengeance by the epic realists, whose disgust, repugnance, hostility, and despair are the very building blocks of their drama.

Epic theater can in Grabbe's case be stretched to cover the actual blurring of the distinction between epic and drama. For Grabbe did not hesitate to put into his dramas extended descriptions of milieu and warfare which were even in his time reserved for the traditional epic. And he did not hesitate to go against the cultural assumption that drama was exclusively concerned with individual life, epic with collective life. Long before Brecht, German critics referred to Grabbe's drama as an epic-oriented drama. Their definition was perhaps more accurate than they realized, for Grabbe did bring to episodic theater that sensibility which we now generically call epic. Reading his *Napoleon* crowd scenes today, we cannot but marvel at their modernism, so alive was Grabbe to what could be done with a line of dialogue, a physical gesture, or a stage picture. And behind all his art there is a plateau of cynical detachment which became fashionable only in the art of our century. What dramatist has kept himself from us by more ironic distance than Grabbe? It may not in fact be an exaggeration to say that *Verfremdung* is the very spirit of his drama.

When we experience the action of a scene in a Brecht play, our reaction is hardly a simple one, and the same applies to Grabbe. At the same time that we respond to uproarious grotesquery, we are conscious of tragic overtones; while we laugh, we *know* that the implications of what is making us laugh should make us quite sad or angry. We realize that the dramatist is exaggerating to the point of caricature; still his characters are disturbingly real. Episode after episode shows what little basis exists for a high opinion of the human species, but rare is the scene that leaves us feeling the driving forces of life are not at bottom relished. Skillful blending of opposites is integral to the power of Brecht's art, and it was every bit as much to Grabbe's. Long before the sardonic playwright from Augsburg created a drama whose form is constantly set off against its content, Grabbe had done the same. Not that this diminishes Brecht's achievement; but it is rarely stressed how much he was anticipated by Grabbe. One wishes that critics who cannot overstate the importance of Büchner to German drama would at least recognize Grabbe's existence.

Perhaps what links Grabbe and Brecht most significantly is the nature of an inner conflict neither could resolve. Both viewed the world as grotesquely impossible. Brecht's solution was communism, but this never altered the nature of reality implied by his drama. Deep down Brecht may well have realized that absolutely nothing would ever materially change the parasitic quality of human life. Turning to Grabbe, we get an idea of his conflict from his powerful need to identify himself with Schiller rather than Shakespeare and his conviction that Schiller created with his spirit. The implication seems to be that Grabbe was very much for the spirit as against coarse materialisms. But he hardly lives up to this image; the truth of the matter is that with all his contempt for material reality, he realized bitterly that such contempt really had no basis. Like Brecht, he could not escape the conviction that material reality is all there is, that it makes irrelevant any outraged attitude one adopts toward it. Here, perhaps, is the ultimate source of that strange mixture of social concreteness and cynical detachment which entered German drama with the emergence of epic theater.

chapter three:

georg büchner

Easy as it may have been for Grabbe to praise Schiller, it was not at all easy for him to say something complimentary about that foreigner named Shakespeare. But one looks in vain for any Schillerian emphasis in Grabbe's best work comparable to that of Shakespeare. This reluctance on Grabbe's part to be truthful about his literary models was not shared by Georg Büchner, who grasped essentials of Shakespearian technique Grabbe never did. Büchner's admiration for Shakespeare is unqualified by ethnic considerations; it is, in fact, the kind of unstinted admiration that had been commonplace among the writers of the *Sturm und Drang*: " . . . still I console myself with the thought that with the exception of Shakespeare, all poets confront nature like schoolboys."[1]

This comment is taken from one of Büchner's letters to his family after his escape from the local police. In another letter, he puts Goethe in the same class with Shakespeare, but he never expressed in a letter how he felt about the dramatist who seems really to have affected him most, J. M. R. Lenz. His prose fragment on the last days of that hapless *Strum und Drang* genius is, therefore, all the more worthy of examination. If we go by the word of one critic,[2] however, *Lenz* is not at all a reliable guide to the aesthetic views of the man whose name gives the story its title; for one thing, the historical Lenz never made the statements per se that Büchner put into his mouth, and for another, the historical Lenz's views were actually at variance with the views of Büchner's Lenz.

Going to the text itself, we find that Büchner pictures Lenz an opponent of the idealism that was coming to the fore in the late eighteenth century; most of all, Lenz is said to object to those who would transfigure reality:

[1] Georg Büchner, *Werke und Briefe*, ed. Fritz Bergemann (Wiesbaden: Insel-Verlag, 1958), p. 390. All through his work one will be struck by the extent to which Büchner learned from Shakespeare. *Danton's Death* recalls *Hamlet*, *Woyzeck* has resonances of *King Lear*. Büchner was quite aware of what the *Stürmer und Dränger* missed totally: Shakespeare's art of creating poetic unities while seeming to exercise complete episodic freedom. Büchner was sensitive also to Shakespeare's way of underlining human suffering by monological intensification and tragicomic contrast. In fact, some scenes in Shakespeare, e.g., that of Cinna, the Poet, in *Julius Caesar*, and the Gravediggers scene in *Hamlet*, are the obvious models for similar scenes in *Danton's Death*. It is no exaggeration to say that Büchner discerned aesthetic refinements in Shakespeare's plays that were critically articulated only in our own time.
[2] A. H. J. Knight, *Georg Büchner* (Oxford: Basil Blackwell, 1951), p. 149.

Dear God has made the world as well as it should be, and we can hardly concoct something better; our sole endeavor should be to copy him a bit. I demand in everything: life, possibility of existence—and then it's good. And it is not for us to worry whether such art is beautiful or ugly. More decisive than both these criteria is the feeling that what has been created is alive. In artistic matters, it is all that matters.[3]

Only in Shakespeare and Goethe does Büchner's Lenz find art so alive: for all he cares, all other writers' works could be burned. Idealistic art "manifests the most disgraceful contempt for human nature." And Lenz goes on to say that with *The Tutor* and *The Soldiers* he had tried to show that art could work with the lowest materials, using as his characters extremely prosaic individuals who were no less human for all their ordinariness: "But in all human beings the vein of feeling is equally strong; only the shell through which it must break is sometimes thicker, sometimes thinner." All in all, Büchner makes Lenz an exponent of what may well be called humanitarian realism. For it is as necessary to be faithful to the actuality of things as it is necessary to love the humanity one depicts. *Liebe* and *Wirklichkeit* go hand in hand.[4]

No doubt, this is Büchner crystallizing his own aesthetic philosophy, and it is in accord with all the random observations on art and life strewn among his letters. But it is also a logical extension of much of what the historical Lenz said in his *Notes to the Theater*. True, literary idealism had not yet taken hold when Lenz wrote his essay; Schiller's classical period was still to come. But most of the fire Lenz directed against neoclassicism was prompted by his feeling that this movement subordinated living actuality to dead rules. What he admired about Shakespeare was the latter's creation of an enormous diversity of characters, all of whom pulse with the same blood. Like Büchner, he insisted that what is characteristic of life should be characteristic of art; art should not pursue ideals of beauty divorced from reality. Not a value judgment of Lenz's major critical work conflicts with what Büchner attributes to his semifictional re-creation. And is Büchner not correct to see *The Tutor* and *The Soldiers* as anti-idealistic works

[3] Büchner, *Werke und Briefe*, p. 94.
[4] "One must love humanity if one is to penetrate the specific being of everything; and one can understand all only when one allows no one to be too ugly or trivial; the most insignificant fact makes a deeper impression than the mere perception of the beautiful. . . . " *Ibid.*, p. 95.

grounded on the assumption that the fates of quite ordinary people
are compatible with great art?

Büchner was as fed up with the theater of his day as Brecht was
with contemporary escapist theater. Again, we know this through a
fictional intermediary, Camille of *Danton's Death*. He speaks with
Büchner's voice when he laments the insensitivity of theater audiences
to anything but imitations of the real thing, their thirst for melodrama
stiffly served up in the most blatant rhetorical style, and their lack
of intellectual sophistication which makes them overrate the commonplace served up ornately. This kind of *Rauschtheater* sickens Büchner,
and for the very reason he was always repelled by idealistic art: it
shifts man's attention from the wonders of the actual world, deadens
his responsiveness to what is really going on about him, makes him
in fact, afraid of the real world by habituating him to a meretricious
substitute. As far as Büchner was concerned, idealistic art was hostile
to life itself.

A key quotation which critics invariably set down on Büchner is
from a letter in which he reminds us less of Lenz than of Grabbe:

I felt as though I were crumbling to nothing beneath the ghastly fatalism
of history. I discern in human nature a frightful sameness, in the human
situation an inescapable power, bestowed on all and none. The individual
nothing but foam upon a wave, greatness sheer accident, the lordship
of genius a puppet show, a ridiculous struggle against an iron law—to
recognize this is the supreme achievement; there is no possibility of
controlling it.[5]

This is eloquent fatalism, but one should beware of making the
passage a summary of all that Büchner stood for, of overlooking the
social conscience behind the nihilistic exterior. In 1834, a year before
the composition of *Danton's Death,* that social conscience had im-
pelled Büchner to risk his life by surreptitious publication of *The
Hessian Courier,* a manifesto which minced nothing of his hatred
for rulers who feed on the resources of the ruled. Could the Büchner
of 1835 have changed that much, granted that he was perhaps the
most precocious young man of modern letters? Our own age should
by now have learned to distinguish between varieties of nihilism, for we

[5] *Ibid.*, p. 374.

have had genuine nihilists breathing down our very backs. Nonetheless, a modern critic calls Büchner "the most uncompromising nihilist of the nineteenth century."[6]

It has been credited to Büchner's cultural advantage that he lived at a time when classicism collapsed in France. The collapse of the French Revolution was an equally significant foreign development affecting Büchner's thought. For him, as for so many contemporaries, 1789 had already become symbolic of the expert manner in which history reneges on its promises. Nothing happening in Büchner's time gave reason for seeing in the Terror anything but the real face of what moves this world. The pessimism of *Danton's Death,* like that of *Napoleon,* is part of a cultural reaction which embraces the life-negating content of Schopenhauer's philosophy and the relished cynicism in Byron's later work.

Of historical works on the Revolution, Büchner seems to have been most impressed with two French versions by Thiers and Mignet, as well as by a comprehensive historical work on the period between 1789 and 1830 by a German named Konrad Friedrich. Not that Büchner set out to dramatize documented fact: *Danton's Death* is not in the vein of a modern *You Are There.* Neither is it the kind of dramatization whose resemblance to historical fact is purely accidental; Büchner always respected fact, and his willingness to appropriate historical text at times without modification attests to this. On the other hand, as analysis will show, the weight of Büchner's personal sympathies falls too heavily on the play and its characterizations to allow us to see it as history before tragedy. And then again, Büchner ranges beyond the Revolution to bring in material which some may find totally irrelevant on a strict historical basis.

Danton's Death has little plot in the conventional sense. It begins at that stage of the Revolution when great expectations have turned into bitter achnowledgments and when Danton's state of mind very likely approximated Büchner's own state of mind as a dispirited revolutionary. Even in Grabbe's *Napoleon,* with its emphasis on how much of history is nothing really happening, there had at least been an exciting sense of impending developments. Here there is almost none of that. From the start Danton is already dead to most of life, and he never really snaps out of it. Whatever happens, happens *to* him; if he has any needs at all, they are for anodynes against life itself. The painfulness of life obsesses him at every stage of the play's action,

[6] Closs, *Medusa's Mirror,* p. 157.

which is divisible into three phases punctuated by the decisive acts
of others. By the end of phase one Danton has been condemned
by Robespierre and St. Just; by the end of phase two he has been
condemned by the mob; and by the end of phase three it is all over.
Through it all, Danton has largely been as passive in relation to
his human enemies as he has been active in vocalizing his feeling
that life has not a speck of meaning.

Brecht would often arrange his plays so as to drive home inescapable
axiomatic conclusions. *Danton's Death* recalls this arrangement. Büchner delineates the various forces which predestine the outcome of
the Revolution; on the one hand are opportunistic leaders avid for
power by any means and shrewd enough to camouflage their ambitions
with radical catchwords; on the other is a segment of the intelligentsia
genuinely concerned about the monstrous character the Revolution is
taking on; and between these two groups, the crowd, easily swayed
by demagogues operating on the assumption that political wisdom
is the art of the gutter. Robespierre and company are quite prepared
to cater to the mob's infantile fantasies, to play father of the people
for all it's worth. But the sincere revolutionaries are not; their main
preoccupation is still to make life at large more livable. Naturally,
their ideals doom them from the start, for while they talk to themselves, Robespierre plots. Danton's clique isolates itself fatally by the
very nature of its members' idealistic makeup. They *must* be swallowed
up.

This impersonal *must* is the crux of a key speech in *Danton's Death*
delivered by Robespierre's right-hand man, St. Just. It is a speech
hard to read today without shuddering, for St. Just's reasoning has
in our own time been translated into the extermination of millions.
What makes the speech doubly provocative is that Büchner himself
almost accepted St. Just's logic. For St. Just seems to bend backward
to avoid sentimentalizing what happens in history, to eschew any untenable separations of the moral and natural. Who would challenge
him on the point that history marches across corpses or that nature
is indifferent to human anguish? As a matter of fact, even Danton
would not dispute St. Just's basic point that nature must of necessity
manifest its relentless continuity.

It is not on the point of determinism that Danton and his opponents
part ways; it is on the implications of that determinism, on the nature
of the forces which control all. St. Just, like Robespierre, maintains
that there is ultimately some constructive purpose to justify the inhu-

manity of the present. He sees history as cold and destructive but also progressive. Not Danton. He sees history as cold and destructive and purposeless. For him, the Revolution is an incurable cancer; for St. Just, it is an invigorating bloodletting. Where Büchner himself stands is indicated by outspoken comments in the text that could not be plainer—comments which belie the idea that Büchner was striving for objectivity but simply could not repress his dislike of Robespierre and company. Büchner consistently exposes how Danton's enemies stand for system at the expense of life, consistently shows himself repelled by the mechanization of life in the totalitarian revolutionary society. Mercier's comment that the system of the Revolution is being constructed out of human bodies, Danton's observation that the curse of the time is that one has begun to work with human flesh—these remarks catch the unpleasant truth St. Just's speech will not confront. To get this across so that no one will miss it, Büchner has Barère say later to St. Just: "Yes, St. Just, go on, spin out your sentences, wherein every comma is a sword stroke and every period a hacked-off head!"

Critics refer to the "conflict" in *Danton's Death*. This may be misleading. The kind of interaction which *conflict* connotes is all but imperceptible here. Danton refuses to act until it is too late, and that is all there is to it. Robespierre gets what he wants, not because he acts, but only because the subsuming necessities which push everyone around decide that for the moment he can play God. Soon enough he will be as prostrate as Danton.[7]

The absence of genuine conflict contributes to making *Danton's Death* as formally significant as it is in the history of epic theater. To say, as Knight does, that the play lacks conflict as well as crisis and struggle,[8] and to say so disappointedly, is not to be fully alert

---

[7] Mayer, emphasizing Büchner's hard materialism, sees the fall of Robespierre assured by his inability to give the masses material satisfactions. But does Büchner really convey such a clear equation between economics and history? Doesn't he, rather, indicate that Robespierre will be cut down by the same dark forces that dispose of Danton? Marxist critics, in general, avoid that part of Büchner not reducible to dialectic.

[8] Knight, *Georg Büchner,* p. 86. In all fairness to Knight, he goes on to indicate that the "one almost inescapable weakness in the drama," namely " . . . lack of action . . . , lack of struggle, conflict, crisis . . . " is inextricably tied up with Büchner's "deterministically viewed universe." But on p. 87 he only confuses things by saying that if Büchner were a strict determinist, he would have no special sympathy for Danton. Perhaps "determinism" has become as ambiguous a term as "nihilism"; certainly, one can believe that everything is determined and still be for certain things and against others. See also

to the anti-Aristotelian vantage point from which Büchner wrote. Like Brecht, he sought a dramatic form to emphasize the extent to which character does not control reality, but vice versa. The result may be less dramatic in the conventional sense, but this is wholly deliberate. *Undramatic* should not become a pejorative here; at stake is the cooled-off concept of dramatic experience which Brecht would champion a century later.

Büchner has no compunctions about dedramatizing events which seem made to order for taut drama. Just as he employs with great slackness an episodic structure devoid of those characteristics which excite suspense and preclude detachment, so he employs dialogue in a fashion which makes our response to stage action something different from our ordinary response to drama. For one thing, much of the dialogue is directed not at our hearts but our heads; only a probing critical awareness makes fully intelligible what is implied by the slick hypocrisies in *Danton's Death.* For another, Danton is so transparently the personification of an attitude toward life, rather than a fully credible character, that our emotional identification with him must of necessity be limited. As a matter of fact, to such an extent is Danton's fatalism echoed by his fellow Girondists that after a first reading of the play it is hard to say who said what. Like Brecht, Büchner does not hesitate to undermine suspense or identification in order to get his audience to think along his own lines. The insights of *Danton's Death* are reiterated with a view to making it less a play about Danton than the justifiability of nihilistic despair.

In line with this, the confrontation scene between Danton and Robespierre is less a genuine clash than an exposition by Danton of his ethical relativism and good-humored tolerance. Robespierre says very little. Only when Danton leaves, shocked at the extent to which Robespierre stands confirmed in his moral infallibility ("My conscience is clean. . . . Whoever told you any innocent person has been struck?"), does Robespierre open up, and in making up his mind to have Danton guillotined, he, like Danton, begins to experience himself as an interaction of impersonal forces (" . . . are we not sleep-walkers? Don't we act as if in a dream, only with greater clarity, definition, and execution?"). What confrontation scenes ordinarily

---

in regard to the lack of conflict in *Danton's Death,* Ronald Peacock's *The Poet in the Theatre* (New York: Hill and Wang, 1946), p. 190: "Büchner is almost innocent of the interlocking clash of purposes which is the working material of the dramatist."

imply, those awaited moments when the sparks of direct personal collision begin to fly, is not at all implied here. What is implied, however, is that Danton is quite right to entertain the cynical notions he does about men and events. For Robespierre has become quite simply a murderer with a Christ complex—and this is the man history has chosen to decide whether Danton shall live or die.

In the confrontation scene Büchner uses dialogue the way he uses it through most of *Danton's Death*—to formulate insight in unforgetable terms. Just as Brecht's plays can be shifted for generalizations which sum up his view of things, so can Büchner's first drama; in both cases one senses characters echoing their creator's basic convictions. It was doubtless Büchner who believed that "conscience is a mirror at which an ape torments himself"; that "we are puppets pulled about on wires by unknown powers"; that "there are only Epicureans, be they coarse or polished; Christ was the most polished." And it is Büchner's own desperate resignation Danton gives voice to at the end:

Death apes birth; we die as helpless and naked as newborn children. In truth, shrouds will be our swaddling clothes. What's the use? The grave is as good a place to whimper in as the cradle.[9]

Danton's Death consists of thirty-two scenes, some quite short, others long; some apparently off the main subject, others posing no problems of continuity; some dominated by a single character, others dense with life; some situated indoors, others in the open air. The seemingly arbitrary flow of these episodes recalls Elizabethan drama, Goethe's *Faust,* and, most strongly, the episodic plays of Lenz and Grabbe. Once again a dramatist strings together a variety of actions without fear of abruptly shifting his focus from one character to another or one segment of society to another. Once again the *Guckkastentechnik.*

Büchner's use of the episodic structure was no less radical than Grabbe's. For both, classical rules existed only to be broken. A case in point is Büchner's panorama, which includes game rooms, gutters, political clubs, apartments, promenade, and field, as well as those places where the victims of the Terror were judged, imprisoned, and executed. Unity of place is out of the question here, as is unity of time and action. Büchner gives us the kind of huge cast of characters which

[9] Büchner, *Werke und Briefe,* p. 73.

takes in representatives of just about every variety of human existence. All in all, he recalls Shakespeare, not Aristotle.

To attribute the many scenes of *Danton's Death* exclusively to Büchner's trying to give a rounded picture of a historical development is to leave something out, namely, his desire, above all, to render a picture which corresponds to his conception of life as a chaotic interplay and alternation of wholly necessary events. Having come to realize that all human activity is equally senseless. Büchner translates this realization into the very manner in which his drama unfolds. Robespierre pontificates, Danton philosophizes, and Simon curses—it all comes down to the same thing; each is equally inevitable, equally absurd, and equally deserving of theatrical representation. This should be borne in mind when *Danton's Death* is called epic theater because of its inclusive content and sequence of relatively autonomous scenes.

Multiplicity of episode allows Büchner to make the content of one scene footnote the content of another. Much more than Grabbe is he alive to the irony obtainable from this kind of structuring. It is ironic that while Danton and his friends are discussing the Revolution in the frivolous atmosphere of a game room, and discussing it in terms of sheer political naïveté, the streets below seethe with violence. The same irony is at work when Büchner juxtaposes a scene in which Danton comes through as meriting the gratitude of all who have a stake in the Revolution with a scene in which coarse citizen soldiers are out for his scalp. This kind of irony reaches a climax in the juxtaposition of the scene at the Revolutionary Tribunal with the scene in front of the Palace of Justice. In the former, Danton eloquently exposes the hollow policies of the Committee of Public Safety to the point where the cry bursts forth: "Long Live Danton, down with the Decembrists!" But by the end of the next scene Danton is finished for good, and here the cry is "Long live Robespierre! Down with Danton! Down with the traitor!" The art of letting events speak for themselves could hardly be carried further, nor the art of letting events serve as ironic comments.

The episodism of *Danton's Death* is thus seen not only to allow Büchner the freedom to go where he wants in order to sketch a valid picture of the Terror but to do his reporting in a context of meaningful cross-reference. It allows him also to insert scenes which are not intrinsic to the major action, such as the Promenade scene and the scene in which Camille and Danton agree that the theater of their time is in the hands of men like the painter David, whose art is antilife. Episodism here also makes for an exceedingly varied mixture of tonalities as Büchner alternates vulgar dialogue with political oratory as well as nihilistic lyricism. One must repeat what was said about Grabbe's use of the episodic form, that it was the only form into which so much apparently diverse material could be squeezed. Like Grabbe, Büchner is concerned mainly with one man whose fate is the most powerful comment on the action in which he is involved, but this major character's fate is not divorced from the life around him. Quite often, in fact, he recedes into the background while we see close up how the forces which will prove his undoing are taking human shape, whether it is in the declamatory speeches of politicians or the jangling complaints of impoverished citizens. Danton, like Napoleon, is merely one factor in a vast impersonal field. That this field conspires against any attempt of men to create a more tolerable world was Büchner's view as much as Grabbe's.

There are in *Danton's Death* echoes of *Napoleon* which make one wonder whether Büchner had read Grabbe's play. Like Jouve, the ultimate nihilist of Napoleon, Danton reduces by a phrase what seems momentous to those around him to something insignificant:

LACROIX: Listen, Danton, I've come from the Jacobins.
DANTON: Is that all?

Like Grabbe's pitiless nihilist Jouve, Danton sees all of life as a pose:

LACROIX: And Collot screamed as though obsessed—
all masks are to be ripped off.
DANTON: That would leave no faces.

A comparison of Jouve's nihilism with Danton's makes us realize how vague the term "nihilism" is. Jouve recalls Shakespeare's monsters, especially Iago; Danton recalls Hamlet by way of Coleridge and Goethe. For Jouve, nihilism means killing; for Danton, dying.

The idea that *Danton's Death* is less in the mainstream of epic theater than *Woyzeck* because its scenes only make sense in the full context of the play[10] deserves comment. The concept of the autonomous scene hardly implies that the implications of that scene will not in some way be clarified, deepened, or reinforced by subsequent scenes. To jump ahead, much as we may realize in the early scenes of *Woyzeck* how badly the odds are stacked against its protagonist, it takes his actual murder of Marie to complete the picture. The scenes in *Danton's Death,* too, require the execution of Danton and his followers to give them their total meaning; but this does not really keep scene upon scene from summing up the situation at a glance. Danton, very much like Woyzeck, is a character whose situation continually makes us aware how impossible the human condition appears to Büchner; repetition of the idea that man suffers in a meaningless world is as integral to *Danton's Death* as to *Woyzeck.*

In one of his letters Büchner defends himself against the inevitable carping of those bound to find the vulgarities and obscenities of *Danton's Death* objectionable;[11] he explains that he was only doing justice to the way things must have been at the time of the Terror—to paint a prettier picture would be to paint a false one. Part of his picture takes in the street life of Paris, and here Büchner is out to shock as nowhere else, to the point where he has given one critic the impression that his delineations of low types imply "comtempt."[12] Street life is shown to have been unspeakably coarse and brutal, the man of the street being depicted as crude in manners, venal in pursuits, and callously animalistic—no idealized common man by any means.

But in all fairness to Büchner, this is only half the picture. If Simon's daughter is a slut, her sluttishness at least keeps her family going. Büchner supplements his stark renditions of lower-class life with reminders of the social conditions which invite such realities. If there is whoring and begging, blame hunger; if anyone is responsible, it is the economically privileged whose money supports the vice

---

[10] *Georg Büchner, Complete Plays and Prose,* trans. Carl Richard Mueller (New York: Hill and Wang, 1963), p. xxiv.
[11] Büchner, *Werke und Briefe,* pp. 399–400. In this letter, Büchner says, among other things, "The dramatic poet is in my eyes nothing but a historiographer, but he surpasses the latter by virtue of creating history for the second time, putting us directly into the life of a period rather than contenting himself with a dry account, giving us characters rather than characterizations and figures rather than portrayals." One discerns here the same emphasis on character and life championed by Lenz. Also, Büchner is quite explicit in this letter on his feelings about Danton's opponents, whom he calls "bandits of the Revolution."
[12] Knight, *Georg Büchner,* p. 91.

of the poor. Like Brecht, Büchner connects concrete sordid fact with
social and economic forces that control events far more powerfully
than any individual. A citizen comments that the summary execution
of an aristocrat is not as cruel as the slow torture to which the members
of the lower classes are automatically consigned at birth.

The realist wishing to convey the texture of everyday life may not
be able to avoid grotesque effects, but he tries hard to do without
them. Here Büchner works quite differently; he cannot put enough
grotesqueries into *Danton's Death*. There is the grotesque attempt
of citizens to hang a young man because he blows his nose with
a handkerchief; the relief on the part of executioners that in the
case of pregnant women extra coffins will not be required; the condem-
nation of Danton because he, unlike Robespierre, seems to enjoy life;
the patriotism of the citizen who offers up his wife to the guillotine
and feels himself a modern Brutus; the bickering of two carters over
who gets a day's pay for transporting victims to the blade; the dancing
of Parisians at the *Place de la Revolution* while Danton and his friends
await their final turn; and the cheerfulness of two executioners as
they scrub and polish the blood-spattered guillotine after another
execution.

These grotesqueries are as shocking as Grabbe's, but they also show
what a difference in psychology separates Büchner from his contemporary. Grabbe employs the grotesque with a matter-of-factness which
has little humanitarian resonance. Sometimes, in fact, he seems to
relish the grotesque horrors of his plays in a way which implies pathology. Büchner, on the other hand, employs the grotesque to make us
feel the anguish of human life wholly at the mercy of impersonalities.
Unlike Grabbe, he is always on the side of the victim. Some of our
own age's grotesqueries, like the gassing of human beings to the tune
of Viennese waltzes, would hardly have come as surprises to Grabbe
and Büchner.

Büchner's stage speech, like Grabbe's, avoids the high-toned rhetoric
associated with German classicism of the type associated with Schiller;
it is, in fact, at the opposite pole from any dialogue which subordinates
language to ideals of dignity and decorum. Sections of *Danton's Death*
consist of the condensed, harsh, aggressive prose which Büchner would
sophisticate into the searing exchanges that make his final drama so
fierce an experience; at times this prose seems literally to shoot out
at the reader, so intent is Büchner on charging language with mimetic
force:

SIMON: You pander, you shriveled-up poison pellet, you worm-rotted apple-brain. . . . You whore's cot, lewdness nests in every inch of your body. . . . [13]

In cacophonous passages like this, language is sheer verbalized aggression. Simon's act of communication is so adrenalized that he may as well be talking to himself—which is, after all, Büchner's point, that most dialogue is really monologue. Even the less primitive characters of *Danton's Death* talk mainly to themselves, for no one listens to any voice but that internal voice which Robespierre feels pulling him along. In Büchner's drama, speech is on the road to the kind of introversion which would become the linguistic hall-mark of Wedekind and Sternheim. People talk *at* or *past* one another, least of all *to* one another—what the Germans call *Aneinandervorbeisprechen*.

Büchner's prose is plastic enough to characterize personalities who, unlike Simon, do not spit out their words. Robespierre's dialogue, for example, is a triumph of linguistic characterization. His measured cadences, studied diction, and protracted elaborations catch the mentality of an impossibly unctuous demagogue. The pronoun "we" comes easily to this voice of the people, and in front of a crowd he is the skillful manipulator who gets just the right touch of paternalism into his confidential admonitions. He tries to appear as the patient savant anxious to explain things coolly and logically to the less gifted and he does nothing so much as to deceive and inflame. Adroitly he employs adjectives like "elevated" and "most holy" to dignify that which he is for, and verbs like "plunder" and "poison" to blacken what he is against. The cheap slogan is his ultimate weapon, and he enunciates it like a momentous truth:

Terror is the weapon of the republic, virtue her strength.

The revolutionary government opposes tyranny with the despotism of freedom.

Vice is the aristocracy's mark of Cain.

Danton's speech is another matter. It is the speech of a philosophical man who has come to a single overriding insight which determines almost everything he says. Whereas Robespierre and St. Just generalize

[13] Büchner, *Werke und Briefe,* p. 13.

the concrete into the portentously abstract, Danton is quick to confront hard fact. His reaction to Robespierre's declaration that "virtue must rule by terror" is that this sentence puts the finishing touches on boards for the guillotine. Unlike his executioners, he is not given to facile phrasemaking, to premeditated oratory, or, most important, to cold mechanical formulations. He may wish to appear detached from life, and to an extent he is, but no one around him indicts life with his passion.

Danton's speeches contain much concrete imagery of the kind that would not become poetically stylish until our own time. But concrete images do not serve here to assure us of the inarguable materiality of the world; they drive home man's inexorable isolation and recall us to Grabbe's repelled alienation from a noxious world. Danton views his body as a "broken fiddle," a bottle emptied of wine, an object which stinks and sweats, a pair of trousers ragged from wear and appetizing to moths, and a pair of worn-out shoes ready to be donated to the begging earth. The down-to-earth metaphor could not be employed more tellingly to communicate despair. Büchner achieves here a heartbreaking pathos without sacrificing cynical overtones. He manages to be lyrical without sentimental chords.

Büchner's linguistic genius is at last receiving scholarly notice.[14] Among his major achievements is his mastery of the paradoxical aphorism which clarifies in an instant significant implications. "Where self-defense ends, there starts murder," says Danton as he sums up the limits of radical militancy. To the plea that time should not be wasted, he says, "But time loses us," a line that could well serve as his epitaph. And when he notes that "we are always on stage even when we are finally stabbed in earnest," we get a haunting anticipation of Pirandello. *Danton's Death* is full of such comments lifting us beyond the action to levels of penetrating insight.

No discussion of Büchner's dialogue can omit mention of his great debt to Lenz. An excerpt from *Danton's Death* will make this debt quite obvious:

Where is the maiden? Speak! No, I cannot put it that way. The young lady? No, that too is out. Woman, Miss! That too, that too is out! Only one more name—I've no breath left to get it out.[15]

---

[14] See Helmut Krapp's *Der Dialog bei Georg Büchner* (Darmstadt: Hermann Gentner Verlag, 1958).
[15] Büchner, *Werke und Briefe*, p. 13.

Like Lenz, Büchner writes dialogue to transcribe the dynamics of a befuddled mind. Like Wenzeslaus in *The Soldiers,* for example, Simon repeats himself idiosyncratically, makes all kinds of overconscious notations, answers his own questions quite seriously, and in general tangles himself up in the labyrinth of his own redundancies. Like Wenzeslaus, also, he interlards his nonsense with classical reference, and one can see Büchner, like Lenz, striking out again at traditional respect for classicism by showing how easy this respect comes to fools. Also, in the same way that Lenz's middle-class characters, for all their politeness, cannot hide the fact that they are anxious for status and self-importance, so Simon is always trying to convince himself that he is not a negligible factor in the scheme of things. Büchner finds the little man as vain as his oppressors.

Büchner projects human isolation by emphasizing time and again that what is repellent to one human nervous system arouses no such reaction from another. Robespierre lives by the cant which makes Danton sick at heart; the average Parisian woman enjoys the guillotining which strikes terror into women like Lucile and Julie; the *Bürger* are only too happy with art that revolts intellectuals like Camille and Danton. Büchner shows human beings not only hopelessly cut off from each other but compelled by some malevolent force to confront one another in irrevocable opposition. Sartre's idea that hell is "other people" is very much a major theme of *Danton's Death.*

The hopeless vision of life articulated by any number of eloquent declarations throughout *Danton's Death* is fully borne out by the events of the play, events which are, so to speak, synopsized by images of stage action which reveal how sensitive Büchner was to theater as a visual experience. What could say as much about the anguish Büchner is trying to convey as the picture of Camille waking up and pulling at his sheet the night before his execution; Julie cutting a strand from her hair to give to her helpless husband; a callous carter pointing to the window behind which the condemned are waiting for their end; Lucile running madly off stage; prisoners lining up at the guillotine and attempting to embrace one another. All these actions interact with the verbal text of *Danton's Death* to reinforce its futile tone, to substantiate its indictment of the gods. In line with this it is not surprising that when Danton reduces the world to chaos and a future nothingness the Jailer enters to take him and his friends to the execution block.

While part of humanity suffers, another part takes itself seriously enough to feel its world is all that counts. This is the world of the *Bürger* who strut through the Promenade scene, which is quite reminiscent of the Faust episode *Vor dem Tor*. Like Goethe, Büchner is all too aware that the bourgeoisie elevates complacency to virtue; like Goethe, he pinpoints this by contrasting the *Bürger* and the Beggar. The *Bürger* are unable to make the Beggar see the value of work; for the latter it makes little sense to labor for a coat when a rag will do— after all, the best things in life are free. This rejection of middle-class psychology is topped off with melodious cynicism:

A handful of dirt and a bit of moss . . .
Is all I'll ever get upon this earth

What is it then, what is it then
That gives man joy in life

Crushed as he is by a thousand cares
And the need to work, work, work
Till the long day disappears.[16]

Büchner uses song once more in the same scene when a Soldier and a girl named Rosalie proceed to tease one another.

SOLDIER:
Dear little Christina, dear Christina mine,
Does the injury in question really give you pain,
Give you pain, give you pain?

ROSALIE (*singing*):
But of course not, Mr. Soldier, Sir,
To be quite frank, I'm eager for some more,
For some more, for some more![17]

Büchner's songs have a dual thrust, commenting at the same time on the emptiness of the bourgeois life style and the emptiness of life itself, a life in which the bestial is perfectly natural. The songs communicate personal despair all the more by interacting with dialogue

---

[16] *Ibid.,* p. 37.
[17] *Ibid.,* p. 38.

that is quintessentially trivial. Büchner's realization that life is in essence unbearably painful accompanies his realization that most of humanity is anxious to deaden its sensibilities with trivia.

The rest of the Promenade scene makes plain why Danton finds he cannot take life seriously. As he puts it: "It's beyond me why people don't stop in the street to laugh in one another's faces. I mean their laughter should boom out of windows and graves so that heaven explodes and the earth turns topsy-turvy from laughter."[18]

This state of mind is justified by the caricatured stupidities on view. A mother lectures her daughter on virtue with a capital V while the latter is fed a salacious item of gossip by a Young Gentleman who enjoys his scabrous work. Another Gentleman is convinced that mankind is moving steadily upward, while his companion is terrified at stepping into a puddle, for the earth's crust is all too fragile. This same frightened specimen cannot get enough thrills in the theater, where he enjoys seeing things blow up. Here Büchner compresses several oblique comments into a single image—the earth *is* a kind of minefield in which one can be blown up at any moment, but the height of naïveté is the bourgeois belief that one can evade the wrong puddles. Only in the relative safety of *Rauschtheater* is the average man willing to confront life. The link to Brecht here requires no further comment.

Though Grabbe experimented far more with the episodic structure than did Büchner, he never exhibited the control of this structure which seems to have come naturally to Büchner. *Napoleon* had scenes which do little more than subordinate the dramatist to the meticulous historian. This kind of dissociation Büchner never manifests, he was quite sure as to what he wished to achieve with every episode; there is never any slackening off into action or dialogue which does not bear directly on his major concerns. And unlike Grabbe, he never changes personality from scene to scene, turning from cynicism to admiration or from stultification to sentimentalities. Büchner is the first epic dramatist who can make even the most banal aspect of the passing scene reflect his version of life,[19] the first who does not yield

[18] *Ibid.*, p. 39.
[19] Pertinent here is Karl Viëtor's point that no one grasped as profoundly as Büchner the relevance of the episodic structure to a deterministic view of life; if man is determined totally by conditions, then drama must focus on the different conditions at work, must be free enough to encompass any factors that influence the human state. See *Georg Büchner Politik. Dichtung. Wissenschaft* (Bern: A. Francke Ag. Verlag, 1949), pp. 155–56.

to the temptation to write episodes which fail to sustain subtle emphases and expectations set up in previous episodes.

As his episodic technique allows Büchner to give us a scene satirizing the immersion of the bourgeoisie in work and their belief in progress, so it allows him to devote an early scene to a promiscuous young woman named Marion. By the end of the scene Danton will be saying what he is always saying, that the Revolution devours its own children; but the substance of this scene shows us that one can be devoured in more than one way. Marion is a victim of pure instinct, a creature as helpless as Läuffer in the sphere of the erotic, the difference being that she worships what Läuffer tried to excise. Brought up as puritanically as the groping adolescents of Wedekind's *Spring's Awakening,* she was unable to control her sexual appetite once she learned the pleasures of its gratification. Her promiscuity brought about the suicide of her first lover as well as the premature death of her mother. But in the long run none of this can matter, for Marion conceives of herself as an irrepressible sexual force. One may well be reminded here of Lulu, Wedekind's own personification of amoral female sexuality. At any rate, Büchner's point here, as elsewhere, is that to the deeper forces vitalizing life, man-made ethical systems are brittle rationalizations. To get this across he gives Marion what amounts to a soliloquy on how she became what she is. Once again he shuts out the Revolution to comment on life itself—life which he sees to be so demonic in nature that it will never do to call him a premature Marxist.

This is precisely what some would make him out to be. Lukacs, for example, pictures Danton and Robespierre as two representatives of ideology and sees Büchner concerned with the question of which attitude is more valid. Danton of course comes off badly; his is the defeated attitude of the inactivist whereas Robespierre acts.[20] The best reply to this invidious comparison is Krapp's.[21] He points out that long before they confront one another it is clear that Danton is not the carrier of any socio-political principle as such. Danton stands for himself while his friends still align themselves with programs. The confrontation scene is merely another link in the chain of Danton's progressive isolation. One might add that the confrontation is not

[20] Georg Lukacs' Danton becomes estranged from the Revolution because it stops attacking feudalism and begins attacking capitalism. The mob scenes supposedly illustrate those societal forces which Danton is unable to comprehend. See *Deutsche Realisten des 19. Jahrhunderts* (Bern: A. Francke Ag. Verlag, 1951), pp. 76–77.

[21] Krapp, *Der Dialog bei Georg Büchner,* p. 136.

between abstract principles but living flesh, not two types of radicalism but two types of human personality. Büchner knows that politics cannot be separated from psychology, that the sick fantasy of a Robespierre is not a negligible factor in the world of power politics.

Krapp has gone on to qualify Büchner's relationship to Brecht. Büchner's drama, he suggests, is not in the mainstream of epic theater because Büchner is primarily involved with what is momentary, in-stantaneous, and immediate,[22] with exactly what Lenz had taken to be the right subject matter for the artist, who must above all delineate what is sentiently alive from moment to moment. The fact that Büchner learned from Lenz does not mean, however, that Brecht could not learn from Büchner. The latter may have been far more impressionistic, but that should not tag him with the adjective "lyric"[23] and thus separate him irrevocably from the adjective "epic." Much more than Brecht, Büchner may be nervously energetic, furious, and intense, but he is not all nervous energy, fury, and intensity. Like Brecht, he splits up his scenes in such a way as to let them make sense as independent comments on life, and they make even more sense when pondered in the context of the scenes which surround them. Exactly like Brecht, Büchner seeks to reinforce methodically the idea that life as we know it is reprehensible.

Danton's Death could well be called a drama of commentary. Char-acter after character verbalizes, not according to the strict requirements of prosaic realism, but in enunciation of Büchnerian insight. Danton is Büchner's leading repository of the kind of cynical wisdom which was to permeate Brechtian drama; like a Brecht character, he has seen enough of this world to entertain no illusions about its unphilan-thropic nature. In Danton's case, however, the only way to act is not to act at all; he has none of the tenacious survival instinct of a Mother Courage. He is doomed by the very knowledge which "saves" those whom it dehumanizes.

[22] *Ibid.,* p. 138.
[23] Lee Baxandall's exposition of the view that *Danton's Death* "is not simply lyric theater," because of the extent to which the spectator is compelled to adopt attitudes and formulate relationships, strikes this writer as valid enough; but when Baxandall goes on to contrast Büchner's play with other "open" plays like *Spring's Awakening* and works by Brecht which he does not name, his discussion is too cursory. He implies that Brecht and Wedekind were "relatively optimistic," but this is a judgment many readers of Wedekind and Brecht would challenge, as they would challenge also the impression Baxandall gives that Büchner is closer to Beckett than to Brecht. See "Georg Büchner's *Dantons Death,*" *Tulane Drama Review* (March, 1962), VI, No. 3, 136–49.

To search for anticipations of Brecht in *Danton's Death* is to dis-
cover uncanny similarities where one would hardly expect them. No
one has mentioned Brecht's *The Measures Taken* in connection with
Danton's Death, but are not both plays about the incompatibility of
humanitarianism and the revolutionary process;[24] if Brecht's *Lehrstück*
has embarrassed the Communists, it is because they realize he has not
refused to dramatize with poignance the same truth that St. Just conveys so rhetorically. Then again, the very nature of Büchner's attitude
of protest links him to Brecht. For Büchner found as much reason
to reject the "ideal of nature and human fulfillment"[25] of the *Sturm
und Drang* as Brecht found to reject the sentimental ideals of the
German expressionists. Both could identify themselves only with extreme positions on the social and economic issues of their time; neither
saw any efficacy in middle-of-the-road liberalism.

On conventional morality Brecht and Büchner speak with one voice,
seeing it as a prop to the status quo, and the perfect smoke screen
for the intrigue of vicious men. It is Robespierre who identifies opposition to his terror with vice and comes out for virtue; it is St. Just,
his partner in political crime, who talks about nature as something
moral and spiritual, and who sanctifies the leadership of the Terror
by comparing it to Moses' leadership of the Israelites. Like Wedekind
as well as Brecht, Büchner is suspicious of what the Germans call
Pflichtmenschen.

Morality is a lie which most people find too expensive to live by.
Danton's Death conveys this Brechtian point in an altercation between
Simon and his wife. The moral outrage of a father aghast at his
daughter's dissoluteness is deflated by the realism of a mother who
would be very much at home in Brecht's world:

WIFE: Judas, that you are! Would you have so much as a single
pair of trousers if the young gentlemen did not take their pants off
for her?[26]

---

[24] Though Büchner rejects what Brecht does his best to affirm: the right to
take life for ideological reasons. Büchner's basic attitude is very much that of
Camus in *L'homme révolté.*
[25] The phrase is Peacock's, and he uses it in the course of comparing unfavorably
Büchner's "protest" with that of his *Sturm und Drang* forerunners, who pro-
tested "against effete rationalism and stifling social conventions." Danton's
protest he finds "morbid and decadent."
[26] Büchner, *Werke und Briefe,* p. 14.

Simon chooses to respond to this with a series of declamations whose linguistic style would sound absurdly false in any context except that of rhetorical classical drama. Nothing seems to have struck Büchner as being as worthless as the idealistic substance of that drama; he finds it perfect material for parody when he is not attacking it outright.

Simon's histrionic reaction to his daughter's whoring, and his wife's remark on the relationship of his trousers to those of his daughter's patrons is as funny as it is serious. One could well call even the tone of all this Brechtian. No frankness is minced to show what it means to be poor, but Simon's wife is not the mouthpiece of a moralist who has forgotten to smile. There is as much sardonic bite to this defense of prostitution as there will be to the defense of crime in a bourgeois society in such Brecht plays as *The Threepenny Opera*. Just as the nihilistic Büchner or Brecht is never very far from the social moralist, so the social moralist is never very far from the satirist who knows no social allegiances.

The respect for actuality which explains Büchner's distaste for classicism relates him to the naturalists of the late nineteenth century. However, Zola would probably have found him as much of a questionable naturalist as he found Strindberg. Like the latter, Büchner never suggests that the conditions of his plays are in the final analysis decipherable and manipulable by scientific logic. Büchner and Strindberg deal with manifestations of the demonic rather than slices of life. It is hard for them to depict any reality without passionate subjectivity.

But far less than Strindberg's naturalistic plays are Büchner's plays continuities of suspense. Here again Brecht comes to mind, for reiteration is as much a basic principle of epic theater as it is of Büchner's drama. Individual scenes are constantly recapitulating the same basic insights, consistently illuminating the over-all theme by still another persuasive variation. This dramaturgy subordinates character to the push of forces that cannot be stopped. Thus, Danton goes to his death as mechanically as Mother Courage goes to her own death in life; the scenes from beginning to end are merely phases of an inevitable progression, a progression toward defeat by a world in which one simply cannot afford to be decent. Some of Brecht's major plays will duplicate this pattern. Rather than complication, these writers give us accumulation, and what accumulates is not the weight of misfortunes which transfigure but of misfortunes which are as painful as they are senseless.

96

Marcuse has pointed out the unresolved tensions of Büchner's art.[27] For all his empiric materialism, Büchner is in the final analysis a mystical pessimist; for all his programmatic realism, he tends toward states of mind which imbue reality with powerful subjective feeling.[28] All of this Marcuse finds paradoxical. However, Büchner is less of an enigma when we realize how much he took to heart the political situation of his own day. He became utterly convinced the only hope for Europe's oppressed lay in direct revolutionary action. Never smug about anything which implied suffering, he refused to allow the evil he witnessed to be explained away either religiously or philosophically. His aggressive nihilism and atheism spring from nothing less than powerful social conscience. Büchner conveys nihilism, but much more he conveys existential anguish at the truth that everything seems to militate against men treating one another humanely.

This anguish explains what some may consider operatically artificial in *Danton's Death,* e.g., the lines spoken by Danton, Hérault-Séchelles, and Camille just before their jailer comes to take them to the guillotine. All three say essentially the same thing: man is a helpless plaything of sadistic gods. Only their metaphors differ; Hérault-Séchelles sees man as a suckling pig slaughtered in such a manner as to be most palatable; Danton refers to children in pain whose condition delights their torturers; and Camille compares the world to a fish bowl in which the death struggle of the condemned affords the gods an amusing spectacle. One may well argue that this is anything but

[27] Ludwig Marcuse, *Die Welt der Tragödie* (Leipzig: Franz Schneider Verlag, 1923), p. 97. Marcuse also makes the point that if Danton were not his own antagonist, *Danton's Death* would be intrigue drama (p. 90). Büchner uses cosmic myths to express his pathetic side, vulgar jokes and grotesqueries to express his skeptical side (p. 100). Marcuse mentions Nietzsche as a writer who, just like Büchner, generates energy from emptiness itself (p. 90).

[28] Subjectivity would seem to link Büchner with the Romantics, but two books exploring this ostensible link show that it is very weak at best: Heinz Lipmann's *Georg Büchner und die Romantik* (Munich: Max Hueber, 1923) and Pier Westra's "Georg Büchner dans ses rapports avec ses contemporains" (unpublished dissertation, University of Paris, 1946). Lipmann points out that Büchner's subjectivity is supplemented by a desire to do justice to the life which envelops his characters. He organizes his drama around a living center; his plays, including *Leonce and Lena,* do not melt into smooth, diffuse transparencies; he does not pursue *Unendlichkeit.* He was not a reactionary absolutist. One could go on and on. The fact of the matter is that he is much more naturalistic than the romantics ever cared to be. Very good is Westra's point that whenever we discern romantic elements in Büchner's work, they are side by side with antiromantic elements. See in Lipmann pp. 99, 101, 136; in Westra, pp. 44, 76.

dialogue and closer to oratorio than drama; but the principle at work here is quite compatible with the principle by which Büchner makes most of his scenes say very much the same thing. Just as his episodes reinforce the same repudiation of any humanistic meaning to this world, so do successive statements by different characters. If we call his larger organizing principle "episodic reinforcement," we can call the principle behind the three prisoners' litany of nihilism "lyrical intensification."

It is hardly possible to list all that Büchner has in common with Brecht. Both find idealism a shameful distortion of life's actualities; both conceive of the world as a jungle-like place; both are extremely sympathetic to the plight of those condemned to anonymous exploitation and persecution; both are aware of man as a social animal whom it is senseless to discuss in isolation from the material forces that make him what he is; both imbue their works with humanitarian feeling while giving vent to a corrosive cynicism; both are aware that the most viable forms of human communication partake of gross hypocrisy; both detest the world as it is and reject the solace of any transcendent element; both are far from Schiller.

Thanks to Schiller, Büchner was for a long time quite uncongenial to German audiences. Unlike Schiller, he has no characters to encourage faith in the responsiveness of history to humanitarian idealism. He has little action that is exciting and suspenseful, and his ironies may fail to get across in performance. Quite often his drama is one of subtle gestures, calling for an acting technique refined only in our own period. Schiller enthusiasts were ready even less for Büchner's attempt to fuse drama into a unitary structure of rhythm, image, atmosphere, mood, and comment. Büchner himself did not mince his low regard for Schiller: "In a word, I have a high opinion of Shakespeare, but think very little of Schiller."[29]

In *Danton's Death* Büchner chose to build his play around the murder of an innocent man by power-hungry thugs claiming to be history's chosen few. *Woyzeck* (1837), the play he left unfinished at his death, is also related to the murder of an innocent man in the name of duly constituted authority, even if that murder does not actually take place in the play as we have it. However, in *Woyzeck* Büchner does not merely present us with a man who is more or less finished to start with; here he shows us the actual process whereby a living

[29] Büchner, *Werke und Briefe*, p. 400.

creature joins the dead. One can say this while fully aware that Büchner never got the chance to arrange episodes of *Woyzeck* into a definitive pattern, and that the German editor responsible for the first coherent version of the play very likely did a sloppy job.[30] Be that as it may, the over-all emphases of *Woyzeck* are clear enough. Büchner made sure of that much.

Danton's Death exhumed the hypocrisy and anguish beneath historical developments; *Woyzeck* does the same with legal developments. Büchner finds the dry dismissal of human values by the law of his day every bit as vile as he found murder by decree during the Terror. Possibly the details of Danton's execution incensed him to the point where he made up his mind posterity should know how senseless the killings of the Terror were—in the same way that he wrote *Woyzeck* to drive home the callous stupidity of a recent German execution. In 1824 the citizens of Leipzig had seen justice triumph with the hanging of an unemployed barber for the crime of stabbing to death his girl friend out of jealousy. A Privy Councilor named Clarus rose to the task of discovering what had made this enemy of society tick and discovered it to be irregular living. This Philistine simplification was more than Büchner needed.

The bourgeois world he puts on the stage in *Woyzeck* offers only two basic types: those who brutalize and those who suffer. Woyzeck is a sufferer whose torments are so vividly conveyed by Büchner that the author succeeded even with his unfinished version of the play in giving the lie to Clarus' pseudo-psychopathology. Lowborn, queer, poor, the odds stacked against him in a society which sees him as infinitely exploitable, Woyzeck lives only for his relationship to a girl named Marie. By the end of the play he has killed her. When he does so, we are least of all inclined to judge him, so close have we been to the texture of his motives. This is a man whose every breath indicts the forces behind life, so completely does some basic disorder cut into his very being. He feels himself hemmed in by dark threatening realities, experiences abysses where ordinary men feel solid ground. Beset by all sorts of fixed ideas, he is an emotional cripple whose obsessive states give way fitfully to flashes of visionary perception in which terror and joy fuse indistinguishably. He is the most intense character Büchner created, the first nobody

---

[30] It would merely be redundant to go into the facts surrounding Karl Franzos' resuscitation of Büchner's neglected fragment. The English reader can get them from Knight, *Georg Büchner,* pp. 115–16.

in the history of drama whose dimensions disprove the view that tragedy is exclusively for the highborn.

Danton had stood apart from events and commented on them with locutions which, in spite of Büchner's conscious revolt against idealistic classicism, strike rhetorical chords. In this sense *Woyzeck* completes Büchner's anti-idealistic rebellion. The world of his last play is lopsidedly evil and stupid to the extent that no Danton is needed to clarify its essence. But more important, most of what happens in *Woyzeck* is portrayed not intellectually but concretely. It is the actuality of the suffering moment that Büchner concentrates on here as well as the actuality of life drearily lived by the morally dead. Büchner sets himself the task of depicting how evil the world is without resorting to heroic intermediaries. Woyzeck's main concern is that of so many a Brecht protagonist, simply to keep his head above water. Büchner finds this no easier for the little man than the originator of modern epic theater.

Büchner is reputed to have said on his death-bed that man cannot suffer enough. This takes on some intelligibility in regard to *Woyzeck*. For horrendous and terrifying as Woyzeck's misbegotten life may be, it is the only life in the play which has dimension, the only one that is not in the final analysis cold and depersonalized. Those who surround him inhabit a relatively empty world in which nothing involves them deeply. They are in their own way as pitilessly driven by forces as Woyzeck; but they have nothing comparable to his powerful inner life. He may well be dizzied by imaginary voids: they are part of a real void which they lack the imagination to perceive. This deficiency of imagination and of the capacity to feel strikes Büchner as the essence of bourgeois psychology.

This psychology is satirized through the caricatured types who enable Woyzeck to make enough money to get by. One of these is a Captain whom we meet in the first scene, and here at the very beginning of the play Büchner projects the grotesque gap in communication which separates Woyzeck from his fellow *Bürger*. Something about Woyzeck exasperates the Captain: this obsequious barber seems always to be lost in his own world; he thinks too much; he has no morals; he does not seem to realize that virtue precedes biology; otherwise, how could he allow himself to lead a married life without benefit of clergy, to the point of producing an illegitimate offspring. Woyzeck's rejoinder that his miserable economic condition should be taken into account, makes little impression on the Captain, who is convinced that goodness is not only possible, it is mandatory. In his own semiarticulate manner, Woyzeck blurts out what the Captain leaves wholly unmentioned: "Money, money!"

But there is no chance the Captain will realize that the very economic serfdom which compels the poor creature in front of him to swallow all his guff makes all talk of morality supererogatory. Like a Brecht character created to underline how ludicrous it is to preach goodness in a parasitic society, the Captain perseveres in his admonitions on sexual virtue. And Woyzeck continues to shave him.

Another employer Woyzeck has to contend with is the Doctor who uses him as a guinea pig. In return for wages which he hands over dutifully to his wife, Woyzeck lives on nothing but peas. Although the Doctor makes sure by this insane diet that Woyzeck is lucky to have any resemblance at all to a normal human being, he still finds his subject's mental processes objectionable: "That Woyzeck—he's philosophizing again." But this cloud has a silver lining; it isn't every day that one comes across such a beautiful specimen of pathology.

Having reduced Woyzeck to a scientific datum, the Doctor is disappointed to no end when this datum spoils everything by urinating upon the call of nature and not by the scheduled requirements of the laboratory.[31] This caricatured scene allows Büchner to vent his revulsion at the kind of scientism which our own age practiced at Auschwitz. To the Doctor, Woyzeck is nothing more than interesting garbage.

There is no question that in his portrayal of the Captain and Doctor, Büchner is less concerned with characterization than caricature; and so it is not surprising that *Woyzeck* has been called a piece of social allegory. But this is not really true, for in spite of the blatant types who drift through the play, the two main characters are not molded to conform to any pre-established social thesis. Woyzeck and Marie suffer from social exploitation, but that hardly sums up what they are. Büchner's antiteleological conception of reality, that whatever exists is sufficient unto itself, was never put into more eloquent practice. As for the stereotype of characterization implied by those who torment Woyzeck, this anticipates Brecht's technique of highlighting the suffer-

[31] The ultimate irony is that the Doctor, who would like even Woyzeck's involuntary muscles to do his bidding, preaches free will like a Schiller hero: " . . . man is free, in man individuality is transfigured into freedom." Juxtaposition of the process of urination with such idealistic pronouncements tells its own story. This is the kind of concreteness which distinguishes the Lenz-Brecht tradition.

ing of some by setting it off against the flat extra-heavy villainy of others. Like Brecht, Büchner suggests that it is not worth delving into the inner life of those who make the world the swamp it is; at any rate, neither of these two dramatists is fascinated by the psychology of evil to the point of minimizing its virulence. One cannot say the same for Grabbe.

Attempts have been made to view Woyzeck as a tragicomic figure. This seems wrong. The response Büchner is trying to evoke is in general quite divorced from healthy human laughter. What Büchner wants to get across is how laughable Woyzeck's behavior must be to the world in which he functions; nothing about him is so intrinsically funny that it is not drowned out by the overwhelming pathos of his predicament. To laugh at Woyzeck the way we laugh at Läuffer is impossible, unless our tastes run to the sadistic; it would be tantamount to laughing at insanity. Lenz's character loses his manhood by his own volition; Woyzeck has it taken away by a society in which he exists to be stepped on. The latter is far less amusing.

In *Danton's Death* Büchner had used song both to comment on the action and to give it overtones of pathos. In *Woyzeck* the songs are even more powerfully incorporated, e.g., the lyrics with which Marie addresses her infant and tries to convince herself that her hopeless social position can become a matter of indifference to her. Here the very act of singing comments on itself as a defense mechanism against painful realization. Woyzeck also sings such songs.

Then there is the song sung at the fair by an old man while his child dances to a barrel organ.

Upon this world there's only flux
And all of us must die
That is, of course, the crux.[32]

The song introduces a grotesque atmosphere, but it does more than that; it says quite explicitly what Büchner always takes pains to put into the mouths of his outsiders, those who have no vested interest in the bourgeois establishment. They see quite easily what the good citizen will never allow himself to see—that in the scheme of things

[32] Büchner, *Werke und Briefe,* p. 155.

man is quite unimportant, that his life is ruled by iron necessities. All his work and progress get him nowhere.

More subtle are the songs by Andres and the apprentices; they comment implicitly on the vast sea of indifference which encompasses all individual human suffering. While Woyzeck seethes with anxiety about Marie, Andres' song reveals a bystander who could not care less. The apprentices sing stupidly about some idyllic scene which is destined to be ever remote from their own drab lives. Such songs add a sinister dimension to *Woyzeck*. It is hard to put one's finger on just how Büchner gets this effect, so naturally does he integrate the songs into the action; the best indication of his mastery in this regard is that on a first reading of *Woyzeck* one assumes Büchner is using song in the casual manner of the naturalist working with folk materials. But the songs comment as forcefully on the world implied by *Woyzeck* as any sardonic Brecht ballad.

As in *Danton's Death,* Büchner digresses from his main plot line for the sake of sardonic comment. At the fair we are back in the kind of racy atmosphere with which Grabbe set the tone of *Napoleon*. Like Grabbe, Büchner uses the unlikeliest types as mouthpieces of bitter insight, a Charlatan and a Booth Proprietor, as if to suggest that life is a circus and humanity nothing so much as menagerie— metaphors which bring Wedekind to mind. The public is treated to an exhibition of animals who would seem to be anything but animals: a monkey who wears human clothes, and an intellectual horse. In spite of these qualifications, the monkey is very much a monkey when he trumpets and the horse very much a horse when it comes to the perfor- mance of his natural functions. Büchner's target is once more the idealist for whom reality is insufficient; he suggests that there is more truth in an animal's spontaneous behavior than in the refinements of artists who keep actuality at a safe distance.

The language of *Woyzeck* is antipodal to that of classical drama. Büchner wishes to transmit Woyzeck's anguish without the slightest coating of artifice, and he wishes to do the same with the instinctual motivation of such characters as Marie and the Drum Major. As in Lenz's plays, the dialogue here comments instantly on much more than its paraphrasable content—it brings out deepest drives at work in the speaker. Woyzeck's dialogue encompasses extremes of apocalyp- tic despair and idiosyncratic rumination. He mutters, babbles, screams, bellows, and howls his way through the play:

A sin so huge and thick—it smells to high heaven, enough to smoke
out the angels. You have a red mouth, Marie. Is there upon it no
blister? How—Marie, like sin you are beautiful—can mortal sin be so
beautiful?[33]
No stopping—no stopping! . . . No stopping, no stopping! . . . Twist
around, roll around! Why doesn't God blow out the sun, so that everything becomes wrapped in lust, man and woman, man and beast? Do
it by light of day, go at it upon one's hands the way flies do!
Woman! Woman is hot, hot—No stopping, no stopping! . . . [34]
The knife? Where is the knife? I left it right there. It betrays me!
Closer, still closer! What place is this? What's that I hear? Something's
moving. Quiet now.— Around over there. Marie? Ha, Marie! Quiet. Everything quiet! What makes you so pale, Marie? What is that red string
of pearls doing around your neck? From whom did you earn that necklace
with your sins? You were black with them, black? Did I make you
pale? Why does your hair hang so wild? Forget to braid your hair
today?—The knife, the knife! Have I got it? So! . . . [35]

Much of this extremely emotional dialogue is accentuated by physical
gestures. Büchner relies frequently on nonverbal communication. A
good example is the scene where Marie is surprised by Woyzeck while
she is in the act of trying on a pair of earrings which Woyzeck
has not given her:

*(Woyzeck steps in, behind her. She jumps up, her hands moving to
her ears.)*[36]

Here Büchner's recourse to pantomime is not in the manner of
the modern director, who cannot resist punctuating anything on stage
with a gesture. Gesture is integral not merely to the psychodynamics
at work but also to Büchner's philosophical convictions. How better
to show man as puppet than to depict him in situations where his
very motions betray how unfree he is. In the moment Marie's hands
jump to her ears, she is nothing but a marionette responding to the
sudden jerks of forces beyond her control. That instant of surprise
illuminates as nothing verbal can.

[33] *Ibid.*, p. 163.
[34] *Ibid.*, p. 165.
[35] *Ibid.*, p. 174.
[36] *Ibid.*, p. 158.

All through *Woyzeck* one gets the impression that Büchner was intent on sacrificing everything to a forceful concision. Hardly a scene could be shortened more than he shortened it, and the language which fills those scenes is cut to the bone as Büchner applies himself to deleting the linguistic matter which troubled or excited individuals will skip over in real life. Where gesture can make a point better than words, words are dispensed with. There is quite a bit of stichomythia and no dearth of lines consisting of a word or two at the most. All of these economies coincide to give an overwhelming effect of perpetual motion. The world literally spins by, everyone on his own mad wheel. The dynamic, haphazard nature of modern life is conveyed even more frenetically than in Grabbe's street scenes.

In *Danton's Death* Büchner had imitated the Shakespearian history play as well as Shakespearian tragedy. His panoramic subject set its own requirements, forcing him to tone down distortion for the sake of historical truth, limiting his ability to follow through on some of the concrete implications touched upon in scenes such as those that Simon and his fellow citizens dominate. In *Woyzeck* these restrictions are gone; here Büchner can pursue the same theme that was to obsess Brecht, that modern society conspires to make life impossible for those without claws. Though *Woyzeck* is not bound by unity of tone as prescribed by Aristotelians, it does maintain all the way through a consistently dismal and chaotic atmosphere in which grotesqueries are only too natural. Even the commentary of this play contributes to our alienated reception of its disturbing content: the Booth Proprietor, unlike Danton, does not sound like Büchner writing to his family but like a sardonic devil with a Brechtian mind. This weirdness which permeates the play makes it far more than an anticipation of naturalism and expressionism; among modern movements, it anticipates epic theater by projecting characters and situations which challenge our total response to bourgeois society and bourgeois attitudes toward life.

Grabbe had employed the episodic structure in order to do justice to the diverseness and discontinuity of history, and to an extent, this was Büchner's reason for using that structure in *Danton's Death*. But in *Woyzeck,* episodism functions more in the way it did in Lenz's plays, to pick up a variety of distinct actions illustrating a central truth about the nature of society and human nature. Seen this way, *Woyzeck's* originality is pinpointed when we note that Büchner's episodic treatment is consistent in a way Lenz's never was. Lenz alternated between scenes devoted to realistic reproduction of milieu and scenes of quick, tense developments; and at times he slackened off into scenes of pure intellectual elaboration. *Woyzeck* betrays no such casual construction; almost every scene intensifies the momentum worked up by previous scenes; episodic reinforcement is carried to lengths it had never approached before. Not for a moment is there any question as to a scene's intrinsic relevance, even if it strikes us as not absolutely indispensable. This relevance stems from Büchner's refusal to dissipate the tension of his story by slowing up scenes in order to conform to documentary realism rather than his own aggressive rhythms.

The accelerated pace at which the scenes of *Woyzeck* fly by is, of course, associated with the tempo of German expressionistic drama, the very drama against which Brecht reacted. However, this mode of structuring a play for maximum economy of its individual sequences was carried by expressionists like Hasenclever to cryptic lengths unanticipated by *Woyzeck*. Büchner's briefest scene has about it nothing arbitrary; even a single burst of dialogue, if that is all there is to a scene, strikes us as having its place in the total statement of the play. Significantly enough, the episodic manner in which Büchner sketches the road to Woyzeck's hell recalls the manner in which Brecht sketches the somewhat similar road of Baal. In the play of that name and in *Woyzeck* the episodes depict the isolation of an individual who by his very nature is cut off from a society that cannot begin to comprehend his apparent strangeness.

As much as Büchner's last play anticipates expressionistic drama stylistically, it does not anticipate its windiness and hysterics, its indulgence in apocalyptic emotion to the point where entire dramas become elaborated, subjective declamations. To his credit, Büchner anticipates not only epic theater, with its emphasis on forces and conditions, but that side of expressionism which, as Sokel puts it, "looked forward to what is most significant and new in the theater of our own time."[37] This is the kind of expressionism which was not taken in by romantic visions, the kind of expressionism practiced by a writer like Sternheim and a painter like Grosz.

Very likely a fair judgment would be that the early Brecht was expressionistic and antiexpressionistic at the same time, sharing the spirit of revolt permeating the movement but not its naïve idealism nor its highly emotional frame of reference. The early Brecht has

[37] Walter H. Sokel (ed.), *An Anthology of German Expressionist Drama* (New York: Anchor Books, 1963), p. xxii.

much in common with the Büchner of *Woyzeck*. Both felt the challenge to write a drama in which humanitarian sympathies would not keep them from confronting the world at its coarsest—a drama in which every temptation to sentimentalize or romanticize would be resisted and every opportunity to underline the hell of life exploited. The young Brecht and the young Büchner were complex mixtures of nihilism and humanitarianism; both assert that the world is beyond pity but neither can keep himself from extending this superfluous emotion.

Most of all, the young Büchner and the young Brecht share an atmosphere. *Woyzeck*, *Baal*, and *In the Swamp of the Cities* all take for granted a grossly unpalatable parasitism as the normal state of mankind. Hardly a character appears in these plays whose skin has not thickened him into a caricature of evil or exposed him to some fellow creature's exquisite torment. The air is charged with volcanic aggressions; it is only a matter of time before someone is raped or killed or taken for all he's got. Life is lurid and grotesque; characters are both monstrous and all too human at the same time; realism blends with antirealism of the most blatant sort; photography interacts with caricature; cynicism dissipates pathos; and, strangely enough, all this dissonance carries lyrical overtones. Finally, the action is always the same: one human being is relentlessly victimized by another until the victor has drawn blood or the victim fallen by the wayside.

The fact that this victimization is not explicable in terms of ideological doctrine but stems from the very nature of what the world is and must always be is the pessimistic conclusion of the early Brecht every bit as much as of the Büchner of *Woyzeck*.[38] Man does not torment man because class is opposed to class; the tormenting is part of his nature. Eric Bentley has said of Brecht's first plays that they are "studies in force, in the domination of man by man."[39] There is one scene in *Woyzeck* which strikes just this chord, the scene in which the Drum Major picks a fight with Woyzeck. Having casually destroyed Woyzeck's only reason for living—his faith in Marie—the Major now adds insult to injury by calling him a filthy name and threatening to pull his tongue out. The men begin to wrestle, and

[38] Brecht considered *Woyzeck* to belong "to a distinctive class of fragments which are masterpieces rather than incomplete works. . . . " *Schriften zum Theater*, VI (Frankfurt-am-Main: Suhrkamp Verlag, 1964), 328.
[39] *Baal, A Man's A Man, and The Elephant Calf*, ed. Eric Bentley (New York: Grove Press, 1964), p. 107.

naturally the half-starved Woyzeck is no match for his enormously strong opponent. In a moment he is beaten and trembling; the Drum Major begins to sing as his victim's last link to sanity is broken. Now Woyzeck will seek only to purchase a knife—the murder of Marie is assured by one man's spitting on another.

In regard to *Danton's Death,* Büchner's significant choice of a hero who refuses to act was noted as symptomatic of his divergence from Schiller. But passive as he was, Danton at least seemed to have the capacity to decide whether he would, like Hamlet, eventually break out of his lethargy to influence developments. Then again, his very position as an important revolutionary figure made even his passiveness equivalent to decisive action. But distant as Danton may be from the active, idealistic Schiller hero, he is not nearly as distant as Woyzeck, who, it is quite clear, belongs among the multitude of nullities who suffer anonymously. In Woyzeck's case, there is hardly a moment in which we are not acutely conscious of the extent to which he is acted upon; even his intellectualizations, if we can call his sudden insights that, expose the terrible psychic pressures which give him not a moment's rest. Perhaps Woyzeck, rather than Danton, is the first truly passive hero of modern drama. At the very least, what his passivity implies concretely brings him closer to Brecht's hapless economic victims than Danton. The latter still breathes the air of a world with grand pretensions, Woyzeck's world is muck.

When Woyzeck is referred to as "hero," it is in the sense of "protagonist" only. There is nothing heroic about him that would associate him even vaguely with elevating connotations. He is a man of no consequence, and what he finally does is of no consequence except to himself and his victim. As far as society is concerned, it will dispose of the matter through its efficient legal processes while enjoying to the last drop the sensationalism of a murder case which breaks the monotony of an excitement-starved way of life. As much as Büchner sympathized with Woyzeck, he resisted every temptation to ennoble or glorify his central character.

Baumann is opposed to the idea that *Woyzeck* is the Büchner play most pertinent to Brecht's epic theater.[40] He says *Woyzeck* is not epic theater at all; for Büchner does not give us a sequence of progression of episodes; he gives us, rather, a stream of discontinuity. What is more, Büchner compels no decisions from his audience, nor does

[40] Gerhart Baumann, *Georg Büchner, Die dramatische Ausdruckswelt* (Göttingen: Vandenhoeck and Ruprecht, 1961), p. 200.

he conceive of man as a process. This kind of taxonomy has little
to recommend it, proceeding as it does from the formal criteria of
epic theater set forth in Brecht's critical writings rather than from
the nature of his plays. Surely Baumann would not deny that Brecht
learned much from both *Danton's Death* and *Woyzeck,* or that the
latter play, with its grotesque types and horribly parasitic bourgeois
society, has a great deal in it that brings to mind Brecht's menageries.
Baumann is far more perceptive when he points out that Büchner's
plays have neither exposition nor development; they conclude as indeci-
sively as they commence; the action really goes nowhere, no solution
whatever being implied for the human predicament.

    Danton's Death and *Woyzeck* are both radical departures from
Aristotelian dramaturgy, departures which point forward to modern
epic theater. This is not by virtue of their rather unconstricted episodic
development, which anticipates Strindberg as much as Brecht, a Strindberg whose mysticism was the very antithesis of Brecht's materialism.
Büchner's two major plays anticipate Brecht because their episodes,
severally and *in toto,* dramatize a vision of life very much like Brecht's.
What Büchner had in common with Brecht as far as dramaturgic
technique is concerned would hardly matter if that technique were
not employed to communicate a certain kind of awareness. One reads
an episode by Büchner in which a character laments the truth that
man is trapped by circumstances; or a scene in which a character
is so trapped he cannot even lament; a scene in which it is made
quite plain that for the poor, morality is a luxury; or still another
scene which pictures with caricatural vividness the kind of philistine
who lectures morality while practicing hypocrisy. Some scenes expose
man's animalism; others reveal his need for money. The intellectual
substance of these scenes, their emphasis on human beings caught
in the act of functioning either naïvely or cunningly in a world which
gives no second chances, their aggressive concreteness and vividness
in areas where so much of literature until recently has refused to
be concrete or vivid—characteristics of this nature secure the link
between Büchner and Brecht, not the fact that their plays share certain
dramaturgic features.

    A modern historian of theater finds Büchner's realism more advanced
than that of our own time.[41] It is not an outlandish judgment. Büchner
did not work by fixed aesthetic categories, did not make the pursuit

[41] Siegfried Melchinger, *Theater der Gegenwart* (Frankfurt: Fischer Bücherei,
1956).

of the prosaic an inviolable literary tenet. For him the prosaic is something to be penetrated for what it implies about the relationship of impersonal forces to experienced life; to clarify these forces he does not shy away from distorting the very reality he wishes to represent honestly. His realism is far from monochromic. At times it is lyric, at other times narrative, but always it is illustrative; it is never realism for the mere sake of verisimilitude. This flexible kind of realism is essentially the realism of Brecht's epic theater, even if Büchner anticipates far more than Brecht.

Lenz had combined the Shakespearian episodic structure with critical social content; his drama exposed the aristocracy's refusal to face up to the human implications of its callous authoritarianism. Lenz criticized the bourgeoisie as well, for its pretensions to status at the price of values. Whatever Grabbe took from Lenz, he did not follow up the latter's scrutiny of society in terms of class and economics; his episodes invariably revolve upon a different emphasis. Büchner, on the other hand, took a great deal from Lenz, not merely in basic writing style, but in the more important areas of viewpoint and approach. Lenz's episodes made visible the concrete social realities of his time and the manner in which these realities exacerbated the isolation of individuals caught between social and instinctual forces. In *Woyzeck,* much of this emphasis remains, even if Büchner does impart an irrational demonism such as Lenz's dramas only hint at. Woyzeck himself is a Stolzius without the bourgeois props—the world suddenly turns on his one link to all that keeps him functioning. Like Stolzius, his isolation deepens until he commits murder, but Woyzeck kills the thing he loves whereas Stolzius murders for justice.

Of the three German dramatists in this study who learned from Shakespeare how to write a play, Büchner was the most Brechtian. Non-Brechtian was Lenz's refusal to recognize that the aristocracy would not reform itself, and non-Brechtian was Grabbe's refusal to recognize that, for all his cynicism, he was possessed by an infantile craving for personified myths. Though Lenz's social conscience is undeniable, it stops far short of the radical rejections made by Büchner and Brecht. Lenz seems, in fact, to have bent backwards to find something fit for salvage. Brechtianism, when not used as a synonym for cynicism, implies an uninhibited disgust for society as it has functioned in our time, a disgust so pervasive that hope for improvement must begin with the complete scrapping of what is. Anything less revolutionary is considered a ruse, and the Brechtian will not be taken in. This loathing of the bourgeoisie to the point where it is seen as a kind of ugly excrescence whose amputation is equivalent to cancer surgery, this all-consuming hatred of the middle-class mentality as mankind's own worst enemy, Büchner shared with Brecht, even if he did not share Brecht's belief in an alternative.

One thing a study of the plays which anticipate Brecht makes clear is that the development of epic theater was no simple linear process. As an example, one might mention Brecht's programmatic commentary, the kind of speech he gives us at the end of *The Good Woman of Sezuan*. Such an appeal to the audience's intelligence in connection with the play's social implications actually goes back to Lenz. Neither Büchner nor Grabbe followed up this method; their commentary precludes rather than invites action on the part of the audience. Only Lenz shares with Brecht the feeling that no matter how terrible things look, a way out must be sought: "What can the solution be?"[42] To the extent that Brecht's thoughtful insertions are ironically juxtaposed with the action of his drama, he may well have been influenced by Büchner and Grabbe, for they devised the technique of having extremely cynical figures express themselves on the grotesque paradoxes of modern life. But if Grabbe and Büchner convey a far more Brechtian tone than Lenz, the latter anticipates Brecht much more in regard to the use of drama as an instrument of social education.

For all their differences, Lenz, Grabbe, and Büchner comprise a well-defined tradition. They share a realism of milieu and atmosphere but do not practice the meticulous realism which prevailed later in the century. They resort to commentary and caricature, ballad and song, episode and gesture. Their dialogue is concrete and vivid. Their plays consist of scenes whose cumulative message is that the world as they know it smells of innocent corpses and broken lives. Each brings upon the stage not just a few major characters but a host of bystanders to reinforce the point that no matter where one turns, it is the same bleak story. Most important, each manifests a personality that is as prone to lyricism as it is to invective. Their episodic plays could not contrast more sharply with the idealistic dramas of the turn of the century, so emphatically do they imply a world of cold, material circumstances immune to idealistic passion. "It is no trick to be honest if one gets his daily share of soup, vegetables and meat."[43] This was said by Büchner, and it could have been said just as well

[42] Bertolt Brecht, *Der gute Mensch von Sezuan* (Berlin: 1955), p. 160.
[43] Büchner, *Werke und Briefe*, p. 463.

by Lenz or Grabbe. What better way to underscore the relationship of these dramatists to modern epic theater than by noting that the hard recognitions which their plays elaborate would today be labeled "Brechtian."

"What is it within ourselves that lies, whores, steals and murders?"[44] This line sums up Büchner. Man is forever crucified; he must suffer and cause to suffer. Büchner manifests no Freudian faith that the forces working themselves out at our expense can be challenged by intelligence; he imputes to those forces absolute hegemony over human nature. Whatever man attempts is suspect; revolutions are noisy masquerades, and when the noise stops, a harvest of corpses tells the real story. No matter what kind of society man evolves, it will be composed of parasites and sufferers, murderers and victims. Remarkably, Büchner had even fewer illusions than that most nihilistic of German writers, Grabbe, and as much social conscience, if not more, as his major influence, Lenz. An extremist in every sense, he gave up on changing the world by revolution and went to work revolutionizing the aesthetics of modern theater, justifying wholly Lenz's belief that this theater need follow no rules except one: to embody truth about man's actual nature.

[44] *Ibid.*, p. 45.

chapter four:

frank wedekind

The realism of the Lenz-Grabbe-Büchner tradition is not a realism of halftones. These dramatists are possessed of a passion to get into their plays what they feel to be the true forces moving the world, and to this end they have no qualms about exaggerating and distorting the reality they are trying to bring to light. Their work abounds in grotesqueries, in situations, imagery, and linguistic forms that are blatantly subjective; their characters are often caricatured to an extent which the scientific pretensions of naturalistic and realistic literature make impermissible. A great deal of their aesthetic technique is directly traceable to J. M. R. Lenz, the *Sturm und Drang* dramatist who wrote under the twin influences of the emergent middle genre and the episodic dramaturgy of Shakespeare.

From Shakespeare, Brecht and his anticipators learned much that suited their antinaturalistic temperaments, e g., the art of constructing a play of highly vivid episodes which when linked together attained panoramic scope; the compatibility of powerful dramatic effects with a context of commentary, whether this commentary took the form of protracted monologues or crisp poeticized observation; and the miscibility of the tragic and comic as well as the prosaic and lyrical. The Shakespearian history play was a perfect model of dramatized narrative in which individual scenes constituted autonomous units of action. Shakespeare offered an approach to character wholly divergent from the balanced psychological approach of nineteenth-century realism.

To a great extent this approach became identified with Ibsen, and it is Ibsen's characters who receive the mockery of one late-nineteenth-century dramatist who avails himself heavily of Shakespearian technique. Quite well known is Frank Wedekind's contemptuous reference to Ibsen's characters as "domestic animals";[1] Wedekind was as convinced as Brecht that, for all his insight and talent, Ibsen had not come to grips with the real determinants of middle-class life, had not penetrated the respectable surface far enough to disclose the wolfish instincts which energize modern society. When he attacks through characters in his plays the divorce between art and life in the drama of his time Wedekind has Ibsen in mind. He questions whether Ibsen

---

[1] Frank Wedekind, *Prosa, Dramen, Verse* (Munich: Albert Langen. Georg Müller, 1960), p. 382.

was at all capable of doing justice to the kind of natures whose portrayal will always escape softhearted idealists. This Wedekind comment on Hilde Wangel speaks for itself:

The author knows such natures only from the outside and imagines what simply cannot exist. In reality, a Hilde Wangel is a superficial creature with a short memory and little perception. Thanks to a lack of any charm, such temperaments are characterized by stunted and banal spiritual functions. Their natures are comparable to shallow water that presents a dynamic surface only because it flows over uneven pebbles. A Hilde Wangel will never send a man upon two scaffolds, in order to see him fall down; for that, another kind of physical and emotional makeup is required. As a matter of fact, she would be the first to faint at the sight of a mouse or a child's bloody nose.[2]

Wedekind's relationship to Lenz, Grabbe, and Büchner, who influenced him more than any other group of dramatists, makes it inadequate to characterize him as a mere antinaturalist, even if much of his art was an angry reaction to that movement. His contempt for the naturalists was focused on their most successful representative, Gerhart Hauptmann, who Wedekind disliked, particularly after Hauptmann saw fit to dramatize some confidential material about Wedekind's family. Wedekind viewed the naturalists as born snoopers who were turning drama into the art of investigation. In his first play, *The Young World,* Hauptmann is caricatured as a compulsive recorder of everything that happens to him; no triviality is too small, no intimacy too delicate to keep him from an immediate date with his notebook. But for all their meticulous procedures, the naturalists were letting what Wedekind considered the most essential aspect of life go unrecorded. What really drives men and women on could not possibly be projected through "men who can make no children, women who can give birth to none."[3] The very naturalism which shocked so many

[2] *Ibid.,* p. 915. The essay from which this is excerpted, "Schriftsteller Ibsen und 'Baumeister Solness,'" gives us also Wedekind's concept of great art: "Beyond doubt every great work of art, *Faust, Hamlet, Antigone,* is symbolic; but by virtue of symbolizing human nature, not abstract concepts; by virtue of trying to crystallize clear and significant standards for life, not by playing hide-and-seek with the reader." See p. 922.
[3] Frank Wedekind, *Gesammelte Werke* (Munich: G. Müller, 1924), III, 136.

in the last two decades of the nineteenth century struck Wedekind as a very pale imitation of what was actually happening.

It has been said that to fully understand Wedekind, the apostle of sexual vitalism, one has to realize that he moved in an atmosphere thick with Nietzsche-worship. Even the more pedestrian type of intellectual was hypnotized by superman psychology. In the air was the idea that great men and Judaeo-Christian values do not mix. Be that as it may, Wedekind, the man, was as powerful an influence on the literary life of his time as Wedekind, the dramatist. He refused to accommodate his plays to Philistine squeamishness, pictured himself as a kind of *Kraftmensch* whose powerful instincts defied the frightened morality of the rabble. He had trouble no end with the censors, but if we go by Brecht's testimony, this never diminished his vitality.[4] On Brecht himself he seems to have left an indelible impression, and the early Brecht projected very much the same kind of artistic self-image cultivated by Wedekind: the writer as sardonic Bohemian who sees through everything and spends his evenings vocalizing bitter insights to the tune of ballads in disreputable cafés. The Brecht of the twenties was particularly anxious to vitiate those conventions which dictate sharp divisions between the atmosphere of the theater and the more low-brow atmospheres of sports events and carnival shows. Wedekind was very likely his model here; even at the height of his fame, he did not hesitate to made needed money "as a cabaret artist, singing his own ballads in the music halls."

A minor early play reveals Wedekind even at the start of his career as a writer whose anti-idealism by no means sums him up. In *The Quick Painter* a struggling artist suffers and suffers until he manages to sell his first painting. The moment he does so, he is quick to exploit the power of materialistic success; aesthetic idealism goes right out the window. Shrewdly, he knows that the girl he wants can no longer be kept from him by a family whose values are entirely materialistic. Wedekind pictures the artist in question as a man who plays his suffering for all it is worth in a world of types whom no art can reach. This may be among Wedekind's worst plays, but it foreshadows what will be expressed with genius later on. He would always take pains to expose pretentious idealists; he would always be revolted

---

[4] Brecht gives his impressions of Wedekind in "An Expression of Faith in Wedekind," the translated title of a eulogy which appeared originally on March 12, 1918, in *Augsburger Neueste Nachrichten*. The translated version is in *Tulane Drama Review*, VI, No. 1 (Autumn, 1961), 26–27.

by the small-mindedness of bourgeois types who see art only in terms of cash. He would bristle at any approach to life not ruthlessly antisentimental, but sheer opportunism never sat well with him.

Lenz's major plays, especially *The Soldiers,* had underscored the need for society to face up to sex as a force that could not be shunted aside by repressive custom. Lenz even went to the point of advocating subsidized sex for the military. Büchner formulated no such programs, but his plays make clear enough that he did not underestimate the power of sex. Thus, Wedekind is hardly the first German dramatist to deal with what he was persecuted for bringing into the open in his own time, and what he was lionized for by the young people of his time. He is, however, the first German dramatist to write plays which articulate an unabashed sexual vision of life, a vision which comes out most powerfully in his Lulu plays. His most famous play, *Spring's Awakening* (1891), also has sex at the center, but it is worlds apart from his later work; here Wedekind is very much the topical dramatist lashing out at contemporary abuses with a reformist zeal that would soon give way to pervasive cynicism.

Spring's Awakening takes a panoramic look at a particular society from the point of view of the adolescent in search of sexual identity. It is not the kind of neutral look the strict realist would approve; Wedekind leaves no doubt where his sympathies lie; he makes quite sure that the implications of his play will not be attenuated by surface detail. Action does not revolve around a single hero or protagonist but a gallery of types such as Brecht would employ to demonstrate individual variations of a basic human dilemma. Wedekind is concerned with institutionalized bourgeois power as misused by those who dictate behavior at home and school, and with the hapless victims of such an arrangement, girls and boys in the process of maturing. Two of the schoolboys could not be more unlike: Moritz is frightened of his shadow and literally perspires at the sexual and academic pressures his society exerts; Melchior looks this society straight in the eye and is quite willing to defy it. Both these boys are driven to the point where suicide seems attractive.

Instead of educating its young to recognize and accept what are perfectly normal impulses, the society Wedekind attacks does the opposite: it promotes sexual fear and ignorance, making almost certain that no one grows to maturity without psycho-sexual damage. The unreasonable defenses erected against erotic awareness block all curiosity about the mechanics of reproduction. Thwarted in their need for

concrete truth, the young people of this society are bound to overdramatize and distort what would fall into perspective in a less repressive
atmosphere. Inevitably, adolescent fantasy begins to take on psychopathic overtones.

Such unhealthy sex is the substance of a scene in which an adolescent
imagines himself as Othello making a final, ritualistic journey to Des-
demona's chamber, identifies himself with Bluebeard on the verge
of disposing of his seventh wife, and, in general, lets his imagination
transport him to pathological realms. This scene comes right after
one in which Mrs. Bergmann, a typical mother, cannot bring herself
to tell her daughter Wendla how babies are made. The implication
is that the kind of prudery practiced by Mrs. Bergmann makes it
all too inevitable for sick, vicarious sex to be acted out by the young.

In his portraits of misguided parents, Wedekind manages to be
cutting without departing from a generally realistic technique. He
works differently in his portraits of schoolmasters, giving away his
highly exaggerative technique by the names with which he chooses
to endow them: Affenschmalz, Knüppeldick, Hungergurt, Knochen-
bruch, Zungenschlag, and Fliegentod. These absurd names satirize their
owners immediately; the schoolmasters are satirized even more by what
they have to say. The opening of a window stimulates them to pedantic
locutions; it is wholly as important to them as the expulsion of a
student for delinquency. These minuscule minds are quite sure that
they speak for the moral order; they defend that order by bringing
to bear the full weight of their authority on Melchior for composing
a treatise on sex. His protest that he merely put down fact falls on
deaf ears. Wedekind pictures Melchior's trial as very much like the
trials we have come to expect under totalitarian regimes. A miserably
defenseless human being is throttled by monsters in judicial robes.

Wedekind utilizes caricature of the most deliberately gross type.
Unlike Lenz and Büchner, his caricatures are not an uneasy blend
of empathetic observation and bald distortion. His predecessors in
the art of sardonic episodic theater refrained not only from prejudging
their portraits of bourgeois types by means of wholly absurd names,
but they were generally careful not to make character an excuse for
mere discharge of contempt. Wedekind, on the other hand, joins hands
with Brecht in refusing to disguise for a moment that same contempt.
We are never in doubt as to what makes the *Bürger* run in Brecht
and Wedekind; both allow their aggressions against the middle class
to spill over into dehumanized portrayals of scourges pure and simple.

Not only in the sphere of sex do inhibition and repression set the tone. The road to intellectual maturity is just as rocky. A severely regimented system of education militates against any kind of normal development; everything is subordinated to iron-tight discipline and sudden-death competition. Those in charge of molding youth have no qualms about the damage they inflict upon the innocent. Their only concern is that the mounting number of students who commit suicide or go insane will not attract public attention.

In short, Wedekind finds middle-class psychology a horrendous blend of hypocrisy, fear, and misplaced aggression. Like Büchner, he cannot resist mocking the pseudo-religious pretensions compelling this class to picture itself as part of a sacrosanct moral order. At Moritz's funeral, a pastor with the Brechtian name of Kahlbauch shields himself from the rain with an umbrella while expatiating on the "inscrutable disposition of His Grace."[5] But the crowning touch of sanctimony comes from Headmaster Sonnenstich when it is his turn to deposit dirt upon the grave:

Suicide, as the most serious offense conceivable against the moral world order, is the most significant proof conceivable for such a moral world order, inasmuch as he who commits suicide confirms the existence of such an order by making it unnecessary for it to pronounce judgment.[6]

Kahlbauch pontificates very much the way Büchner makes almost every *Bürger* and *Führer* who does not experience suffering from the victim's point of view pontificate, and Wedekind adds bite to exposure by having such nonsense expressed over the fresh corpse of a gratuitously destroyed young man. What could be more grotesque than a metaphysical justification of the world's moral order in such circumstances? If Moritz could answer, he would probably be as tongue-tied as Woyzeck.

While Moritz rots, those who killed him talk rot. Some may feel that when the headmaster tries to console the late Moritz's father by informing him that his son had little chance for promotion and would, at most, have lasted another term, Wedekind is simply going

[5] Eric Bentley (ed.), *The Modern Theatre*, VI (New York: Anchor Books, 1960), 141.
[6] Wedekind, *Prosa, Dramen, Verse*, p. 289.

too far. But he is working here very much the way Büchner worked and the way Brecht would work, trying to sum up with a bland grotesquery what his whole play is about. For as villainous as these hypocrites may be, in a way they are beyond good and evil, so ingrained and complacent is their malevolence. One could not for a moment think of indicting them without questioning the kind of society that extends them power and eminence.

Innocent humanity wedged in between instinct and system—one may well be reminded of the vision in *Danton's Death*. But *Spring's Awakening* does not conclude with bloodstained guillotines, even if Wedekind's final scene is among the most morbid of modern theater; it concludes with a kind of Darwinian affirmation. In a graveyard, Melchior comes up against stark reminders of his society's murderous nature: the grave of the girl he impregnated and the corpse of his friend Moritz. At the moment when he sees no reason to go on living, a man in a mask appears to instill in him an unquenchable need to survive. This mysterious intruder is as blatant a departure from realistic technique as the sight of Moritz carrying his head on his arm. *Verfremdung* is a pertinent concept here; Wedekind abruptly demolishes an atmosphere with which we can identify and creates an atmosphere that can only startle us to wonder and reflection. He makes us realize by his grotesque antinaturalism that in essence his play has been about Eros versus Thanatos as much as it has been about adults versus adolescents. In this struggle, specious morality can prove a potent death force, as Moritz realizes too late:

If only you had told me that earlier! It was morality that sent me
to my doom. I seized the murder weapon for the sake of my parents.
"Honor thy father and mother to enjoy long life." That scripture proved
quite ridiculous in my case.[7]

Here Wedekind links up with the Brecht who maintained that to be good in the conventionally idealistic sense is to stupidly invite disaster. Even more coldly Brechtian is The Man in the Mask's comment on Moritz's regretful look back. He declares that Moritz's parents would by no means have gone to an early grave upon their son's failure—the human capacity to feel has very definite physiological

[7] *Ibid.*, p. 310.

limitations. Anti-idealism could hardly be carried to more sardonic lengths; Wedekind translates a concrete apprehension of life into an unqualified philosophy of egoism. No one does anything except to himself, even if he fools himself into believing that he cares for others or vice versa.

Such cynical generalizations must be balanced against the fact that *Spring's Awakening* is above all a drama in the tradition of protest literature. Again, Büchner comes to mind, for like him, Wedekind manifests polar extremes of awareness; he wants on the one hand to contemplate with icy detachment a Godless world, to stand apart in the role of the sardonic, uncommitted observer, but at the same time he cannot transcend a basic commitment to life. In a way he is a composite of Grabbe and Büchner, sharing the former's highly aggressive cynicism, the latter's furiously outraged sense of fairness, reminding us of Grabbe in his overreaction against sentimentalism, of Büchner in his sensitivity to the tribulations of those who exist to be victimized.

To return to the graveyard scene, the technique implied by Wedekind's bizarre final episode is formally related to the manner in which Lenz concluded *The Soldiers*. Programmatic commentary brings to sharp focus what the action of the play is projecting; like Lenz, Wedekind works this out in a series of tendentious remarks. A sequence of scenes showing a particular society to be antilife becomes again the prelude to wisdom. But this is where Lenz and Wedekind part ways; the latter does not have his characters launch into reform proposals. His assult on contemporary society remains implicit; the only solution offered in the final scene to the problem of individual versus society is that one can do nothing more than to hold on to life in spite of its evils. Wedekind's masked philosopher, who is after all Wedekind himself, speaks more with the sardonic intonations of a Büchner or Grabbe mouthpiece of cynicism than with the reasoned calm of Lenz's *Aufklärer*.

In *Spring's Awakening,* what is behind the action is as obtrusively thrust at the audience as it will be in Brecht's epic theater. All through the play, Wedekind sees to it that the sexual basis for what is happening is not blurred. The action is constantly put into perspective by meaningful comment passed off as dialogue. When Moritz asks, "Did you ever stop to think, Melchior, how we got sucked into this whirlpool?" Wedekind is asking us the same question. When Martha remarks that weeds thrive while roses bloom miserably, she is giving voice to Wedekind's feeling that civilization and vital instinct are tragically incompatible; and when Melchior finds no reason for anyone's acting shocked at what is plain fact, he is expressing Wedekind's own resentment toward a society that will not look truth in the eye. It is quite right to sum up *Spring's Awakening* as "the play with a moral."

Wedekind's dialogue takes in an enormous range of sensibility. Headmaster Sonnenstich, for example, typifies the perfect bureaucrat specializing in ponderous formulations: "Notwithstanding the overwhelming fact of a similarity to which recognition has been extended by incontestable authorities. . . . " He comes through almost as absurdly as his fumbling colleague Zungenschlag: "If by the criteria of authority the pr-prevailing a-a-atmosphere leaves little or nothing to be desired, then I would like to put forth the proposal that during the su-summer vacation the other window also be b-b-b-b-b-b-b-b-bricked up!" Against such dialogue resonating with Wedekind's contempt, *Spring's Awakening* contains much that reflects his empathy with sufferers, his sensitivity to the lyricism of innocence. Sonnenstich comes on stage to speak nonsense right after the following outcries by Moritz:

. . . I shall—SCREAM!—SCREAM!—Becoming you, Ilse!—Priapism!— Loss of consciousness!—My strength is being sucked out of me!—This luck-child, this sun-child—this daughter of joy on my road to misery! OH!—OH![8]

What has been said about the style of *Woyzeck*, also applies here. Speech is intended to give the most immediate transcript of mental process, to take us as close as mere words can to the reality of a human being's deterioration. The technique employed here owes every bit as much to Büchner's example as does Wedekind's use of language to vent his rage at pseudo-moralists.

Then there are passages imbued with poetic feeling that convey a rapturous state of mind:

The road is like a fleecy carpet—not the tiniest rock, no thorn.—My feet do not feel the ground. . . . Oh, how I slumbered last night![9]

---

[8] *Ibid.,* pp. 282–83.
[9] *Ibid.,* p. 277.

Even though Wedekind's language is "always a little abstract and more than a little idiosyncratic,"[10] his linguistic talents are undeniable; his speech is as rich with mimetic implications and tonal inflections as that of Lenz and Büchner.

Revelation by monologue is as intrinsic to *Spring's Awakening* as it was to *Danton's Death*—Wedekind availing himself freely of a device frowned upon by scrupulous naturalists. Through monologue we learn of one schoolboy's murderous sexual fantasies; a conventional mother's failure to appreciate the true forces at work in a boy who seeks her help; the powerful psychological change produced in a young girl by her first sexual experience; the utter desperation of a young man who cannot find his way out of the maze of problems his society has manufactured for him; and another young man's utter incomprehension of that same society's stigmatizing him for doing what came naturally. Even when Wedekind gives us ostensibly natural dialogue, he has his characters ruminate in such a way that we get the equivalent of short monologues interspersed throughout the play; he is less concerned with doing justice to the texture of real-life speech than with extending the scope of dialogue to define the nature of the world in which his characters function.

Wedekind's episodic treatment owes much to Büchner, whose *Woyzeck* was also composed of scenes depicting sufferers and insufferables. Like the latter, Wedekind shifts from episodes of pathos and lyrical feeling to episodes of broad and caustic humor, underscoring by alterations of tone the inequities of an impersonal society. Again like Büchner, Wedekind finds society divided into groups which cannot begin to communicate. On a more technical level, both dramatists are realists in some scenes, fantasists in others, and both present a series of pictures culminating in a forceful indictment. Most of all, episodic treatment allows Wedekind to portray society at a kaleidoscope of impulse and repression. Some scenes show youthful impulse in its natural expression; others reveal youthful impulse colliding with censorious puritanism in the institutionalized authority of family, church, and school. *Spring's Awakening* is composed of pictures showing the young as they really are and pictures showing the young as they must be thanks to the power of their elders.

Wedekind juxtaposes scenes for ironic effect, again like Büchner. An alert audience can pick up a great deal merely by the way scenes

---

[10] Bentley (ed.), *The Modern Theatre*, p. 98.

alternate. Thus, Wedekind concludes one episode with the smug know-nothingism of petty professors and begins another with a chance meeting between Melchior and Wendla in the course of which these two young people reveal a complexity unsurmised by their elders; indicates in one scene that adolescents are all too aware how obsessed with sex the adult world is, and in the next scene shows how adamantly sex information is denied those on the threshold of adulthood; proceeds to comment on Mrs. Bergmann's puritanism with a scene of histrionic onanism; footnotes a scene in which Melchior seduces Wendla with a scene in which the former's mother cautions Moritz against impulsive behavior that will not stand to his credit later. Wedekind sets up patterns of ironic relevance from the very start of his play; *Spring's Awakening* is the perfect ironic title for a mosaic of scenes in which the rites of spring are celebrated with the dance of death.

In fact, scarcely a character or aspect of life is presented by Wedekind without dialectic counterpart. The energy of youth versus the inhibitory conservatism of those older is the main thematic contrast of *Spring's Awakening,* but it is merely one contrast among many. One could go on to show the antitheses implied by Frau Gabor and Frau Bergmann as well as by the prostitute Ilse and The Man in the Mask; or how heterosexuality is contrasted with homosexuality, cruelty with sensitivity, system with life, the sensibility of the male with that of the female. Patterns of strong contrast would always show up in Wedekind's theater, and those who explain them as symptomatic of the dramatist's hopeless self-division may have a point; for Wedekind was never able to resolve the larger issues on which he pretended to speak with messianic authority; like the other writers under discussion, he was persuasive in his exposure of the way things were but quite unconvincing on the possibility of something better.

Spring's Awakening is the Wedekind play most unmistakably related to the kind of episodic theater initiated by Lenz. But it is not the only play in which we can detect anticipations of Brecht. For example, the Prologue to *Earth Spirit* (1894) is bound to recall us to any number of cynical prefaces and interpolations of Brechtian theater. Wedekind's spokesman is an animal tamer who does not hesitate to identify theatrical entertainment with the amusements of a zoo in which a brute struggle is the main attraction. Sadly enough, the attraction has begun to lose its magnetism thanks to the competition of other fare, especially Ibsen. Wedekind insinuates a criticism of life by focusing on the harsh economics of theater:

Times are bad!—All the gentlemen and ladies
Who once collected at my cages
Now honor farces, Ibsen, operas and plays
Such fare gets all the kudos of this age.
My boarders are in such need of fodder
That they've begun to feed on one another.
But nothing beats an actor's lot!
The flesh upon his ribs is never threatened
While colleagues starve in times of dreadful need.[11]

He goes on to vent his contempt for the drama of his time:

What do you see in the comedies and tragedies?!—
Domestic animals with well-bred emotions,
Quite content to feast on naught but vegetables
They revel in innocuous commotions,
Like those who prattle—in the pit: . . .[12]

Only his drama constitutes a truly authentic response to the bestial nature of life; only his drama refuses to shy away from an uninhibited presentation of "the true beast, the wild, beautiful beast. . . ." This is the kind of showmanship which Brecht would employ to enhance the shock value of plays like *The Threepenny Opera*. Wedekind may well have taught him the art of attention-getting presentation.

Wedekind's magnificent beast is his most famous incarnation of amoral sexuality—Lulu—and *Earth Spirit* is dominated by her electric presence from start to finish. She lives almost every moment on the level of shameless physical appetite, mesmerizing with a glance the sundry males who cross her path. She serves as the focus for activity which allows Wedekind once again to stress the inextricable connections of Eros and Thanatos. Her sexuality is the inevitable prelude to masculine suicide, whether by deadly weapon or sheer physical collapse. In spite of the corpses that litter her past, she continues to cast her spell upon fresh victims. Only at the very end of *Earth Spirit* does the spell lose its potency, and it is off to jail with Lulu.

For all its resemblance to the more tightly knit variety of play,

---

[11] Wedekind, *Prosa, Dramen, Verse*, p. 381.
[12] *Ibid.*, p. 382.

Earth Spirit is actually a series of episodes. Wedekind does not give us the kind of play whose construction is so unitary and organic that all its actions comprise one single development. Nothing could be further from the dramaturgy which commences with exposition and concludes with residues of climax than *Earth Spirit*. Separate acts treat separate actions. Lulu is shown in terms of the men to whom she is a fatal temptation. Dr. Goll is lascivious and possessive; when he realizes what kind of woman he married in Lulu, he suffers a stroke. Schwarz, the artist, kills himself when he too has his eyes opened; his idealization of Lulu prepared him least of all for the truth. The power-mad Schön who, for all his conformity in the world of bourgeois business, proves Lulu's worthiest opponent, goes the way of all flesh when Lulu pumps five bullets into him.

Again and again, the same essential action recapitulates itself: Lulu, simply by being what she is, changes men into moths near light. The dance of death is performed in a series of grotesque variations, and Wedekind hints at the senselessness of what is going on so tumultuously by indicating it to be merely one small note in a world of dissonance. This is surely the point of footnoting the suicide of one Lulu victim and the agitation of another with the announcement that revolution has broken out in Paris. As in Grabbe's plays, one man's tragedy is quickly lost in the enormous swirl of what is going on elsewhere.

Wedekind prided himself not only on peopling his plays with characters who would not be at home in the living rooms of Ibsen's drama but on inventing for these characters a strange new dialogue devoid of warm human intonation. This dialogue is so mechanical that it often strikes one as the monotonous emission of the same set of signals. Above all, the impression is of characters mouthing what will never find a responsive ear. Everyone seems anxious to speak at the same time, sentences crisscross haphazardly, conversation becomes the alternation of telegram phrases. It is dialogue designed to parallel Wedekind's depersonalization of character in the realm of language.

For all its originality, this stylized speech reflects the kind of verbal mechanisms by which Lenz and Büchner represented mentalities and mental states. Their characters often spoke like puppets tied to a single emotional string and defined themselves by stereotyped speech patterns. What distinguishes Wedekind is that he condenses language to the point where it comes through as the most forceful verbal equivalent of sheer drive. His language transcends self-consciousness, and one often gets the impression of words materializing themselves like circles in water shattered by rock; everything said is wholly automatic. The effect of such dialogue volleying back and forth is of a deadening mindlessness. Wedekind need not even have put any cynical phrases into his characters' mouths; only the morally dead could speak such a soulless language; here the human being verbalizes what Wedekind believed to be his real nature.

Like Lenz, Wedekind can write monologues which comment as much on the speaker as on the absurd world in which he insists on overdramatizing himself. A very unamusing emotional crisis comes through with comic overtones when Schön realizes his house is not a home:

SCHÖN (*alone, looking around*): A real Augean stable. This the evening of my life. Show me a single corner still clean. A plague on my house. The poorest day laborer has a cleaner nest. Thirty years of work, and this is my family circle, my circle. . . .(*He looks around.*) God knows, who's eavesdropping on me now! (*He pulls a revolver out of his breast pocket.*) One's life is in danger here! (*He walks, the cocked revolver in his right hand, to the right and addresses the closed window curtains.*) This my family circle! The fellow has courage!—Might it not be better to blow my brains out?—I'm up against mortal enemies, but this. . . . (*He pulls up the curtain but finds no one concealed.*) The filth—the filth. . . . (*He shakes his head and goes to the left.*) Madness is overpowering my reason, or—exceptions prove the rule![13]

This kind of speech, whose parodistic quality anticipates Sternheim and Brecht, catches the ludicrous atmosphere enveloping *Earth Spirit*. Though a newspaper tycoon who need nod to no one, Schön expects of life the same validation of bourgeois value that inspires clean-living clerks. He goes to pieces because the society in which he rides high is going to pieces. Wedekind's symbolism could not be plainer than when he shows us the magnificent Renaissance home that is Schön's castle invaded by creatures from the lowest depths. These unsavory characters make themselves at home and reveal a vocabulary unburdened by moral assumptions. They have only one aim, to take what they do not have:

[13] Wedekind, *Prosa, Dramen, Verse*, p. 444.

HUGENBERG: Who lives here then?
RODRIGO: We do!

Rodrigo's statement sums up Wedekind's world.

Earth Spirit indicates Wedekind would not have been surprised by what happened in Germany within fifteen years of his death. The play exposes the *Bürger* as utterly incapable of grasping the import of the forces building up against him. Far worse, the *Bürger* actually believes the kind of powers Lulu embodies should be responsive to his need for a nice quiet life. Adrift on a sea of naïve assumptions, the *Bürger* advances slowly but surely to his inevitable demise while spouting moralistic nonsense. Like Brecht, Wedekind cannot get over the farcical disparity between hard facts and bourgeois attitudes; like Brecht, he works this out in farcical situations whose implications are deadly serious.

It has rightly been said that the morality by which Lulu lives is not definable. She comes through as an amorphous force ready to attach herself to the nearest available man; she combines pristine innocence with a colossal capacity for homicide. But precisely because she sails by no recognizable moral charts she magnifies the contradictions of those who invoke morality but chase after Lulu. The technique of personifying forces allows Wedekind to make almost every motion and word of *Earth Spirit* resonate with significance for his dominant theme, that modern society has wholly lost the ability to live in harmony with the very instincts which drive it on, that modern men live by pseudo-sexual values that can bring them only misery.

Like Freud, Wedekind could not overstate the power of sex as the driving force of personality. This emphasis on basic, knowable forces and how they work themselves out in personal terms would concern Brecht as fully as Wedekind, even if the former located these forces in the realm of economics instead of psychology.[14] Brecht, like Wedekind, wrote drama on the assumption that he was dramatizing forces that could not be denied, forces whose recognition the bourgeois mentality could only be shocked into by grotesque visualizations.

---

[14] However, at least one critic speaks of Wedekind in a way which implies he was every bit as concerned with economics as Brecht. In *Frank Wedekind* (Leipzig: Reisland, 1922), Fritz Dehnow takes Wedekind to task for being so conscious of money that he reduces everything to "the need for property." See p. 73, which contains the following couplet to prove Dehnow's point: "Money is freedom and nobility/Peace of mind and human dignity."

Lulu is as much an antitype to bourgeois society as Woyzeck was. Both provoke moralistic admonition from their fellow citizens, whom nothing disturbs so much as an unconventional gesture. Woyzeck's miserable descent into murder and madness could well confirm the *Bürger* in his equation of middle-class morality with Providence, and so could Lulu's. Like Woyzeck, Lulu travels farther and farther along the margin of acceptable society until she is finally ostracized from the company of all except those who live beyond that society's versions of good and evil.

The grisly conclusion comes in *Pandora's Box,* which Wedekind considered organic to the four-act play preceding it. If *Earth Spirit* was dominated by the in-groups of the bourgeois world, this play is dominated by those who have long cast off their civilized masks, if they ever wore any. Wedekind brings on stage human bodies manipulated by anthropoid minds. Rodrigo Quast is all muscle, vanity, and cynicism, quite prepared to do away with others for his comfort; Casti Piani has an eye out for attractive women, so that he can meet his commitments to Egyptian houses of prostitution. They are just two specimens among a collection of swindlers, parasites, and black-mailers into whose company Lulu moves upon her escape from jail. She is lucky to escape from them as well, but not for long. As a prostitute in London, she meets Jack the Ripper, and he is her last customer.

The creature whose vitality and magnetism changed men into swine in *Earth Spirit* is barely recognizable in *Pandora's Box.* She still has admirers, but they are easily outnumbered by victimizers out for the little blood she says she has left. If Wedekind is without illusions on the psychology of the bourgeoisie, he is even more so on the psychology of the sub-bourgeoisie, that class of adventurers and opportunists waiting only for prey. In the realm they inhabit, there are only flies and spiders and the two species are quickly interchangeable. It is a realm whose exploration Brecht would continue, but Wedekind said he saw little evidence of its existence in the literature of his day.

For all the truth of the observation that in the second Lulu play Wedekind casts a less glacial eye on the swirling carnal whirlpool, the author of *Pandora's Box* cannot be accused of having gone soft. In the play, love is made on the couch of a man murdered by one of the lovers; a fugitive prostitute infects her only male friends with syphilis; a lesbian makes the supreme sacrifice of sleeping with a repulsive gymnast in order to win the favors of the prostitute she loves; a white-slaver sings the praises of brothel life; every perversion is taken for granted. The play forces one into a world where the psychopathic response is normal and where all our conventional assumptions are, to say the least, irrelevant. How much *La Dolce Vita* is the life of the cesspool, Wedekind realized long before it became a fashionable insight. Lulu declares: "Is there anything sadder on this earth than a daughter of joy!"

Wedekind was as alive as Büchner to the powerful effects obtainable by nonverbal theater. All through the Lulu plays, meaningful gesture complements self-revealing dialogue. Toward the end of *Pandora's Box,* pantomime contributes to the highly grotesque effect produced by Lulu's taking on three very strange men before succumbing to Jack. The first is Herr Hunidei, whom Lulu finds difficult indeed to figure out:

LULU: What are you trying to say?

HERR HUNIDEI: (*He puts his hand on her mouth and leaves his index finger on his lips.*)

LULU: I don't understand what that means.

HERR HUNIDEI: (*He holds her mouth closed.*)[15]

This goes on and on; the lack of communication exposed between Wedekind's characters was never so shockingly evident. For Hunidei, Lulu is the object of some ritualistic fantasy who would spoil everything by reminding her customer that she is real. And she hardly succeeds in getting across more of herself with her next two men, both of whom reinforce the fact that Lulu is attracting the worst of human deformities. Her fourth man ends it all, and the last we hear from Lulu are her screams; one beast has been pounced upon by another, who kills simply because it is his nature.

The Lulu plays are not panoramic in the sense that they shift about from one locale of action to another in order to encompass what seems to be happening all over. But they do have panoramic scope, for in the course of the two plays we come across characters from just about every level of society, from the affluent capitalist Schön

---

[15] Wedekind, *Prosa, Dramen, Verse,* p. 524–25.

to the artist for hire Schwarz; from the established Dr. Goll to the vagrant Schigolch. The Wedekind landscape takes in procurers, prostitutes, cardsharps, and vagrants as well as representatives of more legitimate pursuits. Wedekind throws all these characters into a proximity which points up how much the underworld is merely a change in degree from conventional society. After killing Lulu, Jack remarks on the poverty of her quarters—not even a towel to be found; his outrage could not be more middleclass.

Diebold has called Wedekind "the tragicomic moralist of the flesh," pointing out that the man who extolled sensuality as a supreme value was never very far from the man who realized sensual living was pernicious. There is truth in this, for Wedekind in no way idealizes the seamy lives of the very persons he pictures as living by his philosophy, those on the periphery of society who prize their animalism too highly to surrender it for civilized status. But, as Diebold himself has noticed, these types are equivalent in the world of Wedekind to the kings of Shakespeare's world; only ancient kings and modern trash have any power to actualize their impulses; only they are not emasculated by convention. The point is that at bottom Wedekind was not quite the simple moralist he tried to picture himself in *Censorship;*[16] there he asserts that he had never presented evil as good and vice versa;[17] the fact is that at bottom he preferred id to superego.

Wedekind is less a moralist than a seeker of value in a world that negates value at every turn. Grabbe sought an exception to the unheroic nature of human life in the stature of mythical leaders, but he knew all too well that greatness is perishable. Wedekind sought an exception to the devitalized banality of modern life in impressive personifications of instinct, but he knew exactly what Grabbe did; his heroic characters soon enough end in muck; by and large they

---

[16] *Censorship* reveals again that Wedekind was a sensualist with a bad conscience. It shows him concerned with the lurid impressions made by his plays. He argues here for religion which is an extension of common sense rather than naïve wish-fulfillment, for religious recognition of the body. All through the play, one cannot escape the feeling that he was in doubt as to the validity of his mission to unite religious and sexual feeling. He seems well aware that the prophet isolated from society may well succumb to the temptation to play God, to translate his own egoism into moral doctrine.

[17] Wedekinds' mouthpiece is Buridan, who defends himself against the charge that his work is immoral: "In none of my works have I depicted good as bad or bad as good. I have never falsified the consequences which flow from human behavior. I have only demonstrated these consequences in their inexorable necessity."

exist to be misunderstood, hounded, or destroyed. It is not unconscious morality that makes Wedekind point this out, but a realistic grasp of life which will not let fantasy obscure fact. For the dramatists who anticipate Brecht, life is seen correctly only when judged by our worst expectations.

In effect Wedekind gives us the same sinister world which Grabbe and Büchner summarized in nihilistic monologues, the same self-devouring world which Brecht would first try to accept for what it was, in *Baal* and *In the Jungle of the Cities,* and which he would later feel it his task to help revolutionize. What distinguishes Wedekind as well as Brecht from Grabbe and Büchner is in part traceable to the cultural fact that the philosophy of materialism was by the end of the century far more firmly entrenched than ever before. Büchner and Grabbe lived at a time when materialism and naturalism were beginning to challenge all idealistic systems, when the very dimensions of the unavoidable, oncoming ideological crisis frightened many into romantic withdrawals. It was an age in which one believed in world-wills, in dark demonic forces, in dialectical systems that were highly abstract. It is no more surprising that the time which produced Schopenhauer and Hegel should produce Grabbe and Büchner than that the time of Marx and Freud should produce dramatists like Wedekind and Brecht. The world of all these dramatists is equally evil, but Wedekind and Brecht are very much of their period when they declare it to be so for sexual or economic reasons.

A more subtle change in theater and attitude between Wedekind and his predecessors is that Wedekind wrote with the realization that his art, for all the resistances it was bound to encounter, might well exert influence on bourgeois thought. He was very much concerned with sexual morality and anxious to contribute to the struggle for a liberalized sexual code. Among other things, his *Music* asserts the rights of women to abortion. The attitude behind his drama may have been more hopeless than he could admit to himself, but it does not approach the fatalistic resignation of Grabbe and Büchner. Unlike them, Wedekind is not primarily concerned with lamenting the unalterability of the human condition; the lurid and sordid world he puts on the stage is intended to show us to ourselves as we really are—and had better not be. Like Brecht, he often seems to say "anything goes" but does not mean it; only a fine moral sensibility could construct the zoos of two-footed creatures given us by Wedekind and Brecht. They sermonize with dung.

Friedrich points out that Wedekind appears to lack "the social pity of the naturalists and the later expressionists," while his subjectivity, violence, and rhetorical style separate him from the documentary emphasis of the naturalists.[18] Interestingly enough, almost everything one can say about Wedekind's relationship to the expressionists is valid about Brecht's relationship to them. According to Sokel, "Brecht showed the Dionysiac essence of Expressionism"[19] in *Baal,* concerning himself in that first important play, as he would later on in *A Man's a Man,* with the value of naked instinct in a frightened depersonalized society. This was precisely Wedekind's concern. Sokel adds that "Brecht made expressionism 'realistic,' " stripping it of "the illusion that the explosive liberation of 'essential man' could be compatible with humanism." Wedekind was just as un-Rousseauistic. This is precisely why one German scholar finds it hard to understand why Wedekind's work did not receive the approval of the Third Reich, whose leaders often mouthed slogans not at all antithetic to Wedekind's championship of instinct.

Undeniable as Wedekind's linguistic influence was on the expressionists, there were definite limits to the extent they could assimilate his wealth of dialogue styles; they simply did not share his passion for pitilessly stripping everything to its core. Brecht, on the other hand, was most receptive to just this side of Wedekind, following him in his use of a diverse mixture of linguistic forms, from Schillerian rhetoric to vulgarized concisions. Like Wedekind, he writes dialogue whose cynical intonations are heightened by the very speech rhythms in which it demands to be articulated, and by imagery which reminds us how much this is a world of tooth and claw. Brecht continued Wedekind's revolt against "literary" theater as well as Wedekind's practice of stylized, antinaturalistic grotesqueries; both poet-dramatists relished the coarsely worded insight.

Aside from the Lulu plays, Wedekind comes through as most Brechtian in plays where he identifies the reality principle with a healthy suspicion of idealistic ethics. *King Nicolo or Such Is Life* (1902) makes the point that in the bourgeois world, power and vulgarity go hand in hand—to be noble is to be isolated and impotent. Quite naïve is the artist's belief that his frustration is sanctified by the holiness of his mission; artists are mere luxury items bought and

[18] Werner P. Friedrich, *History of German Literature* (New York: Barnes and Noble, 1959), p. 244.
[19] Sokel (ed.), *An Anthology,* p. xxix.

paid for by the moneyed bourgeoisie.[20] At the center of middle-class life is a worship of the material and lucrative that holds implications for everyone, without exception. Head-in-the-clouds aestheticism invites disaster.

The world is made least of all for the tender-minded. This is never dramatized more acidly than in *Music* (1906). A young woman is totally victimized by a professor of music who deludes her, impregnates her, impoverishes her, and eventually drives her to the point where she is a step away from insanity. Through all of this he receives not a slap on the wrist from bourgeois authority while his victim has to contend with punitive laws against abortion and winds up in prison. At the end of the play her baby is dead, she in a state of hysterical collapse, while the professor of music steps blithely away from the wreckage to go on with his pleasant middle-class life. *Music* is a vitriolic illustration pattern of the extent to which amoral parasitism thrives in a society where one need only keep up appearances. Small wonder the young woman in question comes to realize her hopeless situation is really quite comical.

If what the Germans call *Sachlichkeit* is attenuated in much of Wedekind's later work, it is quite prevalent in *The Marquis of Keith* (1900). Here a cynical philosophy of life is presented without any overtones of pathos or pathology; the play provides great insight into the polar divisions of Wedekind's complex psychology without the kind of morbid atmosphere which envelops a nightmarish play like *Wetterstein Castle*.[21] Two sides of Wedekind's personality are made

[20] This observation is made in *The Tenor* (1897), a short play in which Wedekind presents modern society as a treadmill of commerce from which no one is exempt. His spokesman of cynicism is the singer Gerardo, who declares that love is a deplorable bourgeois virtue, that there is no success that is not materially rewarding, that only the sick would spend their time on something that did not prove lucrative. For Gerardo, every moment of his life is tied to his trade: he lives quite literally by the principle that time is money.

[21] *Wetterstein Castle* (1910) shows Wedekind trying to be far more explicit about matters he worked more integrally into the action of earlier plays. His art became increasingly one of commentary. Once again we get two Wedekinds: the man in search of an ethos and the cynic without reservations. Wedekind directs his usual fire at the bourgeoisie, but he shows equally that there is no real alternative to commercialized living. Absent is any real exaltation of instinct: Effie, a girl who seeks total sexual fulfillment, is killed to satisfy the perverted lust of a human beast named Tschamper. And upon her corpse another business deal is consummated. The smell of neurosis was never more powerful in Wedekind's work, even if his neurosis allowed him

flesh here: the individual above all eager to affirm his animalism and the individual wholly afraid of life. The Marquis speaks with a Brechtian voice when he identifies religious values with business values—sin is merely bad business. Just as Brechtian here is the constant definition of the action by the explicit commentary of characters whose dialogue takes us straight to their basic attitudes.

Ernst Scholz seeks existential meaning through self-sacrifice, an attitude totally unintelligible to the Marquis, an exploiter par excellence. Life being the merry-go-round it is, the Marquis must beg the man he holds in contempt for some money. He receives instead the advice that he give up his dissolute ways and retire to a sanitarium, advice that begins to make sense when the woman closest to him ends her life. By now the Marquis should be totally destroyed, but he is not, though he fiddles with a revolver. At the last moment, unexpected money falls into his hands and it reignites the old vitality. Why not continue living, inasmuch as life is anything but a respecter of what we tend to take most seriously. "Life is a roller coaster . . . " and one may as well continue to ride; the Marquis makes the same affirmation of life that the Man in the Mask talked Melchior into making. As revolted as Wedekind was by a bourgeois world, he saw as little reason as Brecht not to relish the passing scene; the gusto of their cynicism is a major determinant of their style.

Wedekind is reported to have given an unforgettably convincing performance as Scholz. He may have acted the part so well because it was not wholly a part. For all his conviction that dutiful idealists were sick to the core, he manifested in his own uncompromising aesthetic positions the same kind of self-sacrificial temperament which he painstakingly deplored in his more masochistic characters. Only when we leave the written page to observe Wedekind's one-man fight with censors outraged by his sexual ethos do we realize that when he mocked the messianic zeal of would-be society saviors in plays like *Hidalla or Karl Hetmann, the Dwarf-Giant,* he was actually engaging in self-laceration. He was as torn between commitment to a cause and the cynical view that all causes exist to be seen through as were Lenz and Brecht.

It was not above Wedekind to put a penetrating insight into the mouth of an out-and-out rogue, and it is a rogue in *Hidalla* who

---

to see what must forever be shut to the less troubled. *Wetterstein Castle* is a ghastly vision.

tries to convince the woman he is after how much life belongs to the living: "Oh, Fanny, Fanny—a living scoundrel is much better for your health than the greatest dead prophet." Can one conceive of a more Brechtian declaration of love? Actually, one can take at random any better work by Wedekind and Brecht and expect to find the same relish for the cynical, the same mockery of bourgeois values, the same hard observations on the extent to which neither art nor anything else is sacred in a world where only cash and pleasure counts, the same emphasis on animal instinct driving people on, in short, the same antisentimentalism, the same refusal to be taken in. Neither shies away from social areas exotically remote from the bourgeois living room; both give us a world of individuals against whom the good citizen locks his door. Neither has the least respect for aesthetic criteria which dictate an art of prosaic texture; both spurn the unities and load their plays with explanatory commentary. It is no exaggeration to say they are willfully antinaturalistic. This is not to suggest they are mere carbon copies of one another, but it is to imply that for all their differences, they are kindred spirits. With them, the anti-ideal-istic rebellion in German drama extends to modern times; the force of their work challenges anew the pre-eminence of the Lessing-Goethe-Schiller tradition.

chapter five:

karl kraus

Among the figures who dominated Vienna's cultural life during the first three decades of this century, there was one writer about whom no one had mixed emotions. Karl Kraus (1874–1936) was either loved or hated, praised without reservation or attacked without mercy, idolized or dismissed. For some he was much more than a gifted satirist and little less than a cultural phenomenon;[1] for others he was a biased[2] and destructive chronicler of times which demanded least of all the vitriol he was constantly pouring out. Kraus himself encouraged this polar division in critical thinking. An absolutist in every way, he demolished and championed artistic reputations with an alacrity born of the conviction that he was an infallible taste-maker.

Offered in 1899 a high literary post on *Die Neue Freie Presse,* Vienna's most influential liberal newspaper, Kraus turned it down to found his own satirical periodical, *Die Fackel.* In it he fought for the reputations of writers like Wedekind,[3] whose work he was the first to produce in Vienna, and assaulted, among many other targets, the highly repressive sexual code of his day.[4] His principal crusade

[1] Berthold Viertel describes how he came to realize that Karl Kraus could not be taken exception to merely as a literary personality: "And I was not spared the insight that when I fled from Karl Kraus, I was actually fleeing from the most acute mirror-image of an era and its humanity. . . ." See his *Karl Kraus* (Dresden: Rudolf Kammerer Verlag, 1921), p. 8.

[2] For some it would be no slander to characterize Kraus as a bigot who had it in for Germanic Jewry, since a great deal of his work puts the Jews on the griddle of his satire. From *The Last Days of Mankind* one gets anything but a truthful picture of the Jews' participation in Germany's First World War effort; Kraus takes notice only of Jews who connive for profits and whoop it up for war. A case could be made for the view that Kraus, of Jewish descent, belongs in that tragic company of Germany's stepchildren which numbers Wassermann and Weininger among its self-divided members. Then again, a case could be made for the view that Kraus concentrates on the Jews only because they have the greatest moral tradition to live up to. Such a case is made by Werner Kraft in *Karl Kraus* (Salzburg: Otto Müller, 1956), pp. 80–81. For a less complimentary view, see Emanuel Bin Gorion, *Der Fackel Reiter* (Berlin: Morgenland, 1932), pp. 15–16.

[3] The speech Kraus made at the first Viennese performance of *Die Büchse der Pandora* can be found in his *Literatur und Lüge* (Munich: Verlag "Die Fackel," 1958), pp. 9–21.

[4] Kraus's early *Fackel* essays on Eros denied were collected in two books: *Sittlichkeit und Kriminalität* (Leipzig: L. Rosner, 1908) and *Die chinesische Mauer* (Leipzig: K. Wolff, 1914). In these works, he asserts conviction that the West was inviting a whirlwind of demonic sexuality with its unrealistic sexual codes.

was directed against what he considered to be the modern age's increasing perversion of language, which he viewed as a mystical entity with a life all its own and the ultimate key to what a culture stands for in the moral sphere.

This reverence for the written and spoken word inspired Kraus to polemics in which he saw himself as the vengeful guardian of the living word against all defilers; it inspired him also to write *The Last Days of Mankind* (1922), a panoramic episodic play about World War I that is as much a satire prompted by the pettiness of those who made the war possible as it is a tragedy of European man rushing suicidally into oblivion. It is a play of such epic dimensions and astonishing linguistic brilliance that no critic of its contents can begin his work unapologetically. Nonetheless, the best way to convey what Kraus has done is merely to recite what he put into his Prologue, Epilogue, and five extremely long acts.

The Prologue opens with the hawking shouts of newspaper vendors announcing the assassination at Sarajevo, a piece of news whose reception by the average citizen is remarkably complacent. If anything, the killing of the Archduke promises to improve things: "Everything is going to be better! I tell you, we are heading for a period like that under Maria Theresa!"[5] The imminence of a state funeral such as takes place once in a generation charges the air with excitement, though it is regretted that such momentous developments are not always good for business. Conversation after conversation makes quite clear that the mass of citizens are unable to see what is really going on except through a haze of chauvinistic fantasy; the headlines provide a good excuse to ventilate prejudicial emotion. To the representatives of the press, however, the people of Vienna could not rise to the occasion with greater solemnity.

To what extent prewar Austria was controlled by the force of one petty and impoverished mentality after another is Kraus's subject in the first act. The arrant sentimentalities of *Bürger* on the make are matched by the automated thoughtlessness of officials barking and executing orders in the halls of imperial power: the very texture of Germanic society is an incredibly ritualized hypocrisy. Genuine human relationships have been pre-empted by a rigid pecking order, so that the most important question must always be: Who has final authority? It is only normal for the same man to be obsequious to his superiors

[5] Karl Kraus, *Die Letzten Tage der Menschheit* (Munich: Kösel Verlag, 1957), p. 47.

and dictatorial to his subordinates. In such a power- and status-conscious society, the death of a leading player like Ferdinand is bound to have crucial social consequences as his allies and enemies jockey for advantage. But none of this will become common knowledge thanks to Viennese journalism, which has an eye out only for the transcendent moment. Such a moment comes when the editor of a newspaper orders an associate to describe how devoutly the royal corpses are prayed over. "Make sure you write how they are praying," echoes against the uncontrollable sobbing of the deceased's children. It is the kind of scene the press simply cannot ignore.

The first act makes it laughably obvious that a steady diet of sweet fictions has spoiled the Viennese appetite for cold, hard truth: the very sparks which ignite World War I warm the cockles of superpatriotic hearts, which beat never so wildly as when the death of peace is assured. The refrain, *Serbien muss sterbien,*[6] sums up how the average Austrian feels about his Slavic neighbors. The commencement of the "Great War" is an occasion for rejoicing, whether it be on the part of mobs drifting through Vienna's streets to the rhythms of jingoistic slogans or of sedate citizens who approve wholeheartedly of violence on behalf of the "civilized" Austrian Empire. In this atmosphere a historian sees in the hoodlums out to maul the Jews the very finest qualities that times of stress call for; after all, hooliganism reflects alertness to enemy infiltration.

Kraus handles the dynamics of crowd action with an eye for grotesque comedy that is bound to recall Shakespeare. The crowd is stimulated by a phrase or slogan, echoes it with childish glee, then proceeds to embroider its own set of ridiculous variations. The result is quite comic, and equally comic is the juxtaposition of highly incongruous verbal styles such as the following:

THE FIRST INDIVIDUAL: . . . On this day, thousands and thousands are streaming through the streets, arm in arm, rich and poor, old and young, high and low. The bearing of each person shows him to be fully conscious of the seriousness of the situation, but proud as well to experience with his own body the heartbeat of the great period now emerging.

A VOICE IN THE CROWD: Kiss my ass![7]

---

[6] *Ibid.,* p. 72.
[7] *Ibid.,* p. 75.

All through *The Last Days of Mankind* Kraus will comment on empty rhetoric by placing it alongside words and actions that make the real nature of what is happening unmistakably apparent.

At any rate, xenophobia becomes the national pastime. A citizen inflates a purely private quarrel into something far more serious by accusing his adversary of enemy espionage; the suggestion is put forth in all seriousness to rename the Café Westminster the Café Westmünster; someone falls under suspicion for saying good-by in French; hatred for the enemy becomes part of the Volksschule's curriculum. Accompanying this paranoic vigilance is a basic confidence in the outcome of the war—Serbia will be cleared away with the sweep of a broom.

This bravado is sustained by grossly untruthful journalism. News which does not lend itself to glorified treatment is simply not printed; war reporting becomes the art of pseudo-documentary propaganda. And the military does its part to keep up appearances; when the Kaiser visits the front, he is diverted by a well-planned show. Half the war is photography, officers making sure to get their pictures taken in all sorts of impressive poses. Two of these officers cannot get over the wonderful way executions are reproduced on film.

Although Kraus could not be more explicit about his distaste for street-corner chauvinism and inflammatory journalism than in the scenes where he lets events speak for themselves, he devotes a good share of the first act to explanatory comment. The explaining is done by a character called The Carper, who engages in a kind of moral debate with his emotional antitype, The Optimist. The Carper is convinced that Europe is going down the drain; with the unleashing of war, power has sifted down to the worst elements of Germanic culture; once such a shift of power occurs, things can never return to normal. Unlike The Optimist, he cannot think in slogans; The Optimist sees nothing wrong with vicious types becoming momentarily powerful as long as the overriding goal remains total victory. The Carper foresees only doom. He gives voice to one trenchant generalization after another on the forces which make that doom inevitable:

Duty lies within the sphere of limitless insignificance. Discipline, fulfillment of one's obligations for their own sake is to engage in banal behavior. Thus, the ethos of the moneyed middle class.[8]

---

[8] *Ibid.,* p. 206.

The returning fighters will invade the hinterlands and there the war
will really get started.[9]
All that is happening, is happening only for those who are describing
it, and for those who cannot experience it.[10]
Our life and thought is subordinated to the interests of heavy industry;
that is a heavy burden.[11]
No nation is so alienated from its language, from the source of its
very life, as the Germans.[12]

The more The Carper speaks, the easier it is to recognize his views
as those of Kraus, who, like The Carper, laid the blame for what
is wrong with the modern world on universal materialism; castigated
the Germanic world for failing to live up to its reputation for *Geist*
and *Kultur;* found in the debased quality of modern German speech
the surest signs of a degenerate culture; derided the individual German
for making organization and efficiency ends in themselves, to the exclu-
sion of any real human values; and predicted that no matter how
terrible the present, the future would be a hundred times worse. Kraus,
like The Carper, saw no escape for men who had bound themselves
to a civilization of machinery and had informed themselves by means
of a press that was antithought.

The Carper mentions in his peroration that war will breed parasitism
on an unprecedented scale, and this is borne out in the second act.
There is the parasitism of giant business firms cashing in on the universal lust to kill; the parasitism of black marketeers who do not like
to be reminded of crippled soldiers drifting home from the front;
and, of course, the less obvious parasitism of careerists, who use the
war to solidify professional status and social standing. For these people
the war is a lark, and it is a lark as well for Kraus's favorite target,
the press. The art of misquotation is carried to new heights; journalists
devote their talents to the exaltation of the barbaric; they see, hear,
and speak no evil that will define war as a dirty business. One such
journalist visits Belgrade, and the city strikes her as ugly enough
to have deserved its bombing: unfortunately, its rubble is not photo-
genic enough for her paper.

Even intellectuals, who might be expected to know better, add their
voices to the chorus of support for the war; Kraus does not hesitate

[9] *Ibid.,* p. 207.
[10] *Ibid.,* p. 211.
[11] *Ibid.,* p. 216.
[12] *Ibid.,* p. 200.

to fill his play with living contemporaries who placed their talents at the disposal of the central powers—writers like Bahr, Dehmel, and Ernst. And the church is no better than the intelligentsia; we witness an army chaplain gunning down the enemy with a canon. In fact, war has become so fashionable that opera performances are interrupted regularly for the latest battle reports. In Vienna the populace is afforded the treat of artificial trenches. The bloodthirstiness of the times is perhaps best summarized by a hunter, who enjoys his sport more than ever now that he is hunting Russians. It is hardly necessary for The Carper to emphasize, as he does, that behind all this there looms a rude awakening.

The last vestiges of civilized life disappear and both Germany and Austro-Hungary degenerate into nations that equate the divine with the inhuman. Businessmen are proud to be Germans and are just as proud to worship Krupp. Even children are indoctrinated with pro-Axis sentiment, and they communicate this in their war games. At the universities the vulgarization of war has obliterated all respect for cultural tradition: jingoistic poetry commands the kind of praise once reserved for Goethe; professorial myopia allows one academician to convince himself that, medically and nutritionally, a half-starved people has never had it better. Another professor is worried about the boys at the front—they smoke too much. As for artificial limbs and other such evidences that war is not all honor and glory, they are blocked out by automatically mouthed formulas: "War is war!"

All faiths are anxious to make their contribution. The Christian idea that one must love one's enemy is interpreted to apply only to personal relationships and not to relationships between nations: "In such instances, killing constitutes no sin, but, on the contrary, duty to the fatherland, Christian obligation—nothing less than worship of God!" In such a moral climate it is hardly surprising that a lieutenant shoots a waitress because no wine is left and that a public prosecutor asks the very severest punishment for a woman impregnated by a French soldier. It is hard, indeed, for two officers to understand why the rest of the world will not recognize a *Kulturvolk* when they see one.

Though experts are prepared to stress that Germany is an innocent country fighting a defensive war, and though the Protestant clergy sanctions the war as a moral necessity, The Carper sings a different tune. He will not allow The Optimist to diminish in any way the terrible guilt for the war which all Germans share. Even to blame the leaders is not enough: "No, we alone are the ones who made it possible for such knaves not to bear any responsibility for the games they played. We alone are at fault for having to tolerate a world which makes wars that no one can be made guilty for. . . . Greater cretins than our statesmen are, in fact . . . we ourselves."[13]

The fourth act takes us to that stage of the war in which the slogans that once came from the heart serve to rationalize what cannot be faced. To a child craving food a father can give only the reassurance that the Russians must be starving. And if sheer hunger drives a young woman into the world's oldest profession, she still is not entitled to the sympathy of those who bring her to justice. In the eyes of justice she is a "syphilitic slut." For most of the civilian population there is no choice but to queue up in interminable lines which lead to bureaucratic administrators spouting legalistic jargon: "All persons must prior to departure obtain at the breadbox distribution office the requisite ration-card notice and thereby, in connection with the particular foodstuffs whose sale is limited, as against validation of the ration-card withdrawal notice . . . "—and so on, *ad nauseam.*

At the front, things have reached the point where torture is employed to instill the will to fight: victims are subjected to freezing temperatures which often prove fatal, squashed into filthy pits, or simply beaten to a pulp. The fact that these techniques do not produce a better fighting man annoys officers who use the terms "soldier" and "swine" synonymously. They have no compunction about stuffing men into cattle cars in such numbers that to survive transportation becomes an achievement; the fact that they are sending most of their troops to certain death is the least consideration. Their primary concern is discipline, and the best way to keep starving soldiers from interrupting their marches for a bite is simply to shoot all who step out of line.

Thanks to the continuing press vigilance, this side of the war remains unpublicized. Even in 1917 it is still possible for a Viennese patriot to exclaim: "Everything has become magnificent. Our land is free, our enemies have been beaten back, the troops of Serbia wiped out, the Russian fortresses destroyed." Intellectuals cling to the myth that the Germanic people are in league against the devil in the guise of British jealousy, French hostility, and Russian lust for what can be taken by force. Austria is on a crusade for truth "against the lies of our enemies." If it were not for the enemy, there would be

[13] *Ibid.,* pp. 412–41.

no problems: give Germany a free hand and Alsace-Lorraine would quickly cease to be a bone of contention.

A citizen who cannot force himself to swallow this line is declared medically insane. The Carper is not surprised, for mediocrity has infested every level of Austrian culture. The war is run by mental and moral cretins, to whom one cannot even extend the respect due villains of stature:

Don't get the idea that these cowardly Philistines, who are now taking advantage of the opportunity for power to compensate for their deficiency of manliness by revenge upon mankind, deserve to be considered deliberate tyrants. They are spilling blood only because they can see none and have never seen any; they act in the intoxication of suddenly experiencing the reality of being their own superiors, of being allowed to behave in a way that reflects not what they are but the kind of times in which they live.[14]

Later on, when The Optimist tries to get The Carper to recognize at least one absolute—the greatness of Kaiser Franz Joseph—he inspires a vitriolic denunciation of Austria's monarch:

Never before in world history has a stronger nonpersonality put his stamp on all things and forms, so that in everything that confused our journey, in all the miseries and communication breakdowns, in each and every misfortune we had to cope with—we came across this Kaiser beard. This nonpersonality stood for the innate slovenliness which the here and now had selected as *fundamentum regnorum;* it stood for the grayish doom that afflicted us like a chronic catarrh. A demon of mediocrity has decided our destiny.[15]

A kaiser to match this description appears a few scenes later. Franz Joseph sings in his sleep a series of verses which are surely the last word in the mockery of royalism:

When I arrived upon the scene
The whole thing was a mess

---

[14] *Ibid.,* p. 453.
[15] *Ibid.,* pp. 497–98.

So I decided quickly
It's all the same to me.
The whole thing was a mishmash
Too wild to be described.
What? I should get involved in that?
Am I to be spared nothing?[16]

While the Kaiser sleeps, the carnage continues. If the killing of human beings has become a prosaic fact of life, the killing of defenseless animals can still command respect. A U-boat sends to their doom twelve hundred horses trapped in a torpedoed ship, and the commander responsible is accorded a hero's welcome:

A REPRESENTATIVE OF THE PRESS: Real horses? 1,200 horses, Count?

DOHNA: 1,200—! (*His gestures indicate submerging.*)

REPRESENTATIVE OF THE PRESS (*in confusion*): *Donnerwetter* again!— Real live horses!—Hurrah!— Brilliant achievement!—First-rate![17]

As horrible as the content of the fourth act is, its final image of joy at the senseless killing of innocent animal life sickens as nothing before.

Those who refuse to acknowledge such horror remain worlds apart from those who must acknowledge it at the price of every illusion that man is a civilized creature. But the war that filters through the editorial pages of newspapers and is implied by the pronouncements of political leaders remains a struggle in pursuit of ideals which can be justified only by a peace giving Germany everything she wants. Concrete developments in the area of human anguish remain irrelevant to this crusade undertaken by a nation generous enough to allow its captive peoples to celebrate the freedom of domination. As for those who protest such innovations as gas warfare, their anger only goes to prove how superior such innovations are. Pride in destructive power matches pride in German origin: "—those fellows should never be allowed to forget that we are the nation of Goethe!"

Says one war worshipper: "Wars are processes of purification and cleansing, as well as breeders of virtue and inspirers of heroes." Not

[16] *Ibid.*, p. 519.
[17] *Ibid.*, p. 550.

long after, a lieutenant divulges the opportunity the war gave him to kill indiscriminately and to make a great deal of money. Pictures of men killed carry the caption: "He died a hero's death for the Fatherland." But if a soldier does manage to make it back to Vienna, he is lucky to find a cigarette in the gutter. Small wonder that the wife of a soldier at the front writes her husband, whom she has betrayed with someone ineligible for glory, that he may as well send her all his money: after all, food is free at the front while life is quite expensive back home.

The realization that peace is on its way sends a scare through the tourist trade, but only momentarily: gravesites should prove a lasting enough attraction. Black marketeers lament the end of a good thing: the smell of peace gives them nausea. Those with heavy investments in armament shares feel cheated by history. A businessman tries to persuade his wife that peace is by no means an unmixed blessing; it will deprive soldiers of the one thing civilians cannot aspire to: "As I always say, they've got it made—glory after death in the annals! What've we got? The high cost of living in wartime! They're always forgetting that. . . . "

The Carper's tone is more apocalyptic than ever. The war, he explains, is like no other of history. It has eaten its way into the fabric of all civilized life, damaging irrevocably modern society's potential for sanity, threatening for all time the future of the human race. "The world is going under," he cries, "and no one will know it. Forgotten will be all that happened yesterday; what happens today will not be noticed; and no one will fear what-is due tomorrow. It will be forgotten that the war was lost, it will be forgotten that the war was started, it will be forgotten that the war was conducted. For that reason, the war will never stop. . . . " Reading this today, one can only marvel at how well Kraus foresaw what was to come.

The Carper's lament continues with expressions of anguish at the fate of those swept into a holocaust not of their making. Revolted by the lack of concern of those exempt from combat, he declares himself to have the duty to write in blood what has so far been put down in ink, to bring some measure of justice to the enormous suffering of those fed to the Moloch of the war machine. Gripped by messianic passions, he implores God to listen: "May He receive my blood-drenched frenzies whereby I share guilt at this chaos. May He let it serve as redemption!"

Directly after this speech, we witness a banquet of Prussian and Austrian officers who regale themselves with conversation about such matters as the execution of fourteen-year-olds, the crowding of helpless human beings into baggage cars to the point where many must die. The banquet descends deeper and deeper into rock-bottom barbarism articulated in tones of bland vulgarity. Suddenly, a long series of tableaux in which all the horrors of war crystallize in distinct images and recitations flashes upon a flaming wall: starving victims of war trudge hopelessly along; innocent boys await execution; ravens feast on corpses; the doomed children of the sinking "Lusitania" sing "We're rocking on the wave/We could be anywhere"; an unborn son pleads not to be born into a world where all this is possible. Finally, this phantasmagoria of evil comes to a close; darkness descends. "Then, upon the horizon, a wall of flames ascends. Outside the screams of death." This concludes the final act of *The Last Days of Mankind*.

In a rhymed epilogue, Kraus recapitulates the motifs of his epic play in images and comments explicitly designed to shock. There are recitations by Masculine Gasmasks and Feminine Gasmasks; by hyenas with human faces; by all sorts of human deformities going about the business of milking the war for all it is worth. Once again, war reporters speak the language of the morally blind: "I find it good to stop and stand here. I shall write of this battle without any fear."[18]

Language which reveals the moral infantilism of the speaker predominates to the point where the Epilogue is a cacophony of linguistic perversion. A *Totenkopfhusar* sings:

Schneddereng, schneddereng!
The air here smells so sweetly.
We hussars of the death's head
We do our work completely.[19]

The art of caricaturing figures to the extent of making them revoltingly hateful is carried furthest in the depiction of Fressack and Naschkatz, who try to conduct their parasitic activities in a sea of corpses:

[18] Kraus, *Die Letzten Tage der Menschheit*, p. 734.
[19] *Ibid.*, p. 742.

Should you need something, just ask
Should you need something, just ask
In fact, ask the man you see wearing
      a face for a mask.
By no means be frightened, for soon
      you will realize
We're not human beings, we're merely hyenas.[20]

They proceed to strip from dead bodies what can be salvaged for profit.

In the Epilogue, Kraus crystallizes his indictment in operatically ingenuous fashion. Those to be condemned simply condemn themselves by monologues and comments devoid of humanitarian resonance. The impression of unmitigated monstrosity is reinforced by such gestural imagery as the dancing of hyenas around corpses. The only real tension of the Epilogue derives from the confrontation of Voices from Above and Voices from Below, in which the higher voices speak truth while the lower voices cling to the very falsehoods about to blow up in their faces. Finally, truth manifests itself in a fashion that cannot be denied: a rain of meteors descends upon the earth; rotten mankind is incinerated; the noise of the human beast has finally been stilled. "This was not my wish" is God's only comment, but it makes us realize that Kraus's God is not the sadistic God of Büchner and Grabbe. He is, in fact, the Judaeo-Christian God and can only weep at what man has brought on himself.

The Last Days of Mankind has almost eight hundred pages of printed text, and almost forty pages are needed to identify the characters who appear in its close to two hundred scenes. As the only recent English essay on the play indicates, "It has no hero, no unity of space, time or action. In time it stretches from 1914 to 1919. It takes place on the battlefields of Europe, in stock exchanges and hospitals, in the offices of journals, the lecture-rooms of Universities, the headquarters of armies, and again and again in the streets of Vienna."[21] Its cast of characters includes men and women from every walk of life: kings, dukes, businessmen, ministers, clerics, soldiers, prostitutes, etc. Plot in the conventional Aristotelian sense is absent, and there

[20] *Ibid.*, p. 746.
[21] Erich Heller, *The Disinherited Mind* (Philadelphia: Dufour and Saifer, 1952), p. 194.

is really no suspense. Kraus has simply taken the breakdown of Germanic culture during World War I as a topic to be illustrated by slices of conversation. He shows us through one conversation after another that what people talked about in those fateful years, and *how* they talked, made quite inevitable what happened to them and what is happening to all of us right now.

Like Büchner, Kraus implies that those who twist language to their own purposes are just as ready to do violence to civilization for their own purposes. In Kraus is culminated the tradition of drama in which speech serves not to further plot but to reveal in an instant the forces whose pressure moves the world. No one before Kraus made of the word so irrefutable a revelation; no one possessed the encyclopedic linguistic knowledge which allows Kraus to employ speech patterns that are as diverse as they are authentic; it is hard to imagine anyone going further to show that drama is possible with the most chaotic interplay of dialects, The linguistic revolution begun by Lenz could not be more complete.[22]

If Shakespeare appeared somewhat superhuman to the eighteenth century because of what he could do with character, Kraus appears just as awesome in our century because of what he can do with language. His play contains enough material for a hundred ponderous technical texts. To his credit, scholarship never gets in the way of drama: his characters spring to life with every phrase they utter, and in an instant the vulgarity that has eaten into their souls stands revealed. Whether the language is bureaucratically dense or resonates with the peculiar accents and intonations of colloquial usage, Kraus carries through brilliantly his aim to make language the moral index of a dying way of life. A world literally talks its way to perdition.

A great deal of Kraus's drama is plainly monological: characters get started on some obsessive idea and simply talk themselves blue in the face. And all too often, when there is dialogue, it could just as well be monologue, for the whole point of a conversational exchange is that no one really listens to anyone else, even when to listen means the difference between sanity and insanity. A scene short enough to be reproduced in its entirety will bear this out:

[22] On Kraus's linguistics, see pp. 285–386 of Leopold Liegler's *Karl Kraus und sein Werk* (Vienna: Richard Lanyi, 1920), which points out among other things that Kraus's linguistic approach to art owes much to Shakespeare.

Hospital near headquarters. Cheerful regimental music is audible.

A SERIOUSLY WOUNDED SOLDIER (*whimpering*): Stop playing—stop playing!

ATTENDANT: Quiet! That happens to be the lunch music of His Excellency Field Marshal von Fabini! Do you think he's going to have it stopped on your account?![23]

When Kraus shows us arm-chair patriots discoursing chauvinistically on the war, and then goes on to show us a scene at the front where it is impossible to armor oneself from the truth by verbal fictions, he is saying very much the same thing implied by the above scene. For all the talk in *The Last Days of Mankind,* there is a ghastly silence in the face of the terrible suffering to which the war has consigned so many.

Kraus links scenes to accentuate ironic disparities and to reinforce grotesqueries. A scene in which two philosophy students try to convince themselves that culture is at a level that would have pleased Schiller is immediately followed by a scene which begins:

A PRUSSIAN MUSKETEER (*banging on the door*): Open up immediately, otherwise we'll smash your booth open—we Germans are starved for books!

At the same time that this continuity is ironic, it is also quite grotesque, for the students of the first scene are in essence as ludicrously vulgar as the musketeer of the second. A more tragic note is sounded in the juxtaposition of a scene in which a woman writes her husband that what she has done in his absence could turn into a mere pecadillo if her baby dies, and a scene in which that same husband is shown breathing heavily in a hospital at the front.

A more immediate form of irony is the juxtaposition of pompous speech with something that gives it away in an instant:

Never have our thoughts been so much with those out in the field as at the present time, when snow alternates with rain and frost and when we ask ourselves what is toughest for our brave warriors: the

---

[23] Kraus, *Die Letzten Tage der Menschheit,* p. 452.

red ball of the sun which hangs from a cold February sky, or the water which drips unceasingly and dolefully into the trenches—tuk, tuk, tuk.[24]

The motives behind stultifying speeches of this type are very much those behind the speeches Brecht will give to his outrageous hypocrites: Kraus, like Brecht, wants to project the idea that the world's evildoers are moral pachyderms to whose lips nothing comes more easily than glib rhetoric. Actually, one can go back to *The Tutor* to show that the Lenz-Brecht tradition, aside from its rebellion against idealistic-classical rhetoric in the aesthetic sphere, rebelled also against the inordinate respect linquistic pomposity has always commanded in German culture. The villains of epic theater are least of all plain talkers.

Kraus's prose encompasses extremes of barely articulate vulgarity and highly eloquent moral consciousness. Not the least of his achievements, however, are the versified renditions he puts into the mouths of characters devoid of civilized awareness. After a battle, officers and journalists cannot resist celebrating the slaughter of thousands with poetry whose brutish overtones would prove distasteful in any context. On and on they vocalize their glee at the mangled corpses which cover the countryside, comparing the piles of dead to a good catch of fish. As if this were not enough, Kraus indicates that the singers in question should underline their moral cretinism by illustrative gestures. His predilection for theater which lays great stress on physical expressiveness may well have originated in Kraus's youth, when he witnessed performances at Vienna's old *Burgtheater*. Like Brecht, he favored a highly theatrical style of acting.

This is by no means a minor point. If epic theater in its earlier phases can be related to interest in puppetry as a metaphor for the human condition, epic theater in its latest phases is equally gesture oriented. Brecht would intellectualize this as none of his anticipators did, but one need only skim through Kraus's play to appreciate how meticulously he suggests physical gesture. Speech after speech is rendered in such idosyncratically vivid language, and with such attention to rhythm, intonation, and articulation, that we cannot help imagining a living speaker to the faintest twitch of his face. In Kraus culminates the mimetic approach to dialogue which again goes back to Lenz,

[24] *Ibid.*, p. 347.

an approach based on the idea that characters speak and move in a way that betrays the forces that are pulling them along.

A typical scene of Kraus's play may reproduce the impromptu remarks of Viennese citizens out for a breath of fresh air; the highly studied jargon of a paid employee of the imperial establishment; the hyperemotional reactions of superpatriots to the latest editorial in their favorite prowar journal; the obsequies by a servant to royalty; the discussion of military matters by officers at the front; businessmen's views on the war; one could go on and on, so extensive is Kraus's coverage. But no matter how heterogeneous these scenes may be in terms of social level or linguistic idiom, they all show in their own way that the kind of awareness that could have saved European civilization was almost nowhere to be found. It is found only in Kraus's projection of himself in the play—The Carper, who crystallizes exactly the indictment that the dialogue of other scenes calls for. He is simply a device for commentary.

Every act of Kraus's play begins in the same way, with the shouting of headlines and the desultory conversation of groups moving along in the open air. This technique of capturing the emotional climate of a society from random observations of strollers caught off guard, Kraus may well have learned from Grabbe, who, in *Napoleon,* worked just this way. Like Grabbe, who indicated in his title that *Napoleon* was as much concerned with the final hundred days of the Emperor's reign as with the Emperor himself, Kraus is out to depict the spirit of an era; like Grabbe, he does this by shifting across every level of society, reproducing the texture of a historical period as much through the views of the man in the street as through the views of the high and mighty. Most important, like Grabbe, Kraus shows how totally antithetic to any kind of greatness the very substance of a time can be, though he would hardly share Grabbe's feeling that time itself is the ultimate villain. For Kraus, man sins against the time and not vice versa.

What Kraus achieved with episodic drama is monumental enough to put him in a class all his own; nonetheless, the major features of his truly epic play connect him with the Lenz-Brecht tradition. In a breakdown of his style we find that Kraus's individual scenes are autonomous units of meaning and that they have no prescribed length; he is as prone to mix comic and tragic effects as he is to mix the lyrical and prosaic; he subordinates action to commentary and characterization to satire; he makes of language an ultimate key to the nature of human life: the speech of his characters comments on what they are in more or less the same way that the dialogue of Lenz, Büchner, and Wedekind acts as such a commentary; even the use of visual aids to add a dimension of explicitness to drama, considered by many to be a purely Brechtian technique, is to be found in *The Last Days of Mankind*.[25]

For Kraus, drama was as much a form of moral orientation as it was with the mature Brecht. The world is evil to the core: What makes it so? is the question that both men write plays to answer. Their answers would seem, on the surface, to be wholly different, for Kraus sets himself up as an apostle against materialism while Brecht is an advocate of nothing but materialism. But they are not really that far apart if one traces the evidence of what they put into their plays. The world Kraus puts on stage is peopled with thick-skinned exploiters and infinitely exploitable human material, with pathetic little men and villainous big men, above all, with human beings who have not the faintest idea of what forces really direct their lives. This is exactly Brecht's world, even though he tried to stress that its implications were ultimately antitragic.

Aside from formal similarities, Kraus's work recalls that of the other writers under discussion by its refusal to sentimentalize powerful forces at work to make society hellish. The same moral hypocrisy which Lenz found to be ruling German society in both *The Tutor* and *The Soldiers*, which Büchner transfixed in his portraits of The Captain and The Doctor, and which Wedekind lashed out at in *Spring's Awakening*, Kraus indicts for leading Germany, Austria, and ultimately, the rest of the world, to a common doom. *The Last Days of Mankind* seethes with a hatred for the bourgeois mind that is common to all of Brecht's anticipators; it seethes also with antipathy for those whose catchword thinking permits them to kill with words—and here Kraus is merely picking up where Büchner left off: the tragedy of the modern age is that pseudomoralists like Robespierre and St. Just have proliferated on every social level. Büchner's overriding realization that part of humanity suffers while another part makes that suffering inevitable by its incapacity to feel, is Kraus's overriding realization as well. The clichés that fill *The Last Days of Mankind*, the slick editorial amorality, the pedestrian monologues delivered by hyperserious Philistines, the recourse to language from which authentic human feeling has long been drained—all this stems ultimately from

[25] Especially in the final scene of Act V, beginning on p. 682.

the fact that between the victimizers and victims there is no communication except by cold decree. Danton's nihilistic vision has become more appropriate than ever.

In *The Last Days of Mankind,* characters are not individualized by the criteria of meticulous psychological realism; they are blatantly caricatured into types that embody the very qualities which their creator detests and which he sees to be the dominant qualities of an impossibly heartless society. Kraus's gallery of characters who exist to be indicted includes such constructions as The Patriot and The Subscriber, whose entire psychology is predictable on the basis of the latest editorial in war-glorifying newspapers; their functional names sum up all that they stand for in the play. Other names are even more obviously nonrealistic, e.g., Kommerzienrat Ottomar Wilhelm Wahnschaffe, Hauptmann Niedermacher, General Gloirefaisant, Hauptmann de Massacré, etc.

This brings us to the realization that *The Last Days of Mankind* is an astonishing blend of naturalism and antinaturalism. In spite of the fact that a great portion of the play consists of material lifted straight from life, the effect is unnaturalistic; if anything, the effect is grotesque. Like Büchner in *Danton's Death,* and like Grabbe in *Napoleon,* Kraus can make truth seem more weird than fiction, can show a world of fact to be inhabited by ludicrous marionettes. It is precisely this ability to put on stage a world that is recognizably real but at the same time frighteningly laughable that distinguishes the tradition of anti-idealistic drama begun in Germany by J. M. R. Lenz. Kraus is every bit as much in that tradition as Brecht.

Brecht formulated the concept of *Verfremdung* because he had no use for theater of titillation. Although Kraus never had recourse to the term itself, there is in his concept of satire the same desire to keep art from deteriorating into mere entertainment. What he felt satire should be comes out in an essay on Heine.[26] Kraus thought little of Heine because he felt Heine was, in the final analysis, a tickler of funny bones; had Heine written real satire, he would still be making his readers uncomfortable; the true satirist never loses his power to sting, even generations later. In *The Last Days of Mankind,* as well as in the topical satire of *Die Fackel,* Kraus aimed for the very qualities he found missing in Heine, doing his utmost to make the reader feel that he belonged among those indicted on the printed page. This mode of satire breaks sharply with Schiller's idea that

[26] Kraus, "Heine und die Folgen," *Auswahl aus dem Werk,* ed. Heinrich Fisher (Munich: Kösel Verlag, 1961), pp. 138–56.

drama has a moral effect precisely because it does not make sinners too self-conscious.

Our discussion of Brecht's predecessors has shown that they wrote plays in which a series of events apparently is put down without any attempt on the part of the dramatist to overdramatize their relationship. Nonetheless, the relationship is undeniable, for every scene contributes to an overwhelming impression of human impotence in the face of malign forces. Kraus exploits to the limit this use of the episodic structure to reinforce a sense of futility, even if he sees at work no particular suprahuman demons with a taste for human flesh. For Kraus, the very worst demon of all is mankind's vast stupidity, and he makes its presence felt on every page of *The Last Days of Mankind*.

Büchner and Grabbe exploited, as Lenz did not, the enormous spatial range that episodic drama could accommodate: they were as ready to depict street life as they were to depict what went on behind closed doors. They wished, above all, to convey the life of a society in motion, to make of their drama a comprehensive comment on the nature of all men. It is this aspect of episodic drama that Kraus carried further than anyone else: no one before him or since has built up an episodic play with so many variations on a single overriding theme; no one has shown as conclusively as he did that the grandest of themes—the downfall of a complete civilization—is not too broad for treatment within the same essential structure that Lenz had championed in the eighteenth century as the dramatic structure of the future.

Taking his cue from what he felt was Shakespeare's basic technique, Lenz subordinated plot to the illumination of character, and he found in the grotesque twists of character the surest key to what was wrong with a society in general. What in the final analysis is *The Last Days of Mankind* but a series of character analyses on the basis of the spoken word? And is the relationship between character and society less inexorable than in Lenz? Lenz and Kraus, for all their differences, spoke a common language of the theater, found in *characters speaking* more real drama than in characters interrelating. Both realized that action does not speak louder than words when action is merely the consequence of what words imply. It is true that Lenz concluded his plays with messages of sanity while Kraus's *Walpurgisnacht* of a play ends in the most awful chaos; but this difference is really not one of dramaturgy; rather, it reflects Kraus's conviction that he was, indeed, living in mankind's final period, and that his play would achieve the recognition it deserved only on another planet.

chapter six:

bertolt brecht

If the later Brecht has suffered from the controversy provoked by his critical pronouncements on epic theater, so that there is no dearth of chatter about his failure to make practice conform to theory, the early Brecht has in a way been just as unfortunate. For the Communists, the early Brecht, no matter how talented, must remain untutored on the issues that count, or on the single issue that counts, namely, the dialectics of the class struggle; Brecht himself would look back on his first works as ideologically faulty. But for non-Communists as well, the early Brecht has proved uncongenial, has, in fact, been taken more than once for a superficial nihilist who is always singing the same tune, and a most unoriginal tune at that. Frequently the latter view goes hand in hand with the idea that Brecht developed his theories to rationalize serious artistic shortcomings.

Whatever the merits of these depreciations, the early Brecht is more easily disparaged than defined with precision. Thus, his first play, *Baal,* is to an extent expressionistic, but one would certainly hesitate to leave it at that; what other play so described was written as a specific protest against the superficiality of an unmistakably expressionist work? It is significant that the composition of *Baal* was prompted by the desire to debunk, by that same passion for getting down to fundamentals which would inspire so much of Brecht's later work. And it is significant, also, that the writer whose influence Brecht took it upon himself to counteract won fame and fortune under the same Reich that turned Brecht into a refugee.

Hanns Johst's *The Lonely One* chronicles some crises in the life of Christian Dietrich Grabbe and suggests, at first glance, a tough-minded dramatic biography of that brilliant figure. But though the play contains some acidulous observations about the inability of Philistines to understand why every genius does not enjoy as full and rich a life as Goethe did, it sheds no light on any of the complexities implied by the artist's isolated position in a bourgeois society. In fact, one realizes soon enough that Johst is utterly incapable of saying anything new on this subject, if only because he himself is far more a product of that society than he would like to admit. A writer who inserted into another of his plays a remark on the offensiveness of *Kultur* which was reputedly composed by Hermann Goering, Johst lays bare what is amiss with his own sensibility by the sticky manner in which *The Lonely One* concludes—it is portentously noted that Grabbe's remains are those of a *German* poet. The curtain falls to chords from Beethoven.

Brecht also gives us his major character in an artist at odds with his milieu, one who, in typically expressionistic fashion, conveys his creator's strongest feelings. But Baal has as little in common with *The Lonely One* as with most of the strident theater connected with expressionism. Brecht's hero is not a declaimer of the type so commonplace in the dramas of writers like Kaiser and Hasenclever; he is an asocial cynic whom one could never imagine vocalizing moral outrage. Through him Brecht reveals an antipathy to middle-class attitudes which German drama had not sounded since the emergence of poetic nihilism in the early nineteenth century. Brecht suggests his kinship with that tradition when he asserts that the aim of life is to eat, drink, fornicate, and excrete; he is in that tradition also when he employs as spokesmen for his own views those subbourgeois types for whom society has least use. Philosophizing drifters made themselves felt in Büchner's drama and they dominate what is perhaps the most brazenly nihilistic scene of *Baal*. The God of Nothingness has finally been enthroned, and he is exalted by worshipers who cannot wait to be transformed into corpses, to enjoy the redemption of being forever insensible like stone. Can it be anything but paradise when one has ceased to care that all of nature is caught up in an unrelenting process of decomposition. The dead are in no need of weather reports; they even sleep through hurricanes. Brecht reinforces the depressing effect of such perceptions with appropriately crude behavior. One wretch reaches out for some erotic satisfacton and is informed by the object of his desire that his mouth smells foul, whereupon he retorts that syphilitics cannot be complainers and puts her on his lap. The charnel-house atmosphere intensifies until even Baal, who is far from squeamish, finds this celebration of the death wish intolerable, describing it as an orgy of putrefaction in which worms are eulogizing worms. In *Baal* such imagery is matter of course; here God is extolled in blatantly scatological terms and the Bible used as source for obscene metaphor. *Baal*, like Grabbe's first play, *Duke Theodore of Gothland*, exemplifies perfectly the current psychoanalytic theory on the deeper motivations of nihilism.

Baal is composed of twenty-one scenes that appear to move in no particular direction and generate little suspenseful plot. It is as if Brecht had made up his mind to stretch the principle of episodic reinforcement as far as possible—short of a wholly deliquescent lyricism—so that he was able to transfer appreciable segments of poetry from his first play to his first collection of poetry without any need to establish context. One is far less conscious of what is happening and who it is happening to in *Baal* than of a certain haunting quality, but at the same time Brecht has already made an effort to keep his poetry from becoming nothing more than powerfully evocative. Almost every mood is made to clash with its antitype, and before long one expects passionate moments to usher in cynical recognitions. The fact that ecstasy should introduce disgust is only natural for the protagonist of *Baal*, who finds it as onerous to maintain a specific state of mind as he finds it easy to demolish a human relationship. His erotic life could well be characterized as manic-depressive, allowing him when properly inspired to rhapsodize on love in the following fashion:

And love is like letting your hand bathe in pond water, the seaweed settling between your fingers; like the affliction which makes a tree moan in song while mounted by the wild wind; like drowning oneself in sucked-up wine on a hot day, and her body goes through you like cool wine, drenching every fold of your skin; her joints are smooth like wind-swept plants, and the force of your thrust meets no resistance, and her body turns and turns upon you like cool gravel.[1]

But this is only a temporary emotion. A few moments earlier, Baal had been cold as ice on the same subject, explaining to a young man named Johannes, who is as innocent as Baal is not, that after one has slept with a woman, she may become "a heap of flesh without a face." Pregnancy is an animalistic horror: "And they give birth with monstrous screams, as if being delivered of a new cosmos; but produce only a small fruit. In anguish they spit out what they once absorbed lustfully." This is not mere rhetoric: Baal's powerful aggressions come out nowhere so conspicuously as in his relationship with the opposite sex. Johanna Reiher, Johannes' girl friend, turns out to be one of his victims. After intercourse she asks Baal if he still loves her. Baal's answer: "I am completely fed up." His brutish streak impels him to rape one helpless victim, murder another, and invite two women to bed at the same time. He floats through life in a narcissistic stupor, bothered only faintly by the corpses that litter his voyage, subservient always to the command of his latest impulse. An

[1] Brecht, *Stücke,* I (Berlin: Suhrkamp Verlag, 1961), 34.

outrageous personification of all that the rest of humanity consigns to fantasy, he nonetheless provokes something more than simple revulsion. A measure of our respect goes out to him, if only because he does no obeisance to that world of engrafted social hypocrisies by whose standards he cannot be too strongly condemned. He may be more destructive than his fellow man, but his fellow man is such a small-minded self-deceiver and fear-ridden hypocrite that Baal's unabashed instinctualism has about it something refreshing. Like his mythological namesake, he is ravenous for life of every form, has no compunctions about constantly refilling his cup at the expense of others, finds it perfectly natural to identify himself in cold subhuman terms: "My soul, brother, is the moaning of cornfields rolling in the wind and the sparkle in the eyes of two insects anxious to gobble each other up." In an arena of lethal competition Christian sentiment will not help, and Baal says so with every gesture. For him the world abounds in urine, mud, vomit, dung, and bile; why not enjoy the stench?

"That was circus! The beast must be lured out! In the sun with the beasts!" We are deliberately reminded by Brecht that if he shared Büchner's and Grabbe's Weltanschauung, his sensibility was equally indebted, if not more so, to Wedekind. Circus is a perfect metaphor for the human condition and that condition is best summed up in the sphere of sexuality. For all the differences between them, Brecht's Baal and Wedekind's Lulu are cut from the same cloth, personifying concentrations of primeval drive which modern society by its nature cannot allow itself to accommodate. Carrying this parallel further, one notices that though Wedekind attributed to Lulu an authenticity shared by none of her companions, he made no effort to glamorize the seamier aspects of a life dedicated to the morality of the senses; his ambivalence to that morality proved a rich source of aesthetic tension. Brecht, as well, cannot be accused of letting id worship blind him to what is cancerous about the sensualistic existence. *Baal*, like the Lulu plays, is vitalized by the very force that is tragically dissipated before our eyes.

If Baal recalls Lulu by virtue of his commitment to instinct, he recalls Woyzeck by his outsider's position in a bourgeois society. From the very start of Brecht's play it is as obvious as from the start of Büchner's that the protagonist interacts with that society on the barest functional level. Baal's curt responses to the blandishments of those who would extend him cash for the rights to his poetry parallel

Woyzeck's mechanical responses to the Captain philosophizing in the barber's chair. Both characters prove unresponsive in the company of those wishing to converse with them on a level that takes for granted a mutuality of middle-class interests, though Baal's attitude in his respect implies far more defiance than that of the harried soldier-barber-guinea pig. Put another way, both characters live principally in the hothouse of their own emotional systems, which strike more stable citizens as nothing less than very weird indeed. Eventually their psychic intensities lead them to irrevocable breaks with the society that has not begun to comprehend them, but judges them quickly for crimes that are quite similar—both slash their lovers to death. In Baal's case, the victim is a member of his own sex, and in this connection it might be noted that in three of Brecht's early works a homosexual relationship dominates the action and ends in violence.

Büchner's concern that, above all, drama be alive led him to evolve a prose containing linguistic elements for which neoclassical drama had no place. This prose was as evocative as it was down to earth; it was plastic enough to take in complex subjective experience as well as states of mind expressible in the most vulgar epithets; it availed itself of imagery that was often shockingly concrete and direct, and at times salaciously outspoken. This prose, for all its lowness, was charged with poetic force; it could be true to the idiom of the gutter without doing violence to the sensibilities of the poet. Exactly the same can be said for Brecht's prose; it too encompasses the lyrical and the scurrilous, blatantly coarse vulgarisms and exquisitely delicate impressions, the mean and the beautiful. In Brecht's world, as in Büchner's, corpses that "stink" rot under skies that are strangely beautiful. Eric Bentley's comment that *Baal* revolves around a "state of being" sums up in a phrase that area of style and content which links Brecht's play and *Woyzeck* most closely. Almost any scene selected at random from either play would illustrate this. Brecht, like Büchner, conveys misery, joy, waste, and isolation, life purposelessly unwinding in spasmodic fits of pleasure and pain, aggression and passivity alternating as impersonally as the creative and degenerative cycles of nature. The vision of life in *Baal* as well as *Woyzeck* derives from the intense pressure of personal feeling against the ceaseless continuities of a world in which neither man nor God is merciful. In a manner of speaking, Baal is a sadistic inversion of Woyzeck, relishing the very malevolence built into the nature of things that keeps Woyzeck on the rack.

Brecht's technique of synopsizing by song what may not otherwise achieve full clarity of definition commences with his first play. These lyrical interspersions hardly strike one as choral intermissions to relax by; they reinforce what is scandalous in the text by being every bit as scandalous; their deliberately offensive content is served up in a style of spirited mockery that would later prove irresistible to theatergoers who could not care less about Brecht's deeper social motivations. As early as this it is clear that the most positive thing about Brecht's way of looking at life is the vitality that shines through his despair. The opening ballad takes full cognizance of the truth that the world is steeped in death, but this hardly stops Baal, who is wily enough to feed on the vultures that mistake him for carrion. Brecht celebrates the magnificence of a life force which thrives in the very shadow of Thanatos. Another song glorifies the one place where man's spiritual and physical needs can be accorded proper importance—the toilet. But not all of Baal's songs are designed for raffish effect: "Death in the Forest" describes the agonies of someone so afraid to die he disgusts his closest friends; it will make no one laugh.

The fact that Brecht's first play was, for all its departures from conventional realism, a more truthful look at life than the run of expressionist drama, that it struck a note of directness and irony which separated it immediately from prevailing stylistic practice, is certainly germane to a study of its literary antecedents, if only because Brecht repeats a significant cultural pattern that goes back to Lenz's theatrical innovations in the late eighteenth century. Every writer of the Lenz-Brecht tradition is in protest against his contemporaries' approach to dramatic art; none can ally himself with an established movement except in minor details. Lenz's two major plays may embody certain social emphases thanks to the example of the French bourgeois play and may share certain stylistic traits with *Sturm und Drang* episodic theater, but his work is, for its time, *sui generis*. Similarly, Grabbe and Büchner are not without connections to the German romantics, but they can be grouped with writers like Tieck and Brentano only in very broad cultural terms. How these episodic realists felt about the inadequacies of romanticism is probably very close to the way Wedekind felt about the superficialities of naturalism. As for Kraus, he saw no possibility at all of European theater's accommodating the kind of raw truths with which he stuffed *The Last Days of Mankind*. Similarly, Brecht's *Baal* may have been a *Gegenstück* against a particular play, but it was even more directed against the sickly evasions he felt to be characteristic of almost all that went by the name of modern theater. He was as ill-disposed to photographic realism as he was to the lack of concreteness typical of most expressionist drama.

He was far more responsive to the kind of realism that blended precise observation of actualities with a variety of lyrical and satiric techniques. This is obvious enough on the basis of comparative literary analysis, but even the casual reader could pick it up from Brecht's critical pieces, which leave little doubt as to the dramatists he respected. Thus, his view of German classical theater is conventional enough when it includes Goethe, less so when it includes only the young Schiller, and much less so when it includes also Lenz and Büchner. The latter's *Woyzeck* he described in eulogistic terms, and Brecht rarely eulogized. It was a performance of *Woyzeck* that proved decisive also for Brecht, the theoretician, provoking him to reformulate his ideas on the most effective kind of theatrical presentation and acting style. While his admiration for Büchner has become a commonly noted fact, his relationship to Grabbe receives cursory mention at the most; one hopes that the situation will change as it becomes more widely known that Grabbe in many ways anticipated Büchner. At any rate, it deserves notice that in 1922 Brecht undertook as a project for Reinhardt a new version of Grabbe's *Hannibal*. He never finished it. But it makes an impression that Brecht worked on the one Grabbe play that can truly be said to revolve around a Brechtian motif, concerned as *Hannibal* is with a society so immersed in the pursuit of money that it winds up utterly destroyed. As for Wedekind and Kraus,* Brecht never concealed his admiration for the former as a man and for the latter as a master chronicler of World War I. Much of Brecht's *Fear and Misery of the Third Reich* would be modeled on Kraus's epic play.

One need go no further than *Baal* to find out how Brecht felt about the driving forces of bourgeois life. The businessman Mech, anxious to obtain the rights to Baal's poetry, is presented as a smug bargainer well versed in the art of manipulation, and he reveals with a phrase that he conceives of those who cross his path as animals to be pushed aside. But by and large, Brecht's assault on middle-class values is made in his first play in generalized poetic terms, as he concentrates on giving eloquent expression to those unconventional

* It recently became known that Kraus contributed a few lines to *The Three-penny Opera.*

states of mind which the *Bürger* identifies with eccentricity, if not sheer madness. *Drums in the Night* (1919), Brecht's second play, is a far more specific indictment, a step toward the Brecht who would direct most of his attention to the subject of economic injustice. It is a play that did much for Brecht's reputation among the intelligentsia of the Weimar Republic and won him a major literary prize. The protagonist of the play is an ex-soldier named Kragler who resists every temptation to actively fight a society for which he has very little use and which has even less use for him. Kragler will not move a muscle for any cause promising a better tomorrow because World War I has taught him that all idealistic slogans are false advertisements. Things being what they are, it makes more sense to join the general pursuit of money and comfort than the quest for a new society. Those who enter upon the latter course can expect to have their flesh rot in some gutter.

The embittered returnee is asked what he did in the war. He replies that he lay in filth and stank, and he wonders what his questioner was doing while he lay in filth and stank. He soon realizes he could as well talk to himself; he remains in the commercial world of postwar Germany the same anonymous quantity he was for so long on a remote, corpse-littered field. The gun-carriage manufacturer, Balicke, comes right to the point: "This is no opera. This is *Realpolitik.* There's not enough of that in Germany. It is really quite simple. Have you the means to support a wife? Or have you webs between your fingers?" And Frau Balicke can lecture Kragler as Woyzeck was lectured by his self-appointed counselors of morality: "Herr Kragler! Our Kaiser has said: learn to suffer without complaining!" When Brecht is not focusing on such blatant hypocrisies, he depicts the social upheaval of the Spartakus Revolt through the jerky dialogue of bystanders who remain imprisoned in the sphere of their own preoccupations. All of this to reinforce the logic of noninvolvement, to substantiate the violent rejection of soft thinking that prompted Brecht to place placards among the audience reminding them of their narcissistic romanticism, their desire to use theater for purely escapist purposes.[2]

[2] Brecht's attempts in *Drums in the Night* to reinforce the significance of content by stage techniques which negate the illusion of theatrical performance recall to us the fact that he was greatly indebted to the twin movements of Dadaism and the "Tribunal" theater of Erwin Piscator. The Dadaists relished theater in which every opportunity to nullify illusionistic mood was heartily exploited, though their intentions were by and large to thumb their

Those who wish to demonstrate that the early Brecht does not really change from play to play, point to the fact that Kragler conforms to the type of protagonist who dominates *Baal* and has the last word of *In the Swamp*. That is to say, Kragler is an asocial cynic who trusts his instincts far more than the appeal to any outside authority; in preferring a warm bed to a revolutionary battlefield, he adds another link to a consistent chain of nihilism to be broken by Brecht only upon his conversion to Communist doctrine. But to view *Drums in the Night* this way is to overlook that while it does end on a note of withdrawal, it conveys a more complex attitude all the way through. Brecht is not in this play the nihilist who communicates such an intensely subjective outlook that the final impression is of some strange, private world into which reality intrudes by accident. He is extremely conscious of the texture of postwar German life, especially of the degree to which that texture is reducible to economic competition; and he is conscious of the implications which that competition holds for any sort of individualistic philosophy. When Kragler departs from the scene, he does so in a manner which leaves the audience pondering not the resignation to a rotten world of another disillusioned idealist, but the grossly inequitable nature of that world—and the possibility of doing anything about it. Paradoxically, the later Brecht would want to suggest with his work that such a world could be changed, but he suggested all too often the very opposite. *Drums in the Night* says explicitly that the world is not worth lifting a finger for, but it communicates nonetheless an attitude of deep involvement. The quality of the cynicism is as ferocious as it is because it conceals a simple humanitarianism which Brecht exposes only for moments. One such moment is a waiter's explanation of why he lets himself get involved in the troubles of people like Kragler: "One can't be petty when a man needs help." The impulse to be good, such an intrinsic motive of the later Brecht's work, is already present; and

---

noses at the dictates of tradition and convention. Piscator, on the other hand, after a brief period of Dadaistic allegiance, went on to direct and stage dramas in which political consciousness was wedded to highly documentary modes of production. Though Brecht, the poet, owed little to Piscator, Brecht, the theatrical innovator, owed a great deal to him. A recent attempt on Piscator's part to demolish the very common notion that Brecht deserves exclusive identification with the label "epic theater" was made in his introduction to Rolf Hochhuth's *Der Stellvertreter* (Hamburg: Rowohlt, 1963), pp. 9–10.

if we are to call the Brecht of *Drums in the Night* a nihilistic writer, it will have to be with the same reservations we attach to such a characterization of Büchner.

Alienation is a pervasive mood in the early Brecht's work, whether it is self-imposed by autistic perception (Baal) or imposed from without by an impossibly unfair society (Kragler). But alienation is nowhere stressed so thematically as in the one Brecht play that is loaded with obscurities to the point where it invites cryptography rather than criticism. *In the Swamp of the Cities* (1924) consists of eleven episodes that are even more loosely woven together than many a far less impressive expressionist play; and arbitrariness of scenic continuity is matched by incomprehensibility of action. More than ever, one feels privy to the elaborations of some bizarre Brecht fantasy, and, as usual, the fantasy bespeaks volcanic inner conflict. The homosexual element so recurrent in Brecht's early work is present here as well, though one is far less conscious of it because of Brecht's attempt to give everything a deeper metaphorical significance. For this reason all clarifications of the play come down to exercises of selective interpretation unless one is content with giving that bare outline about which there can be no argument.

Such an outline must note that an exotic Malayan named Shlink literally immolates himself for the sake of breaking down those barriers which stand in the way of human contact. Not only does he fail to make any dent in those barriers; he winds up a senseless corpse for his efforts; the man he hoped to reach, called Garga, steps blithely across Shlink's remains and finds the memory of those events which spelled disaster for the Malayan quite pleasant. And the implication of the play is that he should; for if the world subsists on conflict rather than contact, then the world belongs to winners only. One either survives or falls by the wayside. And that is all there is to the art of living.

The body of the play serves as prelude to this hard realization. Again and again, Shlink offers up pieces of his ego in the hope that he can obtain some human warmth in return. And again and again, he finds himself more deeply imprisoned within his own self. This aspect of *In the Swamp* is given poetic intensity of a kind that is bound to recall Büchner's lamentations on man's inability to achieve genuine contact with anything outside of his own instinctual promptings. In *Danton's Death* it was asserted that humans are equipped with skins so thick that when hands reach out for reassurance, they meet only cold leather—"we are very lonely." Brecht's terminology is not much different when he has Shlink say that skin thickens far more impermeably than leather. Too fragile for survival if they hold on to their sensitivities, men shield themselves with integuments through which no warmth can flow, so that if a ship were stuffed with human bodies, it would freeze from impacted loneliness.

Brecht strove to characterize *In the Swamp* as a play so laden with the blows of direct conflict that it could be enjoyed simply for the techniques employed in delivering those blows. But rather than quintessential struggle, Brecht gives us quintessential absence of struggle, or, to extend his metaphor, shadowboxing; for Shlink and Garga both come to realize that their opponent is imaginary. Struggle in the modern world is simply a writhing of the self within the self. Again Büchner comes to mind, for one of the sad regrets of *Danton's Death* is that those who are about to die cannot even go down fighting, cannot enjoy the release of throwing all their primitive equipment of teeth and nails into a fierce final encounter; what man calls conflict is a melodramatized version of something far more deadly—the monotonous elaboration of a monstrous mechanism built into the very nature of things.

In the Swamp strikes many as the most nihilistic play Brecht wrote, for in no other work was he so intent upon exhibiting life as a purely animalistic experience without a shred of redeeming value. Even *Baal* seems positive in comparison. Life might be hellish, but if lived to the hilt, it is worth living. *In the Swamp* offers no such consolations. Here sex is an exquisite form of humiliation and perversion, essentially an exercise in *Realpolitik* applied to the most intimate area of human relationship; such sex invariably ends in impotence and prostitution. As for the possibility of transcending this cesspool by strength of character, if nothing else, that is exactly what Garga attempts, and he winds up doing the dirtiest work of the play. Our first glimpse of him shows a man who cannot be bought; our last, a man content to sell out his own family. One could go on and on accumulating nihilistic testimony from *In the Swamp,* so obsessively does Brecht recapitulate his basic idea that life has meaning only for those taken in by false idealisms, those Gargas who are fortunate enough never to meet their Shlink. Our first reaction is that this is the vision of an arrant nihilist, but, as usual, Brecht defies simple identification; above all, he impresses us here as being on the way to something else because he confronts so pitilessly what he already is. Having made up his mind to remove the last trace of romantic emotion from the kind of nihilism displayed in *Baal,* he writes a play in which there are no idealistic escape routes whatever. Even wild nature cannot provide succor: the trees are draped with dung. *In the Swamp* reveals Brecht anxious to strip nihilism down to its pernicious essence, even if he was not then able to embrace any other attitude.

Life of Edward the Second of England (1924) was an adaptation of Marlowe's *Edward II* that Brecht wrote with Lion Feuchtwanger. The modern version is, as has been pointed out, coarser and more concise, much more sharply focused on emotional essentials. Whereas Marlowe's play is viewed as one in which he departed from the out-and-out nihilism of *Tambourlaine,* the German adaptation is as nihilistic on the plane of history as *In the Swamp* was in a more cosmic context. Marlowe's play raises various political and social issues and has provoked discussions on his maturing concept of kingship. Brecht's play is quite frankly an homage to the cynical truth that the wolf will feast on lamb when lamb is to be had. Animal imagery only serves to confirm what the action implies—that *Realpolitik* is the art of living by killing. Every major character lives by this insight. Mortimer says: " . . . and out of / Man comes naked beast. / As things now stand, someone must hang." The Archbishop declares that God is always on the side of the victors, and the man who betrays Edward II justifies his deed by explaining that one's own interests come first. When Edward declares that darkness is best of all, he is saying essentially what the Queen does after a burst of wholly unwarranted laughter. Her explanation: "I am laughing at the emptiness of the world."

Edward's refusal to part with his "whore" Gaveston plunges a whole nation into civil strife and serves to introduce Brecht's conception of history as "the nothingness of human affairs and deeds." Such explicit nihilism makes it strange that one critic should note that there is in the play no counterargument to violence for political ends; the counterargument is built into the very texture of the play itself, into speech after speech communicating the utter senselessness of all violence and, for that matter, all action. The whole point of Brecht's adaptation is that those who kill for political reasons and those who kill for the sake of killing are of a kind. This is Grabbe's view of history all over again, and as in Grabbe, the chaotic nature of the historical process is given vivid expression by having momentous events filtered through gutter sensibilities:

Eddie's mistress has a beard on her breast.
Plead for us, plead for us, plead for us!

Eddie fleeces his Gavy from morn to night.
Plead for us, plead for us, plead for us![3]

In concentrating on the painfully concrete way in which historical developments take their toll of human misery, and in suggesting that those in power are indifferent to the anguish they inflict in consequence of their irresponsible attitudes, Brecht anticipates motifs he will be concerned with in later work, just as he anticipates basic elements of technique that will be associated with his concept of epic theater. He is already minimizing suspense where others might be tempted to enhance it; he is already clarifying action by showing it from various angles. The episodic structure allows him to devote major scenes to cogent synopses of content and to reduce identification by shifting from one point of view to another. His concept of the scene as a body of action illustrating, in essence, a single defining action, is operative as well. It may not be inaccurate to see this adaptation as a kind of formal exercise on Brecht's part to determine the suitability of the episodic structure for the presentation of varieties of *recognizable* human experience and varieties characterized less by repetitions of highly emotional states of mind than by a tough-minded skepticism about anything and everything.

It is common knowledge that after his adoption of Communism Brecht's work was marked by a highly contradictory character. But it should be realized as well that from the start his work manifested tensions between polar attitudes; in fact, it is hard to conceive of a play so much the product of self-division as *In the Swamp*. The later Brecht could not resist disintegrating what he was ostensibly trying to prove; the early Brecht is just as ambivalent when he presents himself, on the one hand, as a confirmed nihilist, and, on the other, as someone who could not stand to be a nihilist a moment longer. Brecht escaped such a clash of irreconcilable attitudes only in those plays where he assiduously expunged whatever might cast doubt on the fixity of his commitment, namely, in his most mediocre work. As for his tendency to assume a far more elusive stance in better plays, this has been the focal point of Brechtian criticism in the Anglo-Saxon world and has naturally sparked controversy between those intent

[3] Brecht, *Stücke,* I, 20.

on fathoming his basic motivation and those concerned, above all, to find him spinning a consistent thread of existential-social protest. For the former, the emphasis remains on the emotional dynamics projected by Brecht into characters who incarnate powerful unconscious strivings; the enigmatic Brecht is viewed as being torn between the anarchies of impulse and the compulsions of a superego thirsting for discipline at any price. For some Marxist critics this approach is too much in the nature of a diversion from the main point of Brecht's writing, his confrontation of the true nature of bourgeois life from the first play to the last and a confrontation every bit as intrinsic to *Baal* and *In the Swamp* as to plays in which the socio-economic context is loudly advertised. The crux of the issue here, of course, is related to that much-discussed question of yesterday—the validity of any ideological course of action in view of man's projective nature, his inability to formulate solutions except in the rationalized terms of his own inner conflicts. In Brecht's case that question takes on renewed topicality, so obvious is it from his plays that he sought in communism relief from the pressures of deeply personal psychic problems; and it is equally obvious he was never certain he had found the right cure. One might note that Marxist critics intent upon making Brecht's extremely complex personality a side issue, are acting completely in character. Their refusal to recognize how much the chaos depicted in Brecht's work stems from the chaos in the man himself has its roots in the same ideological conformity which prevented Brecht from understanding why *Mother Courage* was not received in the proper anticapitalistic spirit. The true believer dare not allow himself to know himself.

Brecht was not yet in that category when he wrote *A Man's a Man* (1926), but in the light of what that play contains, it could not have occasioned too much surprise when he finally turned Communist. He was already thinking along lines that converged with Marxist emphases, already satisfied bourgeois individualism would soon be obsolete. And as far as Brecht was concerned, when something is about to depart the stage of history, the astute will put out flags for what is coming—communism was surely attractive to Brecht not just because it promised to deliver a more humanitarian social existence but because, given the absurd contradictions of capitalism, its success was a certainty. As Bentley has noted, Brecht's triumphant return to East Germany after the war proved, if nothing else, that he had guessed shrewdly about his relationship to the future of the party. That guessing was already going on when *A Man's a Man* came out, Brecht claiming to be showing today what would be the rule tomorrow, namely, the process whereby individuals are persuaded to become units of broad collective entities—and becoming such cogs without regrets.

Brecht works out his equation on an innocent named Galy Gay, who sets out one day in a very Kiplingesque India to purchase a fish but never comes home with it. The kind of person who cannot say no, in general, and doubly so when he sniffs a chance to make some money, he winds up replacing a member of the British Colonial Army, whose absence would otherwise prove highly embarrassing to the quartet of soldiers of which he constitutes one fourth at roll call. The crux of the play is the attempt of these soldiers to persuade Galy Gay into a full acceptance of the missing man's identity. They succeed brilliantly, abetted by Galy Gay's eagerness to net a profit. He agrees to claim ownership of a fake elephant in the expectation of selling it, but this proves quite a blunder: it exposes him to military trial as a crook and to a mock execution. Scared out of his wits, he is eager to avow that he is the same Jip whose name belongs in roll call with that of Jesse Mahoney, Polly Baker, and Uria Shelley. With the change of name comes a radical change in personality. The meek packer of Kilkoa turns into a military man who knows no fear.

Brecht referred to this as a happy ending, and those who find that he starts with sound assumptions could well agree. Premise number one is that the continuity of the ego is a fiction; premise number two, that all fictional constructs are to be abandoned the moment they impede one in the struggle to survive. For Brecht this is quite a transvaluation: he has stopped viewing the self as a dungeon from which no escape is possible; it has become more like an automobile part which one replaces as a matter of course when it ceases to do the job. Brecht underscores his contempt for the idealistic ethics of expressionist drama by building an entire play around such a functional concept of ego, concerned as the expressionists were with the importance of their protagonists' moral transfigurations. All too often the expressionist hero sought an exalted state of subjectivity: Galy Gay wants only to make a little money. No declamatory expressionist play was ever built around the brutification of a nonentity. Clearly, Brecht is at this stage intent upon banishing from his work whatever might attenuate his view of life as a cold, hard exercise in materialism. He wishes to propound the same unsentimental rules for living that Wedekind never tired of preaching—rules based on the undeniable truth that reality is a flux which life can come to terms with only by virtue of its plasticity, its capacity to accommodate. The star performers in the circus of existence are those with limbs of rubber; tragic moments do not leave them crushed but merely endow them with an added appreciation of the absurdities with which they have to contend. Soon enough they are back on the trapeze, soaring cynically above those who have never learned morality is something to chat about over soup and to forget while making sure soup will always be on hand. One would hardly expect such an approach to ethics and life to enchant Communists searching for "anticapitalistic" elements in Brecht, and it is small wonder that Schumacher, a leading East German critic, after picking *A Man's a Man* clean for the smallest crumb of revolutionary sentiment, in the end calls the play unconcrete and undialectical; for he realizes quite well Brecht has written the perfect apologia for all totalitarianisms that promise satisfaction of basic needs.

That the malleable shall inherit the earth is a cynical message, and Brecht went out of his way to indicate that this was precisely his message. But as is so often the case later on, he proves disingenuous on the real nature of what he gives dramatic form, failing to mention that one will find in his play serious reservations about what seems to be advocated. Thus, while Brecht does sing a hymn here in favor of depersonalization, he is not without second thoughts on the manner of Galy Gay's rebirth to a new resplendent self. Off stage, Brecht trivialized what brainwashing comes down to in personal terms, but on stage he depicts that process in all its harrowing concreteness: Galy Gay screams his anguish and loneliness while his tormentors wait for him to make the proper gesture of submissiveness. Brecht cannot help suggesting that to carve out a new identity is equivalent to butchering the old—and you cannot butcher an identity without torturing a man. Nor is this the only note of social conscience in *A Man's a Man*, Brecht revealing himself to be prophetically alert to what things have come to when identity is reduced to a mere matter of identification: "A man can be replaced at any time, but there is nothing holier than the possession of a pass." The world is full of Galy Gays for whom the ultimate validation of reality is wholly financial:

A SOLDIER: Do you still have any doubts about the elephant?

GALY GAY: Since he is being purchased, I have no doubts at all.

For those concerned with the psychodramatic aspects of Brecht's work, Galy Gay deserves attention. A mixture of venality, charm, opportunism, naïveté, and a tendency to let himself be victimized, this character seems to embody a good share of the traits commentators invariably refer to in characterizing Brecht's work as one long confession of psychic conflict. Without becoming too immersed in psychological analysis, one can still point out that Brecht does with Galy Gay what he would later do with Mother Courage, creating a character who is on the one hand the quintessence of the kind of money-obsessed personality Brecht despised and at the same time a device through which he expresses his own emotional state. Blindfolded for what he believes to be his execution, Galy Gay becomes just such a device, and it is Brecht on Brecht we begin to hear: "Listen to me! I confess that I don't know what has happened to me. Believe me and don't laugh, I am someone who doesn't know who he is." In Brecht's work, the temptation to caricature will always yield at significant junctures to the temptation to articulate existential despair—even after Brecht had ostensibly made up his mind that thanks to communism, the concept of tragedy was as outmoded as the concept of individualism.

A Man's a Man deals not only with a character who has his identity cut away but also with a character who attempts to regain what he feels is his true identity by shooting his sex away. Bloody Five, a pathologically aggressive sergeant whose name commemorates his use of five defenseless victims as target practice, is as unable as Läuffer was to subordinate his sex life to his career, with the result that he arrives at Läuffer's radical solution. Brecht may well have intended Bloody Five's fate to underscore how much better it is to be a Galy Gay than the jealous guardian of a name, but his emasculation hardly leaves that impression. It merely makes us realize that man must cope with a far more complex set of forces than are encompassed by Marxist doctrine, and Brecht will be forcing that realization upon us in *The Threepenny Opera* and most of his important work thereafter; much as he may have wanted to make of sexual activity an area of human behavior defined by socio-economic criteria, he merely succeeded in restating an insight running through almost the entire Lenz-Brecht tradition—that instinct is an autonomous force which can be explained only in terms of its own momentum. Man is driven by forces he does not begin to understand, and he does not begin to understand either how thin-crusted is the earth upon which he strikes his postures. In making this clear, Brecht employs imagery that takes us right back to Büchner's dangerous puddles.

On a formal level, *A Man's a Man* is an episodic illustration by parable in which Brecht is already utilizing much that will become staple in his later epic theater. Actors step out of character to underline the illustrative nature of the proceedings; moody lyrics make us conscious of universal truths to which all the sound and fury of the moment will have to conform; commentary focuses on the illustration pattern's critical implications; and each scene, though it provides a building block to an interlocking pattern, contributes its share of self-explanatory tragicomic observations on such matters as military values, the importance of personality, the power of money, etc. As he will later on, Brecht loads his scenes with broad social satire, deflating left and right what he smells as fake. A typical thrust is that colonial soldiers drink as heavily as they do to satisfy a consuming thirst for law and order.

The Brecht who will mix comic and tragic effects in order to demonstrate that what seems comic is laden with tragic implications, is already present in *A Man's a Man.* So is the Brecht who will teach by grotesque example that man is his own worst enemy. *A Man's a Man* has all the ambivalence of the plays which we identify most fully with Brecht's concept of epic theater, suggesting on the one hand a cynic who observes the human menagerie with a detached hopeless smile, on the other, a humanitarian who cannot shirk his emotional involvement. It even suggests that most glaring paradox about the later Brecht—his failure to confront the tragic implications of his deepest convictions. Communist critics may not find *A Man's a Man* wholly to their liking, but they can find enough in it to make out a case for it as an arraignment of capitalism. It is just as easy to see it as an arraignment of men in general—precisely the summary Brecht's major plays demand.

In posing problems for those who would like to attach to him a single overriding attitude, Brecht recalls forerunners like Lenz and Büchner whose cynical perceptions and pessimistic outlook combined oddly with an anguished social conscience. Writers of this type are easy to dismiss as cynical nihilists by quoting lines from their works that could not be more cynical without probing the complex motivation behind those lines. In *The Threepenny Opera* (1928), cynical nihilism seems to be the message when it is bluntly stated that morality is only possible on a full belly and that one man's full belly means someone else has been fed on; that no matter what values men say they live by, they live hypocritically; that most men cannot possibly be cunning or evil enough to make a go of things; that even outstanding men are not immune to pure instinct; and, to top it all off, that the worst fools are those who sacrifice personal comfort to make a better world.

But it is wholly cynical to stress that one should not preach morality to those without the means to practice it; that whether we like it or not, our first concern is to have enough to eat; that mankind fails to react to the genuine need of the unfortunate but is quickly enough energized into action by melodramatized misery. The cynical comments in *The Threepenny Opera* do carry a ring of conviction because Brecht finds in the world more than enough to be cynical about; but the cynical tone should not fool us—no mere cynic could write as eloquently as Brecht on the need to be cynical. *The Threepenny Opera* was Brecht trying to confront his audience with the real nature of their world, to get people to realize how much evil is perpetually being taken for granted. Brecht seems to have felt at the time that he could do this no better than by striking brazen antiromantic and anti-idealistic attitudes, by exhibiting modern society as a place where one must, above all, possess sharp teeth if one is not to be plowed under. In this he succeeded far too well, and when one thinks back to *The Threepenny Opera,* one recalls most of all such bits as the whorish laughter shattering the quiet in which a killer like Macheath disposes of another victim, or the venalities which prepare Macheath's betrayal by his dear friend Tiger Brown, or Peachum conducting a lesson in how to look properly maimed for maximum sympathy and minimum revulsion, and so on; one remembers, in short, a society in which injustice is so pervasive that the possibility of a better tomorrow simply does not enter into the picture. While this may have shown Brecht in the grip of a darker vision than he cared to admit, it does not reveal him as the sort of facile cynic that writers like Koestler have tried to make him out to be by focusing on a catchy line taken out of context.

On the other hand, those who accord Brecht the status of a master ironist who resembles Swift in his ability to convince the literal-minded that he is an exponent of the very attitudes he is exposing, should realize they are extending a compliment whose implications are far less flattering. An ironist cannot suddenly reverse his angle of attack in the middle of a work and expect that his audience will make a clear-cut distinction between what is steeped in negation and what is offered in the spirit of constructive social criticism. Brecht wished, among other things, to make *The Threepenny Opera* a piece of forceful anticapitalistic satire; he wanted his audience to share his view that the banker is as much a criminal as the gangster, the public official as much a prostitute as the street-walker, the business world as much a jungle as the most violent section of a slum. But these observations, reflecting Brecht's initial study of Marxism during this period, do not detach themselves from criticisms of a more generalized nature such as fill the body of the play. Rather, they reinforce a predominantly negative tone that can be described as racy and cynical, raffish and knowing, bawdy and mocking, much the same tone in which Grabbe's barkers suggested the world to be a zoo and man quite apish, and in which Büchner's exhibitors mocked man's pretensions to be anything but a member of the animal kingdom. It is as well the tone of Wedekind inviting his audience to receive his plays as zoological studies. In *The Threepenny Opera* we are dealing once more with fauna and we know it from the very start:

And the shark possesses teeth
And he wears them on his face.

Much worse than the shark is man, who can slice up his victim while looking most harmless. The point of Brecht's ballad opera is that man is the only animal whose gift for hypocrisy matches his genius for exploitation—he is bound to taint whatever he touches. Given such eloquent misanthropy, what is the logic of punctuating satire with touches of straight Marxism; or of making characters embody what is incurably wrong with human nature, on the one hand, while endowing them as well with attitudes implicit in the psychology of capitalists. Brecht's equation between the business of crime and the crime of business strikes us as mathematical proof not of the need to change the nature of the conditions under which business is conducted but of the more depressing axiom that society must forever be no better than its members. Determined as Brecht is to make clear that there are no idealistic alternatives, he succeeds only in convincing us that there are no alternatives whatever to the terrible realities that so obsess him. *The Threepenny Opera* concludes by reminding us that we inhabit a dark, cold universe in which the most common sound is a cry of misery.

Brecht's inconsistencies in *The Threepenny Opera* are invariably cited by those who assert he attempted to achieve by theatrical technique what he could not convey by the written word. It is not a criticism one can dismiss, especially since certain elements of style changed very little in the course of his career. He could never resist putting into the mouths of his most pathetic characters apt observations of the kind which are appreciated for themselves, no matter who gives them utterance. Characterization would always carry a substantial load of programmatic commentary, with the result that one begins to find it natural for characters to resonate every once in a while with their master's voice. And quite understandably, one would hardly be able to view such characters simply as examples of what was wrong with the same world they dissect so cunningly. Brecht tried to salvage the illustrative value of such characters by emphasizing that they had to read their lines in a certain way, or move about the stage in a certain way, or define their purpose by acting in a manner wholly at variance with the insights they articulate. But it never worked, at least not for Western audiences—Brecht, the director, is no match for Brecht, the poet. When he makes of characters like Peachum or Macheath sources of irrefutable perceptions, he gives to content a significance that cannot be neutralized by style of presentation.

Least ambiguous are the works Brecht produced immediately after *The Threepenny Opera*. Apparently stung by the impression he had made on a leading critic that he was unconvinced as well as unconvincing on the issues he blended with his entertainment, Brecht makes absolutely certain in *The Rise and Fall of the City Mahagonny* (1929) that no one can carp about the precision of his message. For all its exotic locale, *Mahagonny* takes place in the world of modern capitalism as Brecht saw it; that world, says Brecht, elevates individual appetite to religious heights, enshrining as its holiest commandment "Thou shalt never be without money." Hedonistic experience—and here Brecht clearly has in mind his own glorification of instinct in the early twenties—is the sole resource of those trying to function by the rules of a profit-oriented society while clinging to the idea that they are free men. But in a world where cash decides, the rush for diversions serves merely to underscore that all is emptiness. No amount of sport, sex, or drink will give moneyed sensation-seekers what they really need and what can be obtained only in a system that does not define personal value in commodity terms. In essence a flow of verse set to music, *Mahagonny* is constantly reiterating such an apocalyptic view of the capitalistic ethos. Brecht goes so far as to show a character executed for lack of money, continuing to equate what is matter of fact under capitalism with ultimate horrors. As in *The Threepenny Opera,* he indicts the way things are by seeming to relish their rottenness. Thus he puts on stage boards in which liberty is advocated only for those who are rich, bravery extolled as an attitude by which one adds to the misery of those who cannot fight back, and filth bluntly equated with greatness. Whatever one may feel about the ideological aspects of Brecht's vision in *Mahagonny,* one cannot deny that the vision itself is remarkably powerful; and if future students are bound to turn to *The Measures Taken* to understand the workings of the totalitarian Communist mind, one can expect them to be equally fascinated with *Mahagonny* for revealing why a middle-class intellectual is attracted to Communism in the first place.

Saint Joan of the Stockyards (1930) is an episodic play in which Brecht reveals much the same feeling about Schiller and the high style conveyed in *Danton's Death.* Like Büchner in the Simon scenes, Brecht parodies elevated rhetoric by placing it at the disposal of vulgar thought and by associating it with stark realities to which high-flown poetry has scant relevance. These realities comprise the education of a missionary Christian social worker named Joan Dark who begins with the idea that the world will in time be a better place in which to live—but first, people must change themselves; in the end Joan is confirmed in the belief that nothing is more evil than to attach such importance to personal development. Joan comes to feel that any action which does not have consequences for society as a whole is not worth performing, but that any action which does is commendable, even if that action is violent and, by Christian standards, unpardonable. In fact, so wrong is nonviolence as a basic social attitude that war to the death must be declared on any philosophy which blocks recourse to the gun or club promoting revolutionary change. Believers in a God who might save man the task of hacking his way to something better should have their heads pounded on the pavement till they croak. Joan says all this as she is about to die. But her message gets through least of all to the villain-capitalists Brecht has placed at her bedside: the meat kings of Chicago drown out her attack on all transcendental thinking with noisy idealistic lyricism. The verse patterns of German classicism echo grotesquely not only against Joan's final remarks to the effect that force responds to nothing but force, and people can be helped only by people, but against loud-speaker announcements on the state of a world in which coffee harvests are poured into the sea and banks closed one after another by governments—a world Brecht views to be wholly at the mercy of monopoly capitalism.

In *Saint Joan* Brecht employs the open form to illustrate the fallacy of identifying the forces which keep that capitalism going with reasonable humanity. His intention is to shock the audience into the same ruthless attitude to which the dying Joan commits herself. The eleven episodes are designed to make increasingly untenable any faith in nonviolent progress. It comes down to the ever-growing capacity of Joan to think the unthinkable, to conceive of human beings who will only stop exploiting and killing when they cease to breathe. Thus, in scene 1 Joan preaches idealism while ladling out soup; in scene 2 she determines to add knowledge of what is really going on to her idealistic convictions; by scene 4 she has become acutely conscious of the material nature of spiritual poverty, but the learning process has still not consumed her basic conviction that no man is a total villain; even in scene 9 she clings to that conviction—it leaves her only in the end.

The play is not remotely realistic; its characters are obvious personifications of attitudes, its dialogues and monologues are the antithesis of ordinary speech, and its plot is so obviously schematic and tendentious that we are constantly aware of the dramatist as speech writer. While it can be performed effectively, and was, indeed, so performed on the German radio with actors Fritz Kortner and Peter Lorre, among others, it is a far cry from the disturbing plays Brecht was still to write, those plays in which he would sound chords whose full tonalities he could never explain away with Marxist dogma. *Saint Joan,* for all its serio-comic brilliance and linguistic versatility, is a play in which the cynical intonations move in a single direction; any reservations one might have about the crusade against capitalism are vitiated by the device of having nasty capitalists express such reservations to Joan, who is always quick to show they have no basis in reality. The later Brecht would never be so cut and dried.

Brecht's *Lehrstücke* have been called "miniature epic dramas," but they are epic only in the sense that episodes are employed illustratively.

They have none of the richness of characterization and background detail of the work by which Brecht is known. They are single-mindedly didactic to the point of abstraction, and to describe them by the same phrase used to identify plays like *Galileo* and *Mother Courage* does not make sense. If epic theater is not to become too vague a classification, it should not be employed to refer to plays whose tone and feeling set them sharply apart.

But what *The Measures Taken* tells us about Brecht at the beginning of the thirties cannot be overlooked.[4] Like Büchner, who was haunted by the realization that only killing could usher in a different social order, Brecht stresses in *The Measures Taken* that the road to a better world must be paved by executioners. To be thrown on the corpse heap of history are not just those who stand in the way of progress by their reactionary convictions but even those whose basic decency cannot be called into question. In *The Measures Taken* Brecht is ideologically explicit about the value of individual personality in a way he was not in *A Man's a Man*—humanitarian feeling should never outweigh the larger considerations at work; those whose task it is to wipe out innocents, whose only crime is that they cannot extinguish their capacity to feel, are acting with logic. Individualism and idealism are inexcusably regressive postures in a world where all value is collective. If Brecht heretofore opposed idealistic value systems with a forthright cynical materialism, he now opposes them with a materialism interpenetrated by religiofied Marxism.

The rejection of liberalism in *The Measures Taken* is on view in other pieces written by Brecht at this time in a highly didactic style, but nowhere else is it given such stark formulation. And here one might add that if Brecht showed himself in a key play to be very much aware of what his concept of paradise came down to in concrete terms, he is bound to recall a similar moment of truth in the work of the one modern dramatist about whose greatness as a living presence Brecht had no second thoughts. Could one not say that *The Measures*

---

[4] Reinhold Grimm has observed that in his early work Brecht avoids the realm of tragedy by virtue of his characters' cynical compromises in favor of personal gratification (e.g. Kragler), while in later plays of the twenties and early thirties, collective value blots out just as effectively any real confrontation of ideology and tragedy. The one exception to this is his *The Measures Taken,* and there can be little doubt that, like Grimm and Sokel, those out to stress the tragic implications of Brecht's work will inevitably have to make this the key work in relation to the whole question of Brecht's basic attitudes.

Taken occupies in Brecht's work a position parallel to that of *Death and Devil* in Wedekind's drama? In both cases the intention was to set forth unambiguously what might tend to lose clarity in a play of more complex texture; in both cases the dramatist confronts in concrete terms his belief that there is a solution to the world's ills; and in both cases the results are surprisingly negative. In *Death and Devil* Wedekind showed himself to be tragically aware that there was no basis for his dream of a world liberated by erotic radicalism. The fate of sexual reformers like himself is to be eulogized by weak-kneed candidates for spinsterhood. In a play which should logically have vindicated a faith, Wedekind offers a confession of despair. In *The Measures Taken* Brecht, too, disappoints those who expect of him bold affirmations. Like Wedekind, he cannot hide from himself that death and dehumanization are organic to his vision, that the true landscape of his ideals is barren of the very things for which he is fighting in the first place. It cannot be accidental that Brecht and Wedekind give us leading characters who are obvious projections of their creators and that these characters in the end are mercilessly destroyed all of which may go to show that nihilistic pessimism is least of all an ephemeral attitude and has a way of reasserting itself long after it has supposedly been overcome.

The Exception and the Rule (1930), in which a merchant kills his coolie because he thinks the latter is about to kill him, when in reality the coolie wishes only to do him a kindness, is another play in which Brecht wants to show that the world is too evil to respond to halfway measures. One wonders if that is all it shows. On the one hand, Brecht demonstrates again a world in which those who act on impulse are destroyed; on the other, he shows that those who do the destroying are as much shackled by self-defeating contradictions as their victims. The exploiter, in order to secure his parasitic position, must constantly add to his demands on the exploited. Reason tells him he deserves to be loathed in return, and this awareness brings paroxysms of anxiety—with the result that the exploiter is a kind of split personality, swerving between joy at the superiority of his position and despair at ever being secure enough not to have to armor himself against any genuine human warmth. His survival instincts dictate that for every stirring of good fellowship he must become that much more inhuman, since kindness is bound to be interpreted as weakness. As for the exploited, they are in an equally stereotyped situation. They cannot ever hope to transcend the status to which their masters have assigned them: cast in the role of villains, they must play that role to the hilt every moment of their lives, for to express any unpredictable emotion can be suicidal. They survive, in short, by hardening themselves to the point where they will appear to be just what they are expected to be—and they are expected to be maelstroms of murderous hostility. Quite plainly the one thing that Brecht's world will not allow is the manifestation of humane impulse. Evil is bound to perpetuate itself because all avenues for the expression of anything better have been sealed off. Exploiter and victim appear frozen into attitudes that cannot be altered; the coolie will always cringe, the merchant will always stand above him, whip in hand. It should be clear why one can easily make of *The Exception and the Rule* another key play of Brechtian ambiguity; for some, Brecht is, of course, saying again, "That's capitalism"; for others, his image of the coolie crucified for a humane gesture, after being treated all his life like a pack animal, carries more tragic overtones.

Of the plays Brecht wrote to indict Hitler's Germany and to illuminate the forces that made Germany ripe for Nazism, *Fear and Misery of the Third Reich* (1938) is most memorable. It is a cumulative indictment by episodes and is bound to remind us forcibly of *The Last Days of Mankind*. Each scene of Brecht's play shows Germany as the land of *Richter und Henker* which Kraus asserted it to be. Like Kraus, Brecht displays the types for whom things never go better than when they go worst for men of decency; and like Kraus, he exposes moral cretinism while making vivid the tragic side of rule by force. It might not be at all unreasonable to look upon Brecht's play as a continuation of the social and cultural history dramatized by Kraus; for its dialogue this play also depends on the way individuals really talk; once more the surest guide to a moral atmosphere is the spoken word.

Brecht gives us close to thirty unconnected episodes, and each episode illustrates what a pervasive fact of life the Hitler regime was for the Germans. Religiously, economically, and socially the Nazi virus spreads through the moral fabric of a nation. Toughs of the SA have the power to play God in 1933; and by 1934, judges are prepared to modify their legal outlook now that they know which way the wind is blowing; nuclear physicists make sure that they will not be accused of practicing "Jewish" science; a doctor and his wife realize they are racially incompatible inasmuch as she is of Jewish descent; parents live in dread of the day their children will report them to

discovery of a new truth is of far less import than its subsequent application. Apropos of this, he recalls that the day it was announced the atom bomb had been dropped, he sensed among fellow Californians relief at the imminent conclusion of the war as well as great sadness and distrust. It was Brecht's contention that all scientific break-throughs should meet with an equally ambivalent reaction.

Galileo was thus rewritten to serve as an indictment of amoral science, with the protagonist serving as his own judge and jury. The decisive changes are contained in the single scene where Galileo reveals himself to have written the *Discorsi* under cover. When a former pupil congratulates the old scientist on his achievement while apologizing for having joined those who slandered him as a traitor to progress, Galileo declares that his reputation is wholly in accord with the facts. He capitulated to established authority not because he was once again living by the philosophy that working scientists can do more for the human race than dead heroes, but simply out of fear—and to compound his ignominy, that fear was probably without foundation, since it is now his understanding that the pope was extremely reluctant to have him tortured and since he himself had already become a formidable figure at the time of his recantation. As Galileo's *mea culpa* continues, he firmly refuses to allow his life to be evaluated on any grounds except those connected with his desertion of his anti-Ptolemaic position. He equates that desertion with a negation of all the social principles on which a new age might well have been erected, denouncing himself for emptying science of basic human considerations, for reducing it to a cold technology whose future development could well jeopardize all that makes a civilized life possible.

As speeches go, Galileo's is quite eloquent, and we are bound to recall that Brecht's work is full of such ringing self-appraisals. Galileo, like Joan Dark and the doomed comrade in *The Measures Taken*, comes to realize that at certain junctures of history there is no room for compromise. But whereas in Brecht's earlier plays the schematic nature of dramatic treatment made it natural for a character to be subsumed by his function as spokesman for a particular point of view, in *Galileo* such a transition is far less acceptable. And this is because until the moment Galileo strikes out at himself he is presented as a character whose distinction is precisely that nothing can make him subordinate his lust for life to categorical imperatives. In fact, his scientific activities are simply another expression of the same basic drive for pleasure that makes Galileo a connoisseur of food and wine.

Wholly without illusions about what one must do in a profit-driven world to get by, he has nonetheless decided to function by the rules of just such a world rather than withdrawing for the sake of some abstract ideal. Above all, he wants to fill his belly, and those who use their brain without getting something concrete in return he holds beneath contempt.

Against such a portrait, the speech Brecht wrote to point up Galileo's villainy must of necessity strike us as extrinsic. One cannot build up a persuasive pattern of episodic detail and then expect to add climaxes unprepared for by such detail without confusing the issue. Actually, Brecht in *Galileo* is guilty of the same kind of dissociation observable in the first drama of the Lenz-Brecht tradition. *The Tutor* presented a series of episodes in which it was made evident that Läuffer would be self-destructive no matter what the circumstances; certainly he would not be transformed into a more admirable type by a realization of the ideals propounded by characters who served as Lenz's spokesmen. In *Galileo* the leading character is just as incongruous for the lesson Brecht has in mind, if only because we are fully convinced that Galileo's fear of torture and unabashed hedonistic life style is immune to reformation. Galileo may want to suggest in his final long speech that if he had to do it all over again he would be tempted to immolate himself for a more ethical conception of science; but there is really no reason to take him at his word. Characteristically enough, after Galileo says his piece he sits down to eat goose. And he makes no secret of the fact that he enjoys such eating.

Galileo then is a play in which we find much of the implicit pessimism running through most of Brecht's other work. But some would have us think that it contains also something positive, namely, the search for scientific truth. According to Margret Dietrich, this is the sole human activity upon which Brecht did not cast the shadow of his merciless cynicism. But while episodes in *Galileo* are built around such an affirmation of science as a pursuit, Brecht is not nearly so positive when he decries the fact that scientists are expected only to contribute knowledge and not to care at all whether their contribution will prove constructive in the long run. Brecht was acutely aware that in the seventeenth century, as well as in our own, the search for truth on the part of dedicated individuals was inevitably bound up with the interests of power-hungry institutions seeking to maintain themselves. As always, what Brecht passionately wants to affirm collides with what he bitterly cannot help realizing. At any rate, if one cannot go along with his comment that *Galileo* has nothing to do with tragedy, one can at least credit him with making the Galileo story highly thought-provoking; and Brecht indicated he desired to do just that with his second version.

Sokel has noted that *Galileo* is relatively "cool" theater. Schumacher and Mayer, on the other hand, seem hardly disposed to call the play a good example of epic theater. How one stands on this point very likely depends on where one lays the stress of Brecht's critical theories. *Galileo* is far more documentary in texture than plays like *Mother Courage;* inasmuch as it is in essence dramatized history, a measure of coolness and objectivity is to be expected, and Brecht's theories advocate such qualities. On the other hand, if *demonstration* is made the key concept of epic theater, any thought of rendering history factually is bound to be viewed as a regression to undialectical realism—which brings us once again to the major criticism of Brecht's final version of *Galileo:* it is an uneasy mixture of authenticity and special pleading. For all its coolness, *Galileo* is to a degree suspenseful because the life of the real Galileo warrants such treatment; individual scenes do not achieve the kind of intellectual autonomy that modern critics associate with the type of theater they call epic.

"I always tell myself: you are a virtuous person, a good person, a good creature." The Captain compliments Woyzeck redundantly on the latter's right to be called good but indicates no concern with the economic implications of goodness. This is one way to begin discussing *The Good Woman of Sezuan* (1940), a play in which Brecht, like Büchner, states emphatically that to be good is simply to be exploitable, that virtue is weakness, and that we live in a world where those who determine the semantics of goodness feel no obligation to help make it part of the practical person's vocabulary.[8]

In *The Good Woman of Sezuan* Brecht asserts that no help for this world will be forthcoming from any reservoirs of ethical idealism conceivably present in human nature itself. As the world now stands, it is bound to make those who are evil more so and to swell their

---

[8] Very relevant here is the following Büchnerian comment by Brecht: "We spoke specifically in the name of the wronged and not in the name of morality. One deals here with two different things, since those wronged are often told on the basis of moral authority that they must be content with their lot. For such moralists, people exist for morality and not morality for people." *Schriften zum Theater* (Frankfurt-am-Main: Suhrkamp Verlag, 1957), pp. 71–72. That Brecht should say this in the same essay in which he pokes fun at Büchner's *bête noire,* Schiller, is more than coincidental.

ranks with disenchanted do-gooders. Brecht concerns himself mainly
with the fate of the good; the only person in Sezuan who fits this
description learns soon enough that kindness cripples, that to survive
one must function wholly without sentiment. As the good woman
Shen Te the protagonist is everyone's soft touch; as the no-nonsense
man of action Shui Ta she keeps parasites at arm's length while
improving her lot; as Shen Te she lives for others and finds she
can do so only by surrendering her right to live any kind of decent
life at all; as Shui Ta she lives for herself and finds she can do
so only be stepping on others. Society offers only the choices of self-
destructive goodness and self-protective egocentricity.

Brecht gives us scenes in which he demonstrates how difficult it
is to be a Shen Te in a world made for Shui Tas, as well as scenes
in which we can see for ourselves how swiftly Shui Tas resolve what
proves insurmountable for Shen Tes. Beyond that, episodic continuity
allows Brecht to follow through effectively on the point of departure
for his play: the conviction of three gods that goodness is by no
means ruled out in the world they have chosen to visit. At significant
points of the action the utter irrelevance of any supernatural orientation
to the hard facts of earthly economics is made apparent by showing
the gods' efforts to rationalize away what it is beyond their capacity
to influence. They persist in their glib simplifications while Shen Te
sinks deeper and deeper into the vicissitudes of a life in which nothing
is so impossible as to live and let live. Representing all forms of
evasive idealism, the gods leave Sezuan as complacently as they arrive,
refusing to recognize that life in no way validates their presumptuous
expectations of human virtue.

Highly abstract and concrete at the same time, *The Good Woman
of Sezuan* is a dramatic parable in which Brecht makes certain the
illustrative function of character does not fade from view. The device
of having changes of character symbolized by the putting on of a
mask adds to our impression of the play as a living demonstration
in which character is at all times to be related to economic circumstance.
One experiences little action without its implied lesson. Brecht's conviction that true realism should not aim for mimesis but a clarification
of underlying forces is borne out by *The Good Woman of Sezuan*,
in which what Brecht takes to be the concrete nature of life is com-
municated all the more incisively by techniques that established realism
excludes. What realistic play has focused as relentlessly as Brecht's
on the *economic* contexts of everyday life? When one recalls a play

like *Les Corbeaux,* in which Becque has no more illusions about the power of money than Brecht, one begins to appreciate Brecht for provoking thought where a naturalistic dramatist merely stimulates our sense of self-righteousness. For while we are quite certain we are not the villains of *Les Corbeaux,* we can be equally as certain that all of us, in one way or another, wear the mask of Shui Ta.

When we have finished *The Good Women of Sezuan,* we have much the same feeling that is evoked by Lenz's episodic illustrations. We have witnessed a number of scenes in which a naïve young person is taught by bitter experience that the competitive nature of modern society makes of ingenuousness the most dangerous fault of all. Läuffer, Marie Wesener, and Shen Te all learn that to be spontaneous and trusting is to invite disaster, and never more so than in that area of human experience where one has no wish to be anything but spontaneous and trusting—love. All three capsize on their inability to depersonalize the erotic—in their sexual lives they make the big mistake of simply letting go. While Lenz envisioned specific remedies within society for the amelioration of those conditions that defeated his characters, Brecht suggests in his Epilogue a mixture of passionate social conscience and desperate resignation: "There must be a good one—must, must, must!" Brecht verbalizes what Lenz is always implying silently—that there are no easy answers, if there are any answers at all.

Mr. Puntila and His Hired Man Matti (1941) is a play in which Brecht uses the episodic structure to make another pessimistic comment on the possibility of men ever treating one another humanely. Consisting of twelve scenes, *Puntila* stresses the episodic nature of life itself: it shows human personality to be, in essence, a flow of moods; as in *A Man's a Man,* no ideal continuity splices these states of mind into a pattern that would reassure us of man's intrinsic sanity. Episodic organization is shown to be suitable not only for the dramatization of dissociated history but for underscoring how devoid of meaningful continuity human emotional life can be. Even though Brecht includes in *Puntila* enough action and dialogue[9] to make a case for the view

---

[9] In *Puntila,* dialogue is largely monologue, as Franz H. Crumbach has noticed in his analysis of the play's dramaturgy. Brecht, like Büchner and Wedekind, reinforces a sense of human isolation by conversational exchanges which are usually quite undramatic, with the result that the dialogue says in one way what the reality of the master-servant relationship says in another—that everyone is tied to his own concerns so inextricably that there is no room for genuine human contact.

that he is showing only the psychology of exploiters to be so fragmented, he is no more successful here than in *Mother Courage* in keeping a tendentious play within the bounds of its message.

When drunk, the Finnish landowner Puntila bubbles over with human warmth; when sober, he can treat human beings at best as objects. What he promises in bursts of intoxicated generosity he retracts the moment he is again sober. He is simply not recognizable from scene to scene, so fundamentally is his nature altered by liquor. The only man who is not taken in by his spells of good feeling is his servant Matti, who finally acts out the gesture of revolt which Brecht would like us to generalize into a rejection of capitalism, no matter how progressive. Matti knows from bitter experience that the more human his master appears when drunk, the more impossible he will be upon recovery of his senses. So Matti leaves his master's house, and he explicates his departure with a poem on the need for each man to be his own master. But the play still strikes us as essentially tragic, indicating, as it does, that man's relationship to man can be decent only at rare moments, that the world will inevitably harden everyone into the petty protector of his own narrow interests. Once again Brecht has invested the character who is *bad* with so much vitality and color that we cannot help seeking the clue to his play in the contradictions of that character. One is inclined to remember most clearly a common phrase from Matti's poem of rejection: "Nothing helps. . . ."

Brecht's hatred of parasites and exploiters, his conviction that small people always pay for those on top, sympathy for victims who must remain forever unnoticed in their misery, goodness as a deadly temptation, the prohibitive cost of all that makes life worth holding on to—these and just about every other perennial Brechtian motif can be found in *The Caucasian Chalk Circle* (1945); but they are worked into a story whose development by climaxes and tidy ending one is not disposed to call Brechtian. In *The Caucasian Chalk Circle* Brecht comes close to writing the kind of escapist theater against which he had once inveighed, theater that serves to entertain and reassure rather than so disturb the audience that it is compelled to make decisive reformulations of attitude.

The fact that the later Brecht was much more sympathetic to drama along Aristotelian lines, and apparently far less concerned with teaching lessons in dramatic form, is germane to the reason he began in *The Caucasian Chalk Circle* to dispense with stylistic elements associated with the Lenz-Brecht tradition. Though influenced by Shakespearian dramaturgy every bit as much as by any work covered in this study, *The Caucasian Chalk Circle* does not reflect a radical fusion of Shakesperian form with modern content. If anything, Shakespeare here proves to be too obviously the model being imitated. Robert Brustein has remarked that the play "is not only permeated with the mood and atmosphere of Shakespearian comedy, but also with some of its dramatic conventions"; and Brustein goes on to note that, among other borrowings, there is "the main plot" which "turns on suspense, misunderstanding, and intrigue." Recourse to Shakespearian modes of humor is complemented by boisterous comedy, whose emphasis on the quick laugh has prompted the observation that Brecht never got out of the cabaret. As for content, *The Caucasian Chalk Circle* is the one play in which goodness is not without compensation, and in which the rewarder of that goodness is plainly a wish-fulfilling projection of Brecht himself; Azdak, the memorably whimsical Samaritan of those whose difficulties can only be exacerbated by conventional law, allows his creator to give vent to his usual all-inclusive cynicism without in any way questioning the essential benevolence of that cynicism. Thus Azdak, like Brecht, sees through the contradictions of fashionable moralities thanks to a concrete grasp on life that yields to no system of abstractions. But biographical relevancies do not suggest themselves when Azdak turns out to be an unequivocal force for good. In a manner of speaking, Azdak is Mother Courage and Galileo without tragic qualifiers, this being one instance in which he who does the Brechtian deflating is not, in return, shown in need of the same unmasking. It is as if Brecht grew bored with demonstrating life as something to be lived only at the price of one's illusions, if not one's life. For once, his cynicism and skepticism, his hopelessness and hostility, do not determine the character of our final response. Not that this should be taken to imply that the response itself is powerful enough to merit the analysis bestowed on ambivalent reactions that are evoked by Brecht's best tragicomic work; actually, the nature of that response is not such as to explain why there are those who view *The Caucasian Chalk Circle* as among Brecht's masterpieces.

It was noted earlier that Brecht's episodic theater is built around a core of vivid characterization in a way reminiscent of Lenz, who insisted that Shakespeare's capacity to endow his figures with pulsing blood was his most distinguished aesthetic trait. Brecht was not unaware of Lenz. He payed tribute to him in a poem, *Concerning the*

Bourgeois Tragedy, 'The Tutor' by Lenz, describing Lenz's play as
Figaro on the other side of the Rhine, and noting that what came
through as comedy in France proved tragic in Germany because of
the impotence of the German lower classes. Brecht went on to write
an adaptation of *The Tutor* in 1950. He retained most of what Lenz
put into his play: the Major and his wife are as greedy and status
conscious as ever; they are still out to get labor at the lowest possible
price; and they are still unaware that the tutor is a human being
with human needs rather than a polished robot. In his treatment of
Läuffer's relationship to his masters, Brecht adds concrete details not
found in the original. Thus, we are made conscious of the knife
the tutor uses to convert himself into an asexual creature; and Läuffer's
desire to escape the stifling atmosphere of the aristocratic environment
in which he is not allowed the minimal pleasures of normal social
intercourse is focused on his attempt to get a horse from the Major.
Naturally, such horses are not available for tutors. The end result
is that Läuffer proceeds to take his place in a society that prefers
the puppet to the man:

Only after maiming and castration
Do his masters condescend to recognize his station.
Broken in his backbone. And now he'll be an expert
In making spinelessness the major aim of education.[10]

For Brecht, Läuffer is the archetypal German intellectual, who is
quite prepared to remodel himself in the image most reassuring to his
superiors. How ironic that this same judgment is rendered by present-
day German intellectuals on Brecht himself.

For Lenz, Shakespeare had charted the path modern drama should
take. Brecht, too, considered Shakespeare a giant, going so far as
to call him "a great realist," and crediting him with sophistications
all too often missing in modern bourgeois drama. When adapting
Coriolanus, Brecht was quick to point out that modern depictions
of proletariat psychology suffer in comparison with Shakespeare's. It
was Brecht's opinion, also, that even when Shakespeare wrote perfunc-
torily he wrote extremely well. But Brecht was by no means as enthusiastic about the content of Shakespeare's work as he was about

[10] Brecht, *Stücke,* XI, 213. See also Brecht's essay on his adaptation, "Über das
Poetische und Artistische," pp. 274–87, in *Schriften zum Theater,* VI.

its episodic form. The content he found revoltingly archaic; and he foresaw the day when plays like *King Lear* would be looked upon as examples of sadistic entertainment—for what civilized person would have the heart to watch a tragic hero being slowly cut to pieces? Shakespeare's depiction of a world in which human beings are isolated from one another by inexorable forces that defy comprehension makes him the contemporary writer par excellence for a great many readers: for Brecht, it simply makes him outdated.

Here a paradox emerges. Lenz extolled Shakespeare as the playwright-thinker who had modernized the episodic structure by infusing it with a naturalistic view of life. Conversely, Lenz belittled classical drama because the Greeks conceived of life as ruled by supernatural fate. Brecht, in contrast, defines his sense of what is modern by using Shakespeare as a negative example. He finds Shakespeare to be, in his own way, as obsessed with fatalistic action as were the Greeks of Lenz's finding. This might lead us to assume that neither Lenz nor Brecht would be responsible for plays in which human beings are pictures enmeshed in situations that underscore how little freedom of action life on this earth affords. But, as we have seen, they wrote just such plays.

We have been talking of a Lenz-Brecht tradition, and the fact that the dramatists in question do constitute a tradition is borne out by resemblances noted throughout this study. One can mention here that they share not only the basics of an attitude toward existence but a specific way of fashioning a play to convey that attitude in the most persuasive manner. They all de-emphasize Aristotelian plot in order to demonstrate episodically that man is wholly at the mercy of forces that reassert themselves with monotonous inevitability. For Lenz, these forces are social, for Grabbe and Büchner they defy definition, for Wedekind they are sexual, for Kraus, immoral, and for Brecht, economic. In the plays of these dramatists there is as much thematic similarity as one could hope to find in any group of writers linked by kinships of sensibility and temperament. Invariably they show us a world in which only hypocrites and exploiters are at home, a world that is a veritable hell for anyone with reverence for life or truth.

They are so fiercely hostile to the way things are that they do not hesitate to break through the restrictive criteria of a prosaic realism. They stage grotesquery after grotesquery and do not shy away from caricatural portrayals. They are not content to dramatize— they wish to teach; and commentary, both in prose and poetry, pervades their work. They have the satirist's passion for irony and the poet's conviction that the rhythms and intonations of verse are best suited to convey irony in the most concise and effective manner. Their approach to dialogue could well be termed novelistic, for they wish at all times to relate the spoken word to the texture of a specific society, to make of the manner in which characters speak an eloquent indictment of all that a society stands for.

They share the same essential inner conflict. On the one hand, they are impatiently cynical, out to convince us that the world is simply verminous; on the other, they rage prophetically against injustice and pettiness. From Lenz to Brecht we meet a strange breed of writers whom one can justifiably call idealistic cynics, men far too skeptical to believe that evil men can ever be anything but evil, but, nonetheless, so disturbed by this evil that they can hardly keep their violent feelings in check. As it is, their plays would delight any researcher of the art of drama as an outlet for aggressions. In their plays, men are castrated, beheaded, cremated alive, strangled, brainwashed, shot, etc. And while this is happening, the rest of the world spins blithely by, having its own good time. Though all the dramatists of the Lenz-Brecht tradition communicate eloquently in play after play their revulsion at such a world, one cannot help feeling that in their deepest selves they realize their way of responding to reality is a futile emotional indulgence. A world so bad cannot possibly get better. "Nothing helps . . ." could well serve as the theme of the Lenz-Brecht tradition.

appendix

Introduction. In 1928 a noted historian of drama asserted that Shakespeare's episodic history play had exerted minimal influence on the development of modern theater; that same historian then mentioned as drawbacks of the history play that it is not suspenseful except to those who know "the course of history" and that it is held together not by a firm plot but at the most by "the presence of such characters as Richard III or Hotspur."[1] Perhaps it was still too early to appreciate what Brecht had learned from Shakespeare's histories, and perhaps it was necessary for Brecht to be appreciated in this regard before one could give Lenz, Grabbe, and Büchner their due. At any rate, we now realize that the episodic play grounded on a more or less anti-Aristotelian approach deserves singling out as a significant cultural development and that this kind of drama derives its unique identity from the very omissions which have so often been held against it. When I say "we," I actually mean those who have read the key works which constitute the bridge from Lenz to Brecht. Unfortunately, Lenz seems to have been wholly neglected by English and American translators and neither Grabbe's *Napoleon* nor his *Hannibal* can be read except in German. The same is true of Kraus's *The Last Days of Mankind,* and here the outlook is no brighter than present actuality: no one honestly expects this mammoth work to be translated *in toto.* In view of this, it was felt the reader of *Brecht's Tradition* would welcome selected exemplary scenes whose style and content were pertinent to the text's discussion. It is to be hoped that full translations of *The Tutor* and *The Soldier* as well as of Grabbe's historical dramas will in time be available and thus render superfluous at least part of what has here been added.

[1] Donald Clive Stuart, *The Development of Dramatic Art* (N.Y.: Dover Publications, 1928), pp. 220–21.

Introduction to Scenes from THE TUTOR. The protagonist of *The Tutor* can take no step except in the direction of disaster. As to where the responsibility for Läuffer's succession of very bad mistakes lies, there is here the same dichotomy of views that attaches to any play whose social critique is presented in psychological depth. The scenes that follow should allow the reader to draw his own conclusions. In the first scene, Läuffer has finally gained employment, but only because his services can be had for next to nothing: the Major's Wife lets him know right away that his wages will be half of what he had been expecting. Läuffer does not protest: he swallows this affront so quiescently that his masters will certainly be encouraged to try more of the same. The Major's Wife enjoys chatting with Läuffer when he goes out of his way to feed her vanity, but the atmosphere cools swiftly when the tutor gives expression to opinions not designed for flattery. As this first scene shows the Lenz from whom Büchner may well have learned something about the caricatural portrayal of those who take for granted that the life around them exists for them to exploit, so the second shows the Lenz from whom Büchner definitely learned something about the delineation of involute emotional processes. Running from the Major's wrath, Läuffer winds up in the company of the eccentric schoolmaster, Wenzeslaus, who bombards him with nonsensical digressions bound to reinforce the tutor's conviction that he lives in the worst of possible worlds. Wenzeslaus cannot contain his admiration for Läuffer when the latter puts an end to his fertility, but, as the third scene shows, Wenzeslaus is soon disillusioned about the religious significance of his guest's self-emasculation: Läuffer, the eunuch, is quite prepared to become Läuffer, the husband. These scenes reveal Lenz's ability to suggest tragic realities in comic encounters, his talent for refracting what is wrong with a social scene through grotesque twists of character, and his mastery of a dialogue that is extremely realistic and satirical at the same time, dialogue that would prove highly influential on German dramatists who could never content themselves with a realism devoid of the poetic and didactic. Lenz's synthesis of Diderot and Shakespeare will be doubly appreciated by anyone who takes the trouble to read a sampling of the hyperdramatic works put out by his *Sturm and Drang* contemporaries.

the tutor

Act I, scene 3

MAJOR'S WIFE: I have spoken to your father, and we came to an agreement; your salary will not be three hundred but one hundred and fifty ducats. In return for that, I must demand Mr.—what is your name?—Mr. Läuffer, that you keep yourself in clean clothes and bring no shame to our home. I know you are a man of taste; you came to my attention when you were still in Leipzig. You must know that today the world is most concerned with how a man conducts himself.

LÄUFFER: I hope Your Grace will be satisfied with me. To be sure, I never did miss a ball in Leipzig, and I can boast of well over fifteen dancing masters.

MAJOR'S WIFE: Really? I must have a look at you. (LÄUFFER rises.) No timidity! Mr. . . . Läuffer! No timidity! My son is bashful enough; give him a timid tutor and it's all up with him. Make an attempt to compliment me by minuet; just a try-out, so that I can see for myself. Now, now, that will do! At least my son won't need a dancing master! An additional pas, if you don't mind. Things will definitely work out; everything is bound to work out if you make it your business to attend one of our socials. . . . Are you musical?

LÄUFFER: I play the violin, and if need be the piano.

MAJOR'S WIFE: All the better: should we go to the country, or should Miss Milktooth choose to visit us; up to now I was forced to sing something whenever the children felt like dancing, but things are looking up.

LÄUFFER: Your Grace, you overwhelm me. Where in the world could one hope to find a virtuoso able to match with his instrument the voice of Your Grace.

MAJOR'S WIFE: Ha, ha, ha! The fact of the matter is that you've never heard me . . . Just wait; do you know this minuet? (She sings.)

LÄUFFER: Oh . . . oh . . . pardon the enchantment, the very enthusiasm which is overtaking me. (He kisses her hand.)

MAJOR'S WIFE: And I have a sore throat to boot; today I must crow like a raven. Vous parlez français, sans doute?

LÄUFFER: Un peu, madame.

MAJOR'S WIFE: Avez vous deja fait votre tour de France?

LÄUFFER: Non madame. . . . Oui madame.

MAJOR'S WIFE: Vous devez donc savoir, qu'en France on ne baisse pas les mains, mon cher. . . .

SERVANT (coming in): Count Wermuth. . . . (He enters.)

COUNT (after a few wordless compliments sits down next to the MAJOR'S WIFE on the couch. LÄUFFER remains standing embarrassedly.): Has

Your Grace seen the new dancing master who has just arrived from Dresden? He is a Marchese from Florence, and his name is. . . . Honestly: in all my travels I know of only two who surpass him.

MAJOR'S WIFE: That is really something, only two! To tell the truth, you have aroused my curiosity; I know how delicate is the taste of Duke Wermuth.

LÄUFFER: Pintinello . . . isn't that the man? I saw him dance in Leipzig, at the theater; he's nothing special. . . .

DUKE: He dances—*on ne peut pas mieux.*—As I say, gracious lady, in Petersburg I did see a Beluzzi who surpasses him: but this one has a lightness of foot, something so light and divine in his posture, arms, turns—

LÄUFFER: At the Koch Theater he was hooted out of the house at his last appearance.

MAJOR'S WIFE: My friend had better be careful! Domestics are not to participate in the conversations of persons of rank. Let him go to his room. Who asked for his opinion?

(LÄUFFER *retreats a few steps.*)

COUNT: I suppose the new tutor—for the young gentleman of the family.

MAJOR'S WIFE: And the graduate of a first-rate school.—Now, why doesn't he make himself scarce? We're talking about him, and he knows it—all the more reason for him not to be present. (LÄUFFER *leaves with a stiff compliment.*) It's absolutely tragic how money can't buy something decent any more. To think my husband wrote three times to the professors over there, and this turns out to be their best man. Just take one look at his clothes, you'll see what I mean. Imagine, two hundred ducats of travel money from Leipzig to Insterburg and a yearly stipend of five hundred ducats—and what on earth are we getting for it?

COUNT: If I am not mistaken, his father preaches around here. . . .

MAJOR'S WIFE: That I don't know—possible—I never cared to ask—come to think of it, I believe you're right: his name's Läuffer too; at any rate, he's polite enough. He's a real bear, at least his growling has kept me out of his church.

COUNT: Catholic?

MAJOR'S WIFE: Of course not. You should know there are no Catholic churches in Insterburg: what I mean to say is he's Lutheran or Protestant. Yes, Protestant.

COUNT: The dancing of Pintinello is. . . . Would you believe it, my dancing has set me back some thirty thousand guilders. But I would not hesitate to pay twice that sum if only. . . .

Act III, scene 4

(WENZESLAUS *and* LÄUFFER *are dining at an uncovered table.*)

WENZESLAUS: Tastes good eh? Couldn't compare my menu with the Major's, now could you? But at least when Wenzeslaus chews down his salami a good conscience helps him digest it, but when Mr. Mandel ate roast capon in Champignon sauce, his conscience kept the stuff from going down. You are a—tell me, Mr. Mandel—don't take to heart my being so blunt—it's truth I'm after, and truth is like pepper in a cucumber salad: it adds spice to the conversation. But to be frank, isn't it low of me to take money from you—of course, if I were an ignoramus, a man with nothing to teach those I am supposed to teach—but to waste your time—why, you've given me—wasn't it as much as a hundred ducats? God Almighty, I never saw such a heap of cash in one pile. More, one hundred and forty—and are you to get nothing for it? Am I just to stick it in my sack?

LÄUFFER: But you don't really know how much you've done for me. Perhaps you can't know. Have you ever met a slave before? Oh, freedom, precious freedom!

WENZESLAUS: Oh, stop it! Who's free? Freedom, no less! Take me, I'm tied to my school and I'm tied to God and conscience. Both must be satisfied.

LÄUFFER: Just that—but imagine having to satisfy the whims of a master a hundred times worse than your pupils?

WENZESLAUS: Of course—but in that case he would have to be as much above me as I am above my pupils; what chance is there of that? Especially among noblemen? Maybe you've got something there—that scamp actually wanted to get into my room without permission—he was nobility. Why, can you imagine if the shoe was on the other foot, and I tried the same thing with Mr. Count—But good gracious, you're not eating; you look like a man taking a laxative. Tell me, couldn't you do with a glass of wine? Actually, I did promise to give you some, didn't I? But I have no wine in the house. I'll tell you what, tomorrow I'll get some more, and we shall be drinking Sunday and Thursday, and even more if Franz the organist drops in. But don't despair, we do have water, yes water, even the Greeks knew the value of water. It's water I brought from school, and, for your information, I smoke a pipe after meals and take a walk in the fields; do that, and you have no trouble sleeping, you sleep better than a potentate. Surely you'll join me for a smoke?

LÄUFFER: I'll try it; but I've never smoked before.

WENZESLAUS: But you do ruin your teeth, don't you? Why, I've been smoking since I left my mother's breast; I changed the nipple for the pipestem. He, he, he! It's just what you need against foul gas and just as good against evil lusts. Shall I reveal my diet: mornings I restrict myself to cold water plus pipe, school's over at eleven, and then right

back to the pipe till soup's on: Gottlieb is the equal of any French
cook, and I assist myself to a wedge of roast meat, with vegetables,
of course, and right back to the pipe, school again, and then busy myself
writing lesson plans till dinner, at which time I usually eat something
cold, perhaps a salami, with salad, of course, a piece of cheese doesn't
hurt, or something else for which we have the Lord to thank; and
don't think I omit my pipe before going to bed.

LÄUFFER: Oh, God! I've landed in a tobacco den—

WENZESLAUS: And there you have it, the recipe for getting fat
and heavy, the recipe for happy living. Death I never think of.

LÄUFFER: How can the authorities be so irresponsible? They
have a duty to make your life more comfortable.

WENZESLAUS: Oh, stop it, that's the way things are. You have to adjust:
after all, I am my own boss, nobody's on my back. I put in more
than a day's work each day. I'm supposed to teach my pupils to read
and write; but I also teach them math and Latin, and I teach them
to read with intelligence and it's good things I teach them to write.

LÄUFFER: And what do you get for all that?

WENZESLAUS: What do I get?—Is he going to leave that piece of salami
uneaten? Where else could he get such superb salami? If he's not waiting
for anything better, then he may well go to bed with a hungry belly
the first time in his life—What do I get for it? That, Mr. Läuffer,
is a very stupid question. Forgive me. What do I get for it? It's God's
reward that I get for it. But . . . but . . . but . . . (*tears the toothpick
out of his mouth*) just what is it we have here? Is it possible? A man
of your stature should be so little concerned with what is good and
bad for his body? Toothpicks are dangerous; as a matter of fact, it
is sheer suicide playing with a toothpick, sheer suicide, the very destruction of Jerusalem, that's what toothpicking does to your teeth. All right,
it happens, something happens to get stuck in your teeth (*takes water
and rinses his mouth out*): that's the way to go about it, that's exactly
the way to go about it; why, it does honor to God and neighbor
to do it that way. Lose your teeth, and you wind up an old leash
dog who can't keep his jaws straight; lose your teeth and your toothless
mouth will fail to give birth to words: you'll have just your mouth
and nose to rattle with. The conclusion follows: neither beast nor man
will have the power to make you out.

LÄUFFER: This fellow will carp me to death—the damn thing is he's
right—

WENZESLAUS: Well, how're we doing? Something wrong with the
tobacco? I'll wager it won't take long to make you smoke like
a chimney. I'll do a job on you, and make a man of you like
you've never been.

Act V, scene 10

(LISE *walks in with a songbook in her hand.* LÄUFFER *does not notice her. She looks at him without speaking. He jumps up, wishes to kneel, becomes aware of her and looks at her confusedly.*)

LÄUFFER (*approaching her*): You have stolen a soul from heaven. (*He touches her hand.*) What brings you here, Lise?

LISE: I'm here, Mr. Mandel—I'm here, because you said there would be no church—because you—so I'm here—I'm here to ask if there will be instruction for children tomorrow.

LÄUFFER: Ach!—See these cheeks, you angel! How they burn with an innocent flame, so damn me if you can—Lise, why is your hand trembling? Why are your lips so pale and your cheeks so red? Why are you here?

LISE: Will the children have instruction tomorrow? That's why.

LÄUFFER: Sit down here next to me—lay aside your songbook— who pins up your hair when you go to church? (*He seats her on a chair next to his.*)

LISE (*wishing to rise*): Please forgive me; my bonnet is probably crooked—there was such a wind as I came to church.

LÄUFFER (*takes both her hands in his*): Oh, you are really—Lise, how old are you? Have you never in your life—what is it I wanted to say—have you never been courted?

LISE (*soberly*): Oh, certainly, Mr. Läuffer, in fact just last week. And you know, the Shepherd's girl, Grete, she was so jealous that she kept saying: I don't know why any man makes such a fuss over that simple girl, and then there was an officer. It's not even three months since I went with him.

LÄUFFER: An officer?

LISE: Really, and a very distinguished one at that. Let me tell you, he had on his arm all of three sripes; but I was just too young for him, and my father was against it—he doesn't like a soldier's life.

LÄUFFER: Would you—oh, I'm insane—would you—oh miserable ass that I am!

LISE: Certainly I would. With all my heart.

LÄUFFER: Enchantment!—(*He wants to kiss her hand.*) But you don't even know what I'm trying to ask.

LISE (*pulling her hand back*): Oh let it go, my hand is so dirty—Pfui! What are you doing, Mr. Läuffer? But I do prefer the intellectual type: since early childhood, men of learning have always attracted me; they're so well-bred, so polite, not puf paf, the way soldiers are, although I have nothing against that type either—I just can't resist their uniforms with all those gay colors. Of course, if intellectuals were to dress like that—why, I'd just die, Mr. Läuffer.

LÄUFFER: Allow me to close your mischievous mouth with my lips (*kissing her*). Oh, Lise! If only you knew how unfortunate I am.

LISE: Oh, pfui, sir, what are you doing?

LÄUFFER: Just one more time and never again for eternity! (*He kisses her.* WENZESLAUS *enters.*)

WENZESLAUS: What's this? *Proh deum atque hominum fidem!* How now, you false, false, false prophet! Ravenous wolf in sheep's clothing! Is that the care you owe your flock? To seduce the very innocent you are to guard against seduction? It must needs be that offenses come; but woe to that man by whom the offense cometh!

LÄUFFER: Mr. Wenzeslaus!

WENZESLAUS: No more! Not a word more! You have shown me your true faces. Out of my house, seducer!

LISE (*kneels to* WENZESLAUS): Dear Mr. Schoolmaster, he has done no evil.

WENZESLAUS: He has done you more evil than lies in the power of your worst enemy. He has seduced your innocent heart.

LÄUFFER: Guilty—I plead guilty—but can any man withstand so many temptations? Why, if one were to rip my heart out of my body and to mutilate me organ by organ, so that only a single blood vessel remained, that traitorous vessel would beat for Lise.

LISE: He's done me no harm.

WENZESLAUS: Done you no harm—Heavenly Father!

LÄUFFER: Haven't I told you that she is the most lovable of creatures who have ever graced Creation? I've impressed that upon her lips. I have sealed this innocent mouth with my kisses, that same attractive mouth which would have magically seduced me to the commission of great crimes.

WENZESLAUS: And this is no crime? What is a crime to young people these days? *O tempora, o mores!* Have you taken the trouble to read Valerius Maximus? Have you taken the trouble to read the article *de pudicitia?* There you will find Maenius, who took the life of his freed slave, because the latter had once kissed his daughter: *ut etiam oscula ad maritum sincera perferret.* Can you smell that? Can you taste that? *Etiam oscula, non solum virginitatem, etiam oscula.* And Maenius was just a pagan, at that: what should a Christian do who knows that marriage is a divine institution and knows at the same time that the blessedness of a match is poisoned to the root, that neither man nor wife will find joy or consolation in such a match, which is in essence a profanation against the very heavens—away I say, away from sight, villains! I'll have nothing whatsoever to do with you! Why not betake yourselves to a sultan and hire out as caretakers of his harem? That would suit you, all right, but you'll not be shepherds of my flock. You mercenary! You ravenous wolf in sheep's clothing!

LÄUFFER: I want to marry Lise.

WENZESLAUS: Marry? Oh, come off it—and she'll be happy with a eunuch?

LISE: Oh, yes, it would make me most happy, Mr. Schoolmaster.

LÄUFFER: Oh, unfortunate me!

LISE: Believe me, Mr. Schoolmaster, I'm not going to let him get away. Take my life—I'll not let him go. I like him, and my heart tells me I can like no one else that much.

WENZESLAUS: So—why, it —Lise, you don't know what you're saying— Lise, I can't explain it to you, but marriage with him is out of the question—impossible.

LISE: Why impossible, Sir? How impossible if I want to and he wants to, and my father wants it too? You see, my father always said to me, that if I was to marry an intellectual—

WENZESLAUS: But—can't you get it through your thick skull—he can't do anything! God forgive me, but you must listen!

LÄUFFER: Maybe the young lady has no such expectations. Lise, I'll never be able to sleep with you.

LISE: Well, at least he can stay up with me, even if we only spend the day together, laugh together, and kiss hands once in a while—For by God! I like this man! God knows, I do like him!

LÄUFFER: You see, Mr. Wenzeslaus! It is only love she's after. Must a happy marriage cater to animal drives?

WENZESLAUS: Oh, come off—*Connumbium sine prole est quasi dies sine sole.* . . . Be ye fruitful and multiply yourselves, that's God's word. Where there is marriage, there must children be too.

LISE: No, Mr. Schoolmaster, I swear to you, in my life I can do without children. Children, no less! That's all I need. My father has ducks and chickens, and that's enough to feed day after day; to add children. . . .

LÄUFFER (*kissing her*): Lise, you are a goddess!

WENZESLAUS (*tears them apart*): Oh, come off it! What's this supposed to be? In front of my eyes?—All right then, crawl together. I don't care; after all, it is better to marry than to burn.—But things are over between us, Mr. Mandel, things are over; gone are the big hopes you inspired in me, you and your heroic courage. Good Lord! A capon will never be a saint, it's not the same thing, not by a long shot. I actually thought he might make another Origen—*O homuncio, homuncio!* That takes a man of different stripe, a man of basic purpose and principles, only that kind of man could become a pillar of our sinking church. A very different man, indeed! Who knows what may still happen? (*He leaves.*)

LÄUFFER: Let's go to your father, Lise. If he is willing, then I am the very luckiest man upon the surface of the earth!

Introduction to Scenes from NAPOLEON OR THE HUNDRED DAYS.
The best scenes in *Napoleon or the Hundred Days* depict the confused
state of French life before the Emperor's final return, and no scene
does this so brilliantly as the one with which the play begins. A cross
fire of acrid remarks defines the frustrated hopes, aspirations, and ambitions that played their part in precipitating the French Revolution and
its Napoleonic aftermath. Grabbe's principal spokesmen are two displaced
ex-soldiers named Vitry and Chassecoeur, who make it perfectly clear
that they live on memories of the recent past—though their reminiscences
encompass much more than glory: an unforgettable point made by Chassecoeur is that all pictures of war that neglect the actuality of the suffering moment are fake. The first scene has many such striking observations,
and they must be taken into account in any discussion of Grabbe's attitude
toward war, an attitude that struck Hebbel as so adolescent that he
called Grabbe "The Noncommissioned Officer." Vitry and Chassecoeur
are not alone in their sense of dislocation: it is shared by the Old Milliner,
who has lost three sons in the bloodbath that began in 1789; by the
Old Officer, who for military service across the globe has been rewarded
with dismissal; by the lawyer Duchesne, whom the dynamics of history
leave completely bewildered—how can twenty-five years of radical
progress be nullified by a few lines of newspaper print? Even aristocrats
like the Marquis von Hauterive find the time out of joint: a true nobility
of blood has been corrupted by an influx of commonness. All of this
is given a firm cynical lining by the exclamations of various bystanders
whom Grabbe employs in a fashion we now would not hesitate to call
Brechtian.

When Grabbe finally brings Napoleon on stage, it is to show an
exile who regrets having interposed himself between the momentum of
the French Revolution and a future prepared for by the unremitting
thrusts of the guillotine. Apparently he was not great enough to usher
in the golden age. But it takes no more than an account of the demoral-
ized situation in France to bring out the chauvinist and *Führer* in Napoleon: "As if nations could be weighed and counted! The world is most
fortunate when the greatest nation rules all, powerful enough to maintain
everywhere itself as well as its laws—and who is greater than my French-
men? . . . Europe, that childish old man, is in need of a rod of correc-
tion . . . and who could brandish it better than I?" In the second scene
here given, Napoleon finally arrives in Paris, where the mob holds sway
murderously while Louis XVIII totters. Directing the killing is an executioner named Jouve, who would as readily decapitate an emperor as
a king, but who calls on Parisians to light up their windows in Napoleon's

honor when the latter goes by in all his military potency. On what
this scene implies about Grabbe's thinking on the relationship of history
and revolution, there is a divergence of opinion similar to that associated
with a Brecht play like *The Days of the Commune:* Grabbe, like Brecht,
is credited by some with knowing that, in the final analysis, revolutions
can be betrayed but not stopped—does not Jouve say that the caps
of the Jacobins will outlast all else? To which one might reply that
this same Jouve tells the crowd to cut off the Master Tailor's ten fingers
simply for the fun of it—and directly after the gruesome deed Grabbe
announces through Vitry that the Revolution was made by the same
types who are now sorry the tailor had only ten fingers. For that matter,
what was Grabbe's point in composing this scene except to demonstrate
once more that behind the symbolic façades we erect between ourselves
and reality there is little to respect. Napoleon comes home to a land
where the Jouves will always be an essential part of the landscape.
That contempt for the mass of men which Grabbe made no effort to
hide in his letters is very much on display here: the crowd can as
easily be manipulated by the opportunistic Master Tailor—who feels
the Emperor's return will be good for his trade—as it can be mesmerized
into an instrument of murder by demagogues like Jouve who encourage
men to express their basic nature.

napoleon or the hundred days

Act I, scene 1

(Paris. Beneath the arcades of the Palais Royal. Huge crowds surging about in confusion, among them citizens, officers, soldiers, charlatans, youthful chimney sweeps, and others. Those who speak remain in the foreground.)

VITRY: Cheer up, Chassecoeur, the world's still with us—I can hear her this moment—over there on the second floor, the noise is something awful.

CHASSECOEUR: So?—I heard nothing.—What's it all about?

VITRY: The old cannon thunder has stopped up your ear. Can't you hear? How the money is rolling, how they're squabbling with each other—they're gambling.

CHASSECOEUR: Oh, my carbine, if I could only use your butt to smash their brains and coffers!

VITRY: Yes, yes, Father Violet[1] was playing for the world, and we were his croupiers.

CHASSECOEUR: Blood and death! If only we were still!

VITRY: Easy now, easy—in beautiful France each spring brings a fresh bloom of violets, joy and love—Father Violet, too, will return.

GALLERY BARKER: Here, gentlemen, you can get a look at Louis XVIII, King of France and Navarre, known as the Desired One.

MENAGERIE BARKER *(situated opposite to the* GALLERY BARKER*)*: Here, gentlemen, you can see one of the last of a dying species of pigeons so fat they can't walk straight—their beaks like two spoons—from the Isle de France and Bourbon off Madagascar; it's long been the desire of naturalists to inspect and dissect this bird.

GALLERY BARKER: Over here you can see the whole House of the Bourbons—Monsieur, the Duke of Angoulême, his son, the Duchess, her husband, and so on.

MENAGERIE BARKER: Here you can catch a look at the long orangutang, wholly domesticated and religious, though he still bites; also the baboon, with a similar disposition, as well as the long-tailed monkey, a bit wilder than the other two, and called an ocean cat because it crossed the ocean to get to us; also more conventional apes of the *Linné simia silvanus*—for that matter, the whole species of apes, as you'll never see them in action in the botanical garden or in the Tuileries.

A POLICE OFFICIAL: Man, you are insulting the King and the Princes.

MENAGERIE BARKER: How, sir, when I merely exhibit apes? I'm exercising my privilege.

---

[1] One of Napoleon's nicknames.

(*Someone screams.*) Save him! Help the unfortunate fellow!

CHASSECOEUR: What's going on?

VITRY: Someone's crashing to the gutter from the second floor, and his brain is dirtying the clothes of those standing around. Probably a gambler who's lost everything.

CHASSECOEUR: Or someone thrown out of the window by those playing with him—because he's cheated or won too much.

VITRY: Your guess is as good as mine.—The crowd is trembling and afraid to go near him. I'll jump to his aid.

CHASSECOEUR: Pah, let him lie there.

VITRY: Friend, suppose he has a wife and child who must go hungry without him?

CHASSECOEUR: That wouldn't bother me. I have to go hungry—Why shouldn't the whole world keep me company by starving at my side.— Vitry, think of us! When we sacked and pillaged Italy, Germany, Spain, Russia, and God knows what other places, caressed and ravished thousands and thousands of women in these countries, threw heaps of money into the street for children to play with, because every moment more came into our hands—did we ever imagine the day would come when we'd be out in the cold, without four sous between us, robbed of our pay by these spongy, seawatery, tubercular—

VITRY: Bonbons, or whatever they're called. Don't know the precise name.—But listen! The little chimney sweep.

YOUTHFUL CHIMNEY SWEEP (*with his marmot and bagpipes*):

La marmotte, la marmotte,
Avec si, avec là,
La marmotte is here.
From the Alps—
Sleeps through winter,—
Wakes in summer,—
Does its dance in Paris.
La marmotte, la marmotte,
Avec si, avec là,
La marmotte is here.

PEEP SHOW BARKER: Ladies and gentlemen, if you please, over here!—A bit better than a miserable marmot—the whole world can be seen right here, as she rolls and breathes.

YOUTHFUL CHIMNEY SWEEP: Why are you so nasty to my little pet? It is every bit as good as your peep show—(*to his marmot*) poor thing, you look downright troubled—the coarse man has insulted you—oh, my sweetheart, be happy, cheer up—no one believes what the nasty man is saying—I'm going to give you two thick sweet carrots for lunch. But please cheer up!

PEEP SHOW BARKER: Spectators, look over here!—Welcome!—Allow me to first wipe the glass clean—so—please step forward.—There you see the great battle of Moscow—here, Bonaparte—

CHASSECOEUR: The name's Napoleon!

PEEP SHOW BARKER:—Bonaparte upon his white horse—

CHASSECOEUR: You lie! The Emperor was on foot and gave his orders from afar. I stood not twelve steps away from him as his orderly.

PEEP SHOW BARKER: And here, ladies and gentlemen, you see the great and noble Field Marshal Kutusow—

CHASSECOEUR: The old dullard who knew how to capture the lion, but not to hold him. If he and his men had advanced only four thousand more feet per day, not a Frenchman would have made it out of Russia.

PEEP SHOW BARKER: And here you witness the crossing of the Beresina!

VITRY: Why, I helped build the pontoons for that!

CHASSECOEUR: Beresina! Ice and the shudders of death!—I was there too—this must be seen! (*He goes to a peephole.*) My God, how wretched! Vitry, take a look!

VITRY: I'm looking. This is rubbish! Why, at that time my stomach was wholly empty, and I stood three feet deep in water while hostile enemy cannon hail flew overhead. You gave me a whiskey—

CHASSECOEUR: It was my next to last—

VITRY: How silly it looks here—one can't distinguish between the engineers, guardsmen, or front lines—and how few corpses and wounded men!

CHASSECOEUR (*to the* BARKER): Man, can you depict frost, hunger, thirst, and screams?

PEEP SHOW BARKER: No, sir.

CHASSECOEUR: Then all that painting is so much garbage.

PEEP SHOW BARKER: Ah, and there you see the brave but beaten French fleeing across the Beresina.

VITRY: Sir friend, the blows which we suffered there I could take on my back without risk of its turning blue.

CHASSECOEUR: Right, Vitry!—We were only eight thousand men, surrounded like wild game in nets, but we beat our way through sixty thousand rascals and escaped.

VITRY: And they called it a victory!

CHASSECOEUR: Those poor Russian devils haven't any idea what a real victory is.

PEEP SHOW BARKER: And here, ladies and gentlemen, the great battle of the nations at Leipzig—look closely: there you have the old gray moss-covered towers of the old city—there the old guard on foot, at the head the drum major with his large baton, which he throws into the air with a zest that scorns death itself—here the old mounted guard, fixed in the yellow cornfields like an arrow to be shot forth.—There the brave first-line troops already in action. Here the Prussian fusiliers with their short winged horns—

VITRY AND CHASSECOEUR: Oh, Prussians and ammunition!

PEEP SHOW BARKER:—and there in the rain, in the place called Gallows—which he indeed deserved—the bloodsucker, himself, that wretch of a Corsican nobleman, now on the run from the deserved wrath of his legitimate sovereign, Louis XVIII, the dastardly Bonaparte—

VITRY: Who says that?

CHASSECOEUR: Scoundrel, he was worth more than all your Louis—at least he paid full wages.

VITRY: I'll not let the Emperor be insulted! A shambles of this peep show!

PEEP SHOW BARKER: Help! Help!—Conspiracy!—Gendarmes!—The talk here is of emperors.

VITRY: Yes, and kings are trembling!

MOB (coming): Emperor, emperor—is he back again?

PEEP SHOW BARKER: How should I know? They've smashed my showbox to pieces. The cost is fifty francs.

VITRY: Plead with the Angoulême to reimburse you.—From now on this will not be your territory.

CROWD (breaking loose toward BARKER): The bum—tear him apart—

A GENDARME (arriving): Peep-show man, off with you—you're inciting a riot—

PEEP SHOW BARKER: I praise the King.

GENDARME: Then you need abuse no one else.—Get!

CROWD: Wonderful! Long live the police!

AN OLD OFFICER IN CIVILIAN DRESS: Chassecoeur!

CHASSECOEUR: I know that voice from the pyramids, as we planted our tricolor high above Cairo's minarets, the Nile rolling to our feet.—My captain, I haven't laid eyes on you since Egypt.

OLD OFFICER: I've fought since in St. Domingo, Germany, Cattaro, then in Swedish Pomerania, and finally at Riga and Montereau.

CHASSECOEUR: Well, I spent most of that time in Austria, Italy, and Spain, winding up in Russia and Germany. And at Montereau I fought, too, perhaps close to you.

OLD OFFICER: Chassecoeur, we've both made a botch of our careers—I remained captain, and you, it appears, lance-corporal. On top of that, we've been let go from service.

CHASSECOEUR: True—you and I have as much right to pose as marshals as Augereau and Marmont to be emperors like Napoleon.

VITRY: La, la! The waves of fate carry some aloft and hurl others to the bottom. As long as the heart is in good shape—it's the fish bladder that heaves us in whatever direction we want to go—till we croak. (*He speaks to a prostitute passing by.*) A kiss, my child!

OLD OFFICER: What's that you're carrying near your chest? Is it something to eat? Give me a piece.

CHASSECOEUR: Captain, it's not for eating, but it does satisfy me once in a while and may do the same for you.

VITRY: Now he's starting with his damned little catch-words, which affect me nonetheless.

CHASSECOEUR: It is an eagle of the guard, which I saved as it was about to sink out of sight beneath thousands of corpses at Leipzig's Elster Bridge. And—otherwise let the devil fetch me (*if he exists*)—the sun, to which he flew, will soon return.

OLD OFFICER: I believe it too: to be sure, now it is night and fools imagine the light will stay extinguished. But his greatness can no more disappear than that of the sun up there, and he shall return.

VITRY: If only! Here I throw my last sous in the air! Long live—but quiet—(*He puts his hand on his mouth.*)

CHASSECOEUR: You could have saved your few sous. What good does it do us for the Emperor to return if in the meantime we've starved?

OLD OFFICER: Who is that man, comrade?

CHASSECOEUR: He's from the young guard on foot, third regiment, second company, his name is Philip Vitry, and he thinks like me.

OLD OFFICER: He strikes me as merry enough in spite of his misery.

VITRY: That I am, sir. Things are not going well right now. But for future opportunity I have two hands to strike out with, and if no hands, two feet with which to dance.

If misfortune should arrive
Scare it off with a loud hurrah,
Kill a king for breakfast
And sup with thoughts of the Emperor!

Chassecoeur, let me embrace you!

CHASSECOEUR: Ach, leave off your interminable tomfoolery!—He jumps and laughs while we clench our fingers in the palms of our hands out of anger—as if they were crushed worms—and my teeth gnash right along—Angoulême could well look for a confessor if she should come my way—

OLD OFFICER: Comrade, hope—

CHASSECOEUR: Choke! Nothing but trash, as far as the eye can see.

OLD OFFICER: Including the six thousand dismissed officers of the great army, who like us surge back and forth in this heap.

CHASSECOEUR: No. I see and esteem them highly. But that even they should be part of this flotsam!—See, there is one of them—and to be sure one who burns with wrath, not sad and quiet like you—

OLD OFFICER: Friend, I have a family—

CHASSECOEUR: Yes, indeed—but that one over there has none.—One knows who he is by his threadbare, stringy overcoat which he agitates so angrily, by those old military gaiters with which he makes his appearance, as if he were stepping across corpses, by his eye dark as blood—in the midst of these dregs of high and low rabble where one is no better than the next. Death and hell, this one is made of sterner stuff than the new royal house troops, to whom the victors of Marengo must now present arms. This one did not chase after Bourbons when they were on the run—this one's forged in the battery fires of Austerlitz or Borodino!

VITRY: Brother, what a day when our lancers burst through the eastern gates of Moscow on the way to Asia!

CHASSECOEUR: Yes, then one could still expect to carouse in the treasure vaults and harems of Persia, China, and East India! Ach, the world strikes one as wretched as if one had already experienced it six times and been six times broken on the wheel.

(*The emigrés* MARQUIS VON HAUTERIVE *and* HERR VON VILLENEUVE *arrive.*)

MARQUIS VON HAUTERIVE: Not the old Palais Royal anymore, dear friend. All changed—

VITRY: And therefore quite worse?

MARQUIS VON HAUTERIVE (*after reflecting, with contemptuous look*): Yes, my friend—worse. (*He comments to* HERR VON VILLENEUVE, *with whom he goes to the side.*) How impudent the rabble has become.

HERR VON VILLENEUVE: By my sword, they'll return to their old ways!

MARQUIS VON HAUTERIVE: That will not be easy. Herr von Villeneuve, can one help feeling that since the eighties the world has gone to pot? Not only have bourgeois *Dames d'atour* begun to appear at court, but they are even said to be so bold as to seat themselves on stools in the King's presence!

HERR VON VILLENEUVE: Disgraceful, horrible! By God, if Louis XVIII were not my native king, I could challenge him to a duel for being so weak and soft. But this must all be slander spun out by antiroyalists to degrade the King.

MARQUIS VON HAUTERIVE: Herr von Villeneuve, what do you say to the upstarts we are getting as princes and dukes and their wives, especially Ney's wife, the so-called Princess of Moscow?

MONSIEUR VON VILLENEUVE: She is not worth talking about.

MARQUIS VON HAUTERIVE: What tasteless clothes, what impudent behavior, what vacuous conversation, what arrogance!—Doesn't this woman know we are well aware she is the daughter of a baker?

MONSIEUR VON VILLENEUVE: My dear Marquis, we owe all that to the fact that Marie Antoinette, of blessed memory, was much too prone to mix with the canaille and seduced the King into similar conduct. For France, nothing good will ever come from Austria!

MARQUIS VON HAUTERIVE: Ach, the good old days—the smart, elegant salons of that time—now teeming with common cattle!

MONSIEUR VON VILLENEUVE: Things must be different, different, and they shall be different, Marquis, by my coat of arms! We have been robbed of our old estates and rights—and every court must rule for the return of our property, since we never relinquished it. Think, monsieur, of my pretty country seat, La Merveille near Tours, along which the Loire meanders so pleasantly, in whose yew-shaded walks we two enjoyed ourselves so much with the women of the area in the friendly autumn of 1783, through the dwindling sunsets; in which even as a child I never failed to give the first flower of spring to Adelaide, Viscountess of Clary, my departed but never to be forgotten loved one—to think all this now belongs to a tight-fisted factory owner! The high hedges have been torn down, steam engines now roar in the greenhouses, and potatoes have pushed themselves into the spots reserved for my precious tulip bulbs!

MARQUIS VON HAUTERIVE: Well, Blacas d'Alups and Angoulême will help us out and—(HAUTERIVE and VILLENEUVE move off.)

VITRY: Both those emigrés! What coattails, what cheek pouches, what obsolete French faces and ideas, what specters from the good, old, and very ridiculous days!

OLD OFFICER: They know nothing about the bloody years of the Revolution, Philip Vitry—that is over, but they survive, in the same way that it happens a mountain torrent ceases to spurt and some stray grass remains and therefore considers itself stronger than the floods that submerge it still and tear apart the banks. They haven't put a straw blade's distance between themselves and their mad pride, and Louis XVIII himself dates the start of his rule twenty-five years back—

CHASSECOEUR: One could die laughing!—At the time he would like to imagine he was in charge, we were shooting his cousin and accomplice, Enghien, as we were officially ordered; and I myself tied the lantern to his chest in order to improve my aim that night.

OLD OFFICER: Oh, that I should have grown so old and not fallen in battle before the entrance of the Bourbons in Paris! (*He turns to a woman renting chairs.*) Madame, may I sit down? My feet are very tired, but I cannot afford to pay for a seat.

WOMAN RENTING CHAIRS: A look at you tells me you are an officer of the great army. Command at will my chairs.

NEWSBOY: Something important! Important! From the Palais Bourbon, the Chamber of Deputies! Get your journals right here!

MANY VOICES: Over here!—Read it aloud!

THE OLD MILLINER: No, over here, newsboy—over here—your important reports belong upon this table!

NEWSBOY: On those decrepit old planks?

THE OLD MILLINER: Respect it, fellow! This table is classic—on this spot fell first the spark which ignited the world. Here I sat on the twelfth of July of the year seventeen hundred eighty-nine, in the afternoon about half past three; it was sunny and, still young and gay, I sold a bride from St. Marceau a few little things. We joked about the price and thought of nothing but the wedding day. Then in came a man with wild flowing locks, fiery eyes, heart-shattering voice—it was Camille Desmoulins—tears were in his eyes, he pulled two pistols out of his pocket and shouted: "Necker is dismissed, another Bartholomew's night is upon us, take arms and select your cockades, so that we will be sure to recognize one another." And since then, he, as well as the mighty Danton and terrible Robespierre, have gone to the guillotine; since then, the Emperor illuminated this world with such a radiance that one had to shield one's eyes, and he, too, has vanished like a will-o'-the-wisp; three of my sons have been taken by battle—much, much blood and countless sighs the Revolution has cost me, but it has only become that much dearer to me for all that—and it was at this table that I read the most important newspapers!—Yes, it is my last and only pleasure!

CROWD: Yes, brave little mother, he shall read at your table!

VITRY: Indeed he shall! That moment experienced on the 12th of July, 1789, at half past three in the afternoon, was worth more than all the centuries which may prove to be its besmirchers.

NEWSBOY: Gentlemen, it's not necessary for me to do my reading here.— There comes someone who will make everything clear enough.

LAWYER DUCHESNE (*dashing through the mob to* THE MILLINER'S *table*): Attention, attention, and take care that I don't burst your ears open with my news! Everything, everything is being threatened; stupid, impudent hands are boldly at work seizing the storerooms of fortune's wheel.—In the Chamber of Deputies motions are being made against the purchasers of nationalized estates—

MOB: Ha!

CHASSECOEUR (*laughs*): They're not doing much better than we are, eh?

DUCHESNE: Cloisters are back with us, and they're in the process of outlawing those who participated in the Revolution; one can expect serfdom to follow—

(MARQUIS VON HAUTERIVE *and* MONSIEUR VON VILLENEUVE *have come back and move closer*).

MARQUIS VON HAUTERIVE: Well, monsieur, things might not be in such bad shape after all.

MONSIEUR VON VILLENEUVE: Exactly how I feel.

CROWD: "Not in such bad shape?"—"Exactly how I feel?" To the ground with this old aristocratic scum, these cowards who are proud of their stupidity!

MONSIEUR VON VILLENEUVE: Dumb we may be—proud certainly—but France's nobility has never bred cowards.—Just try something—let's draw our swords, marquis, and die like men.

MARQUIS VON HAUTERIVE: Gladly—for God, for my king, and for my rights!

MONSIEUR VON VILLENEUVE: And for the women of our youth!

VITRY: By now they must all be old bags!

MONSIEUR VON VILLENEUVE: Swine, you've pronounced your own sentence—death by a sword in the neck. (*He wants to run Vitry through.*)

VITRY: I doubt that—but as for you, your necks shall be spared. (*He disarms them.*)

CHASSECOEUR: Vitry, don't be a fool!—Allow me here and now to give both dogs a thrust under their ribs—no one will notice as they croak.

VITRY: No, these fellows may be rotten, but they possess courage—which I value above all—long live bravery, even among French emigrés!

CROWD: Long live bravery!

MONSIEUR VON VILLENEUVE (*to* MARQUIS VON HAUTERIVE *as they distance themselves*): Who would have believed, Marquis, that the rabble could have such feeling for courage and honor?

MARQUIS VON HAUTERIVE: Ach, it is more a momentary convulsion than genuine feeling.

DUCHESNE: That whole crew, including the King's Chancellor and Lawyer D'Ambray, the invalid, do they realize we stormed a world? Haven't they been taking this great nation for a silly child? Not us, but the grace of England—

CROWD: Down with the beefsteaks!

DUCHESNE:—the grace of England does deluded King Louis thank for his crown—France's crown! Why, it is a crown so lustrous and massive that even a giant who could more easily swing Neptune's trident than His Majesty's Navy would have a hard time keeping his head from being crushed by it! And this too:—when the King leaves us our rights, he doesn't call that justice, but says that the absolute power which he has by virtue of God and blood—

CHASSECOEUR: Fighting blood, not female blood, confers nobility.

DUCHESNE:—is being subjected to limits.—Limits! Limits!—If they would only guard against using such a word: Louis XVI stood in the way of the limits set by his people and found himself and all his courtiers squashed to a bloody pulp!—How is it possible that three lines of orders published in the *Moniteur* can take away in a day what it took us twenty-five years to achieve? Are the people nothing? Or do they belong to the inheritance of a few favored families?

THE OLD MILLINER: That's just the way Camille Desmouslins spoke, my son!

VITRY: Here come the gendarmes!

DUCHESNE: Let them come, friend. I must speak out and proclaim the truth. Blessed are those who are blind and imagine they can see, but cursed are those who can see and notice how the blind delude themselves. The King is good, but the rabble of carrion-flies out of the time of the Pompadours darkens his eye.—Behind Russian and Prussian bayonets they hope to break the nation's back with edicts for their own ambitions—but wait!—

CHASSECOEUR: Only not for too long, monsieur.

DUCHESNE: The evening of all our days has not yet arrived, and if it had, then a colossal starfish bathed in the waves of his native Mediterranean would arise with renewed splendor and quickly drive away the night!

VITRY: That star wears a green uniform, the epaulets of a Colonel, a white vest, white trousers, a small sword, and keeps his arms crossed in battle.

CHASSECOEUR: We easily make up for them with ours!

GENDARMES: Agitators!—You're under arrest.

DUCHESNE: By what law? Free speech is nowhere forbidden.

CHASSECOEUR: Free eating would be better.

CROWD: There comes the Duke of Orleans!

CHASSECOEUR: Of the whole race of Bourbons he's the most tolerable. But he's got the usual crooked nose.

MANY OF THE CROWD: Extend him respect!—He is the son of *egalité* and fought for France while his father tumbled on the scaffold.

DUKE OF ORLEANS: Gendarmes, who are you arresting there?

A GENDARME: Subversive speakers, my prince.

DUKE OF ORLEANS: Then release them, on the spot! (*It's done.*) Woe to the land that has something to fear from speeches and speakers.

CROWD: Up with Orleans, formerly king!

DUKE OF ORLEANS: The latter, never—but always your friend. (*He goes off.*)

MANY VOICES: What a first-rate prince!

CHASSECOEUR: He'd chase you off if he were king.

CROWD: Ha! There comes the Duke of Berry as well!

CHASSECOEUR: On foot, from a review of his house guard, those old sugar loaves of nobility, who hide their rifles when it rains. Oh, the battle of the three emperors at Dresden!

VITRY: To be sure, it was pouring, and we drove them into mountain caves, like cattle to stable.

CHASSECOEUR: Take a look there at the big white crest of feathers which that youth has on his head! It offends my eyes!

VITRY: Friend, that is the helmet plume of his ancestor, Henry IV.—His family mouths so much about that crest, I'm afraid it's bound to get dirty.

CHASSECOEUR: Henry IV? Who was he? What did he do?

VITRY: He was King of France and routed a few thousand rebels several times.

CHASSECOEUR: That pigmy!—Did he do nothing else?

VITRY: Ask the scholars, I know nothing more.—Berry's noticing you, sees the slashes marked on your face.—He wants to talk to you.

CHASSECOEUR: He wants to use me for one of his coups against the people. But he's mistaken, this saucy brat of a duke. I haven't been dealt with in a fashion to incline me to meet him halfway.

VITRY: And if he should now promise you something?

CHASSECOEUR: Consign it to garbage! They only keep their word as long as they're forced to.

DUKE OF BERRY: Old, brave comrade—

CHASSECOEUR: Thanks. Not that I know of us ever having fought together, Your Majesty.

DUKE OF BERRY: Where did you get those honorable scars?

CHASSECOEUR: Their names will tell you: this one's called Quiberon, that's where we pushed the emigrés into the sea—this one's called Marengo, there we pounced on the Italians—this one—ach!

VITRY (*to himself*): Ach, Leipzig!

CHASSECOEUR: And when the weather or times are bad, as right now, these scars hurt terribly.

A MEMBER OF THE DUKE'S ENTOURAGE: Man, who are you that you dare to speak that way?

CHASSECOEUR: Ach, dear, gracious sir—who I am or who I am supposed to be, I know not, but who I was, I can tell you (*holding himself proudly erect*): a mounted grenadier of the Emperor's Cavalry, Second Squadron, close to the Cross of Honor.

DUKE OF BERRY (*to his escort*): Quiet, don't irritate old wounds. (*He turns to Chassecoeur.*) I'll arrange for you to get care in the Dome of Invalids.

CHASSECOEUR: I have no need of that yet, Your Everlasting Majesty.

DUKE OF BERRY: Then content yourself with my intention.—Long live the King!—

CHASSECOEUR: Hm!—

 (*All are silent;* DUKE OF BERRY *and entourage leave.*)

OLD OFFICER: If the Bourbons are truly in such a bad way, as now—

VITRY: Then they are soon bound to fall.

OLD OFFICER: The people don't seem to care in the least whether Bourbons are sneered at or complimented.

VITRY: All the worse—the people don't know them.

CHASSECOEUR: Therefore, they know someone else all the better.—Come, let us see where we can hunt up something to eat.—(*He stamps with his foot.*) Oh! damned pavement, which bears so many knaves! (VITRY *and* THE OLD OFFICER *leave.*)

YOUTHFUL CHIMNEY SWEEP (*with marmot and bagpipes*):

La marmotte, la marmotte
Avec si, avec là etc. etc.

Act III, Scene 1

(*Paris. Place du Grève near the street lamps. Afternoon. Crowds, some with nothing to do, others busy. In the foreground,* CHASSECOEUR, VITRY *and a* MASTER TAILOR.)

VITRY: It just isn't fair, Chassecoeur! At night we are awakened by suspicious talk, Ney is gone with his troops, Angoulême is supposed to be already on the road to Bordeaux, and there you have a small emigré with his bags packed—. Adieu, my lord!

THE EMIGRANT: We shall return, Herr von Nameless! (*He talks to himself.*) Oh, fire, sword, scaffolds!—All of rebellious France should go up in flames and blood! (*He exits.*)

CHASSECOEUR: Who knows where this emigré will now do his begging? As for Angoulême, once in Bordeaux, she'll want to pray to become another Virgin Mary, to have her kid without help from her husband, since he can't help her that way in the least.—The devil take them all!

MASTER TAILOR: My lords, my lords, the Duchess Angoulême and Berry are riding out of the city; also Monsieur Blacas d'Aulps and Monsieur d'Ambray have been wearing their travel furs for a quarter of an hour.

CHASSECOEUR: Convulsive worm, who are you?

MASTER TAILOR: Lord Human Being, a clothing manufacturer from Paris, who shall, if you insult my honor, run you through with this needle seventy-seven times before you can get in a single lick with your sword!

CHASSECOEUR: I am already trembling.

TAILOR'S WIFE (arriving): Husband, my dear husband, at last I've found you—oh, back to the house! Even our street is full of noise and motion! It's said the Emperor has returned.

CHASSECOEUR: Can it be?—Oh!

MASTER TAILOR: Dumb, infamous wife, talk more quietly (He lowers his voice.) If he did come back, it would do much for France's honor and my welfare.—Go, get as much needle and thread as you can! We shall soon be making uniforms!—I am staying here only to learn what Paris is thinking—this is the place to find out. Go on, I'll be right with you.

TAILOR'S WIFE: Right away? Is that certain?

MASTER TAILOR: Do you think I would leave you and my little worms alone in time of danger? (The TAILOR'S WIFE leaves.) Jesus! Holy Ghost! There comes the King! And look at the coat he's got on! De anno 1790.—Taste, taste you are going under in an ocean! Thank the English for that!

A WOMAN FROM HALLE: Ach, God, I am crying—how impressively things are going in the Chamber of Deputies.—All the deputies want to sacrifice themselves for the King—

VITRY: Do they act upon their wishes?

WOMAN FROM HALLE: They would for sure, if he hadn't departed so quickly. And how he spoke! Tears, I tell you, tears in his eyes! He wiped them off with a cambric handkerchief embroidered with lilies—ach, the lilies are watered bitterly by such drops.

VITRY: There is Mr. King stopping with his coach in the crowd.

CHASSECOEUR: He'll proceed to babble a bit, and at this distance we won't even hear it—those few who do will hardly grasp what he means.

VITRY: Which should only increase their respect for him.

MANY OF THE CROWD: Quiet! Quiet!—The great monarch!

MASTER TAILOR: If the King would just not get up, if he would just remain seated and keep his coattails covered, for they are the most horrible coattails in the universe. Spread wide apart! Is that French? It isn't even English—it is barbaric! The man by his clothes—he who dresses absurdly, is absurd—it is all over with our beautiful country!—As surely as there would never have been a Revolution if crinoline, wigs, and powder had not gone out of fashion—such things literally keep people from getting under each other's skin, or in each other's hair—so certain is it that royal dignity cannot be maintained when the King exposes by his coattails something that is, to be sure, enormously large but not in the least majestic.

(The King is heard speaking.)

WOMAN FROM HALLE: Ach—that is heart-breaking—

CROWD: Long live the King!

(The coach moves off.)

MASTER TAILOR: What did he say?

WOMAN FROM HALLE: Oh, sir, what tongue could repeat it? His people had given him the most moving proof of their love! A few traitors had spoiled France's fortune! He wants to stand at the head of his troops. Oh, the true son of Henry IV.

CHASSECOEUR: That old gout-ridden ass at the head of the troops?

MASTER TAILOR: All very good, my lady, but why then does he run away, given so many proofs of love and so few traitors?—People, people, don't permit your wisdom to be betrayed by your pity and generosity! The King is heading for Vienna to donate France's finest provinces at the Congress of Vienna! In exchange, the Russians are to help him oppress all non-emigrés! That has long been in the works!

CROWD *(raging)*: The damned hypocrite of a Bourbon! After him—catch him, put him in chains!

MASTER TAILOR: Absolutely right—and if he bleeds away, he does so in the presence of our true hearts! *(He comments to himself.)* That means ruined clothing and a profit for my business.

A NUMBER OF VOICES: He is already gone—gotten clear away!

AN OLD WOMAN: Curse to your heart's content—he was nonetheless a good man.

CHASSECOEUR: Yes, he preferred roast beef to oven screws.

VITRY: You are drawing his portrait. What's going on?

VARIOUS VOICES *(bursting in)*: Napoleon has landed—

CHASSECOEUR: Vitry!

VITRY: Chassecoeur! The little violet has bloomed!

MASTER TAILOR: Those two are jumping up as if for a dance!

THOSE JUST ARRIVED:—and he was hanged near Chalon-sur-Saône.

CHASSECOEUR: Who says so?

THOSE JUST ARRIVED: The *Moniteur* and the *Telegraph*.

VITRY: Easy, Chassecoeur.—If both say so, then it is a double lie. Why would the King run away?

OTHERS (*bursting in*): The Emperor is in Fontainebleau!

MASTER TAILOR: Thunder and hail!—Ney's army?

THOSE JUST ARRIVED: Has gone over to the Emperor and provided him with its marshal!

MASTER TAILOR: The poor Bourbons!

VITRY (*to* CHASSECOEUR): From now on, stop trying to reason things out— that's not necessary anymore—think only of your weapons.

CHASSECOEUR: They're at the workshop, shining bright.

VITRY: Mine too!

MASTER TAILOR (*to someone next to him*): Watch carefully, I'm starting a revolution.

THE PERSON ADDRESSED: By what means?

MASTER TAILOR: Fool, by means of this cobble stone—I glance and glance and glance at it.

YOUTHFUL CHIMNEY SWEEP: "*La marmotte*"—(*He stops and indicates the* MASTER TAILOR.) What's up with that man?

OTHERS: What is he looking at?

STILL OTHERS: What's happening?

(*A huge throng collects around the*
MASTER TAILOR.)

MASTER TAILOR (*in an undertone*): Hm—Hum—Oh!

PEOPLE: Great God! What is it?

MASTER TAILOR (*muttering*): Danger—Paris—the Seine—aristocrats—

SOMEONE IN THE CROWD: What is he saying?

ANOTHER: Don't you understand? The aristocrats want to undermine Paris, to blow it to bits with gunpowder from Vincennes, to take out their people and cut off supplies!

WOMAN: We unfortunates! Oh, our children!

MEN: Weapons! Weapons!—Break open the arsenals!—Weapons! Weapons!

A CITIZEN (*arriving*): Gentlemen, it is true—they want to get their people out—I have a shovel here—it was found on the banks—proof enough!

CROWD (*up front*): The shovel—oh, the shovels!

CROWD (*further back*): They're mining the Seine—ten thousand shovels have been discovered!

CROWD (*in the back*): Up! Up! We want to resist for life, wife, and child, or whatever else may be!

MASTER TAILOR (*to himself*): The last part is a real joke—"whatever else may be!"—They don't know what they want, so they'll take whatever they get.—But I do know what I'm after—a new government, new clothes! (*He speaks half to himself.*) The bread—God, the bread—

CROWD: Kill the bakers and millers! They've been bribed by the ministers to make us starve! There's no more bread in the city! Bread, bread, bread!

MASTER TAILOR: How hungry they've suddenly become!—But—oh, who's coming here?—Woe! The suburb of St. Antoine! This collection of humanity may afford me some amusement, but neither they nor I will escape the monster of Having Nothing and Mr. Rising Taxes!—Ach, life was so wonderful under Louis XVIII.

SOMEONE NEXT TO HIM: You, too?

MASTER TAILOR: To be sure. Otherwise, could I joke so boldly? (*He starts to listen.*) Heaven! Already that old, wild *"ça ira"*—my blood is chilling! It's getting white as snow!

ST. ANTOINE SUBURBANITES (*arrive singing*):

Ah! ça ira, ça ira,
Suivant les maximes de l'Evangile,
Ah ça ira, ça ira, ça ira,
Du legislateur tout s'accomplira.

A CITIZEN: What's the point of that today?

MASTER TAILOR: *Ça ira,* sir, is another way of saying "Off with the head of whoever we pick on." The content doesn't matter, the meaning and effect remain the same.—We unfortunates!

VITRY: Yes, Chassecoeur, something like this you never saw in Russia— these fellows have neither trousers nor mercy—their pickaxes are nastier than those of the cowardly Cossacks!

ST. ANTOINE SUBURBANITES:

Ah! ça ira, ça ira, ça ira,
Celui qui s'élève, on l'abaissera,
Célui qui s'abaisse, on l'élèvera,
Ah ça ira, ça ira, ça ira,

Le peuple armé toujours se gardera,
Le clergé regrette le bien qu'il a,
Ah ça ira, ça ira, ça ira,
Par justice la nation l'aura,
Ah! ça ira, ça ira, ça ira.

MASTER TAILOR: What orchestral accompaniment! A tattered bear conductor with a drum and a filthy youth with a triangle! Well, operas, you'll never compete with this!

ST. ANTOINE SUBURBANITES:

Pierrot et Margot chantent à la guinguette,
Ah! ça ira, ça ira, ça ira,
Réjouissons nous, le bon temps viendra,
Ah! ça ira, ça ira, ça ira,

MASTER TAILOR: How gladly I'd run away—damned curiosity! The whole thing's too fishy—oh, there is Jouve, the head chopper from Versailles and Avignon, once more in charge, a large red cap on his head— haven't seen him in twenty years—and there they go, carrying a whore on their shoulders—in her youth she was Goddess of Reason when God was demoted by the Committee of Public Safety— and now she's here again, much older.

ST. ANTOINE SUBURBANITES: Up with Reason!

OTHERS: To hell with her!

STILL OTHERS: And may heaven fall apart!

STILL OTHERS: Let the devil be God!

ALL: That he should be, brave fellow.

JOUVE: That he is, brothers, but for that very reason slandered and oppressed—(He questions the MASTER TAILOR.) Scum, why do your eyes wink?

MASTER TAILOR: Out of joy, sir, that in France even the devil is accorded honor and justice.

MANY SUBURBANITES: Jouve, leave him alone—he's not that bad—

JOUVE: That means he is bad enough—he who is not for us is against us—this one I know to be a scoundrel, full of courage when he has nothing to fear—the kind who carries a flag white on one side, and tricolored on the other, depending on which way the wind blows.—Look how he begins to squirm—now he'd like most to get away to his house, to hide with his family behind the oven, occasionally sneaking to the shutters to get a safe look at what's tearing the street apart—so that he can go right ahead and babble in perfect security about his experience—such cowards are more disgraceful than public incendiaries—tailor's tatters, for that is what you will soon be, out with your courage, scissors, and needles—I've a sledge hammer here—defend yourself or croak!

MASTER TAILOR: Oh no!

JOUVE: Down! (*He knocks him to the ground.*)

SUBURBANITES AND OTHERS: Ha! Blood! Blood! Blood! See, see, see, there it flows, there it flames—brain, brain, there it spurts, there it smokes—how magnificent! how sweet!

JOUVE: Tailor's blood and tailor's brain—we need better blood than that—he who has no red cap can use the blood here as a hairdye, till we get nobler stuff. (*Many suburbanites do that.*) Forward—set fire to the Tuileries!—Long live freedom!

ALL SUBURBANITES: Long live freedom!

ONE SUBURBANITE: There comes the National Guard!

JOUVE: Go and tell their ringleaders that they had better turn back on the spot and go home like good little boys; otherwise I shall chop off their heads in the style I taught them in 1789 at Versailles—before they can open their mouths to scream, they'll decorate the floor.— (*The man addressed by* JOUVE *goes off*).—He who is a solid patriot, follow me! Chop this traitor of a tailor's fingers off and stick them into your mouth as cigars of the nation!

MANY SUBURBANITES: Over here with his fingers! Ach, he has only ten!

JOUVE: Patience, there are more than enough traitors—we'll catch thousands yet. Should the King or Emperor fall into our hands, they'll add to the catch.

CHASSECOEUR: The Emperor?

VITRY: Quiet, comrade—the Revolution made the Emperor and us, but what you see around you made the Revolution and the Emperor.

JOUVE: What upstart dared to interrupt me to ask about the Emperor?

VITRY: Now, you're in for it, Chassecoeur.

CHASSECOEUR: A member of the Emperor's mounted guard.

JOUVE: Gentlemen, this specimen gives himself a title—string him up on the lamppost!

SUBURBANITES: Hang the traitor up on the lamppost!

VITRY: Please, please, spare him, you heroes of the Revolution—

SUBURBANITES: Ah—

VITRY: Beautiful, most beautiful Goddess of Reason, put in a word for this poor fool—It is appropriate for Reason to pity those without sense.

GODDESS OF REASON: Jouve, let this fool be foolish. He was born that way and trained to be so in the army—he cannot be different.

JOUVE: As you say, Goddess.—But, my dear member of the Emperor's mounted guard, let your weak mind grasp this nicety: if you don't want to be beaten to a pulp, keep your mouth from insulting French citizens.

CHASSECOEUR: Hell—

VITRY: Easy!—The Emperor is sure to be here soon.

LAWYER DUCHESNE (*arriving*): Gentlemen—

VITRY (*in an aside to him*): Mr. speaker, quiet—those standing around will not understand what the devil your pap is all about, and unlike your acquaintances in the Palais Royal, they do not admire what they cannot fathom; they'll simply do away with you.

(GENDARMES *on horseback arrive.*)

CAPTAIN OF THE GENDARMES: Scatter, rabble!

JOUVE (*to one of those beside him*): Sneak up behind the captain's horse and pull him down from the back—I'll jump him from the front. (*The man goes.*) What do you wish, sir?

CAPTAIN: Just peace and quiet.

JOUVE: That you will have, in two minutes.—People, do you have good and strong rope? This fellow is fat and heavy.

CAPTAIN: Rebellion! Shoot them! At them!

JOUVE: Who is stronger, a gendarme or a Frenchman? You'll not charge today, citizen gendarmes, but your miserable captain shall hang on the lamppost, as surely as my friend is pulling him this instant from his horse.

CAPTAIN: Save me, comrades!

JOUVE: You'll find your comrades in hell!

(*He strikes down the captain's horse.*)

SUBURBANITES: Up in the air with the fellow! Up and away!

CAPTAIN: Disgraceful—do what you want, but don't hurt my neck too much! (*He is hanged.*) Ach! (*He dies.*)

JOUVE: Where are the other gendarmes?

A SUBURBANITE: They've scattered.

JOUVE: They behaved wisely! (*He is listening.*) Whose trumpets?

CHASSECOEUR AND VITRY (*also listening*): Ha!

CROWD: Over there, endless cavalry!

SEVERAL: Are you familiar with the clinking Kalpaks made of tin and steel? They're Polish lancers.

JOUVE: Nothing's out of order, brothers—they merely wish to take us by surprise in the name of the long dead Emperor!—Those drums over there?

SOMEONE JUST ARRIVED: Ney's infantry, with tricolored shakos.

JOUVE: Satan, what's on the other side?

THE MAN JUST ARRIVED: Artillery, covered by Milhau's dragoons.

JOUVE: How did the little corporal ever manage to arrange things so quickly?—He's really a more capable fellow than Mirabeau, Robespierre, or myself—too bad he's a tyrant! What's to the left? And behind us?

THE MAN JUST ARRIVED: Left is the guard on foot with the old parade music, behind us the mounted guard—as far as the eye can see, nothing but bear caps!

CHASSECOEUR AND VITRY: Our comrades, our comrades!—Shoulder to shoulder with them—now rabble, start shaking!—

(They rush over to the guardsmen passing through.)

JOUVE: Suburbanites, quiet!—We're not playing anymore with Louis's gendarmes but with *him*. He is a rotten fellow but he knows what he's doing. Paris was in his chains before she even knew he was approaching—

A SUBURBANITE: There's a bitch of a coach—surrounded by dragoons—what do they want with that miserable thing? I'd like to get a closer look.

JOUVE: The eye that looked out from the coach belonged to the man from Austerlitz.

A NUMBER OF VOICES: Another two coaches with the Emperor's coat of arms.

JOUVE: Full of princes and princesses of the Emperor's house.—Where there is carrion, there you have crows, otherwise let hangmen figure out where these people are suddenly coming from. *(He persuades himself.)* I must now stop playing imperator and adjust myself to the prevailing fashion as long as it lasts. Tomorrow I'll again be wearing an elegant tailcoat. The caps of the Jacobins will in the end prove to outlast all else. *(His voice grows loud.)* It's getting dark! Inhabitants, lights in your windows in honor of the Emperor and our nation!—Women of Paris, must you be reminded? Our people have long been waiting to receive tricolored cockades from your beautiful hands.

(The windows light up. Women rush to them and throw lots of cockades to the crowd.)

CROWD: Hail to the women of Paris!

A SHOPKEEPER *(steps with his wife out of a cellar)*: Dear wife, make sure that the white cockades which they're throwing away are picked up early tomorrow morning and packed away carefully in a trunk—I did just that a year ago with the tricolors, have, in fact, three trunks full of them, and mark how quickly I'll dispose of them now. *(He calls.)* Here we have tricolored cockades, a sou a piece!

JOUVE: Dog, you dare to sell the colors of the nation?—You're just what my mood is after! (*He turns to his people.*) Take away his cockades! (*Again he speaks to the shopkeeper.*) In return, I'll provide you with a free tricolor: watch, this fist moves clenched to your nose, and you are going white—now that same fist tightens around your neck and you turn blue like the sky—and now I stomp your head, and the blood makes you red.

SHOPKEEPER'S WIFE: God, oh God!

JOUVE: The goose is fainting—go ahead and rape her if she's worth doing it to, but make sure it's in the name of the Emperor!

ALL: Hail Jouve, and again hail!

JOUVE: Bear leader, sound the fifes and drums, triangle player commence tinkling! (*They do so.*) To the Tuileries! (*All go off.*)

Introduction to a scene from THE LAST DAYS OF MANKIND. The scene from *The Last Days of Mankind* gives what is possibly the most memorable diatribe ever aimed at the Germanic world. Since it is a scene of pure commentary, there is really no need to situate it for the reader; and to summarize it is merely to realize how much what Kraus has to say is attenuated by paraphrase. At least, the scene should indicate that those who assert that no modern dramatist, before Brecht, sacrificed drama for commentary as Brecht did are unacquainted with Kraus's epic play. Toward the conclusion of the long dialogue that follows, The Carper—who is always Karl Kraus in the way that Mother Courage is sometimes Bertolt Brecht—reveals the basic principle that determines just about every exchange between himself and The Optimist: The Optimist is merely a provider of cues. And what The Carper attacks is very much what Brecht so often makes the target of his quick-thinking realists: untenable idealisms, war and militarism, the commercialization of modern values, German nationalism, and the egregious hypocrisy of a culture quick to identify itself with a glorious intellectual past and equally quick to arm itself to the teeth. And it is worth noting here that Brecht, the Communist, remained to the end a great admirer of Kraus, even though Kraus saw in communism merely one more symptom of the disease that The Carper diagnoses so apocalyptically in *The Last Days of Mankind.* For that matter, Kraus seems to have been just as unsympathetic in later years to less radical groups like the Social Democrats. The only man in whom he had any faith during the worsening crisis of the thirties was Chancellor Engelbert Dollfuss. It is as if once face to face with those terribly evil times which he had foreseen long before anyone else, he could not allow himself to recognize how absolutely right he had been in saying: "The returning fighters will break into the hinterlands and there the war will first get started. . . . "

the last days of mankind

Act I, scene 29
(THE OPTIMIST *and* THE CARPER *in conversation.*)

THE OPTIMIST: You cannot deny that the war has brought with it
a spiritual upswing, along with happy consequences for those who must
always be looking death in the eye.

THE CARPER: I don't glorify war because it must now let its eyes be
looked into by so many poor devils, who can only be elevated to metaphysical heights by gallow's duty—not to mention that in most cases
this never works.

THE OPTIMIST: Those good become better and those evil, good. War
ennobles.

THE CARPER: It deprives the good of their faith, if not their life, and
it makes those evil, more so. The contrasts of peace were sufficient.

THE OPTIMIST: But aren't you conscious of the spiritual upswing in
the hinterlands?

THE CARPER: As for the spiritual upswing of the hinterlands, I've taken
no more notice of it than of gutter dust whirled up by revolving brooms
before sinking back where it came from.

THE OPTIMIST: Nothing is changing then?

THE CARPER: Oh, yes, dust turns into filth, because the spray truck
soon follows.

THE OPTIMIST: You do not believe then that since the beginning of
August, when our boys pulled out, things have gotten better at all?

THE CARPER: Beginning of August, yes, that was the date they pulled
out, when mankind's honor was given notice. It should have been challenged at the world court.

THE OPTIMIST: Do you wish to deny the enthusiasm with which our
brave soldiers pulled into the field and the pride with which those staying
behind glanced after them?

THE CARPER: Certainly not; just to maintain that the brave soldiers
would rather change places with those proudly glancing after them than
those proudly glancing after them with the brave soldiers.

THE OPTIMIST: Do you wish to deny the great solidarity established
by the war in one magic stroke?

THE CARPER: That solidarity would be even greater if no one had to
pull out and all could content themselves with proudly glancing.

THE OPTIMIST: The German Kaiser has said: "There are no more
parties, there are only Germans."

THE CARPER: That may be right for Germany—elsewhere people may
nourish another ambition.

THE OPTIMIST: But why?

THE CARPER: It goes without saying that as regards nationality, elsewhere they are not Germans.

THE OPTIMIST: Has anyone seen mankind rot away in time of peace as you have?

THE CARPER: Such rotting is carried over into war, war is infected with it, degenerates through it, and the infection in more intense form survives for peace. Before the doctor cures the pestilence, it has taken both him and his patient.

THE OPTIMIST: Yes, but is not war better than peace for a mankind so constituted?

THE CARPER: As that is so, so it is certain that peace will follow.

THE OPTIMIST: But I would tend to think that war makes an end of evil.

THE CARPER: War propagates evil.

THE OPTIMIST: War as such?

THE CARPER: War such as this. It derives its potency from the deteriorating circumstances of the day—its bombs are full of their germs.

THE OPTIMIST: But at least there is the return of an ideal. Doesn't that imply it's all up with evil?

THE CARPER: Evil thrives best behind ideals.

THE OPTIMIST: But examples of sacrificial courage must continue to have an effect beyond the war itself.

THE CARPER: Evil makes its effect manifest through and beyond war—it fattens on sacrifice.

THE OPTIMIST: You underestimate the forces of morality that war sets into motion.

THE CARPER: Far from it. Many now compelled to die can, to be sure, kill others as well, but at least they are exempt from the possibility of profiteering. But such deficiencies are compensated for by the others who glanced after them with pride. Those over there are the sinners of yesteryear; these here, fresh arrivals.

THE OPTIMIST: You are confusing the superficial appearance of a big city with the healthy kernel.

THE CARPER: It is the fate of the healthy kernel to become a superficial appearance. The direction of cultural tendencies is toward the world as big city. In a second you can turn a Westphalian peasant into a Berlin black marketeer, but the reverse does not hold true, and there is no way of going back.

THE OPTIMIST: But the possibility of a recovery is signified by virtue of there being once again an idea and one for which even dying is possible.

THE CARPER: One can go so far as to die for something and still not achieve health. In fact, one dies not for an idea but of it. And one dies of it whether one lives or dies for it, in war or peace. Because one lives on it.

THE OPTIMIST: You are punning. Just what idea have you in mind?

THE CARPER: The idea for which a nation dies, without having it, without having anything from it, and from which a nation dies without knowing it. The idea of the capitalistic, hence Judaeo-Christian, destruction of the world, which resides in the consciousness of those who do not fight for the idea but rather live for it and therefrom, those same ones who, if they are not immortal, wind up dying of diabetes or obesity.

THE OPTIMIST: If, then, such an idea is being fought for, who will win?

THE CARPER: It is to be hoped that it will not be that culture which has abandoned itself most willingly to the idea whose success depends on the very power structures who found the idea exclusively fit for their needs.

THE OPTIMIST: I understand. The others, the enemy, would then be fighting for another idea?

THE CARPER: So one hopes. Namely, for an idea; namely, the idea of liberating European culture from the pressure of the other idea— specifically, of liberating themselves and turning back on the road they realized was dangerous.

THE OPTIMIST: And it is your belief that such an idea is within the ken of the hostile powers who actually represent undisguised commercial interests and whom the world knows to be partisans of commercial jealousy?

THE CARPER: The history of the world repeats itself with us every day, hence far too oft, to require its authority from the Entente. No, statesmen are never conscious of an idea, but the idea lives so long in the instinct of nations that it is bound to manifest itself one day in the action of statesmen, in another appearance, with a wholly different motive. One should gradually accustom oneself to recognize that what is called British envy, French lust for revenge, and Russian rapacity, is an aversion to the brazen tramping of German sweat-feet.

THE OPTIMIST: You do not believe then that there was a well-planned surprise attack?

THE CARPER: Oh, yes.

THE OPTIMIST: Then how—?

THE CARPER: A surprise attack takes place as a rule against those who are attacked, much more rarely against those who do the attacking. Or we can call it a surprise attack if the attacked are taken somewhat by surprise, and an act of self-defense if the attacked party is just a touch surprised.

THE OPTIMIST: You are fond of jesting.

THE CARPER: I seriously consider the European federation against Central Europe to be the last act of which Christian civilization was capable.

THE OPTIMIST: You are then evidently convinced it was not Central Europe but the Entente which acted in self-defense. Suppose, as it looks, this defense will not be crowned with success?

THE CARPER: Then this traders' war will for the present be decided in favor of those endowed with less religion, in order to be converted in a hundred years into an open religious war.

THE OPTIMIST: What do you mean by that?

THE CARPER: I mean that Judaicized Christian Europe will have to surrender at the bidding of the Asiatic spirit.

THE OPTIMIST: And with what weapons would the Asiatic spirit force this to occur?

THE CARPER: By force of arms. With the very idea of quantity and developed technology, by which alone the idea and internal spirit of Central Europe can be gotten at. Quantity China has already, the other weapons she will acquire. She will Japanize herself in good time. She will experience what England is experiencing today on a smaller scale, adopting militarism in order to be done with it.

THE OPTIMIST: But England is not being done with it.

THE CARPER: I hope, yes. And: that she will not herself be finished thanks to militarism; and that she will not purchase a material victory at the price of spiritual impoverishment. Otherwise Europe would be Germanized. Militarism is perhaps a condition by which a European nation is conquered after conquering thereby. The Germans have had to relinquish their foremost position in order to be the foremost military nation of the earth. May it not be so with others, chiefly, the English, whom a nobler drive for self-preservation has kept from universal conscription. Universal force for the sake of self-defense is not only a desperate measure but also a dubious one. England, like Germany, might well wind up conquering herself. The only race strong enough to survive a life of technology lives not in Europe. So I see it on occasion. May the Christian God make it otherwise!

THE OPTIMIST: Aha, your Chinese; the race most unfit for war!

THE CARPER: Certainly, today they are missing out on the achievements of modern times, perhaps because they have already gone through them in a prehistoric time unknown to us. But they will easily enough boast those achievements again as soon as they need them in order to wean Europeans away from the same. They too will engage in tomfoolery: but with a moral purpose. That is what I call a real religious war.

THE OPTIMIST: What idea would this help to victory?

THE CARPER: The idea that God did not create man as consumer or producer, but as human being. That foodstuffs are not the purpose of life. That the stomach should not prove too much for the head. That life is not founded on the primacy of moneyed interests. That man is situated in time in order to have time and not so that his legs carry him anywhere more swiftly than his heart.

THE OPTIMIST: That is early Christianity.

THE CARPER: Christianity it is not, because it was not strong enough to resist Jehova's revenge. Its promise was too weak to assuage ravenous earthly hungers, which took there and then their heavenly compensations. For this species of mankind does not eat in order to live but lives in order to eat and even dies therefor. Brothel and slaughterhouse and in the background a lonely pope wrings his hands.

THE OPTIMIST: All right, then, in a word: the idea.

THE CARPER: All right, then, in a word: the idea.

THE OPTIMIST: But is not German militarism the one conservative institution standing in the way of those tendencies of the modern world which you despise? I am surprised a conservative thinker should speak against militarism.

THE CARPER: I am not at all surprised a progressive should speak on behalf of it. You are quite right: for militarism is not what I mean but what you mean—the power-means which whatever spiritual direction is dominant employs for its success. Today it serves, as it in turn is served by the press, the idea of the Jewish-capitalistic destruction of the world.

THE OPTIMIST: But in the pronouncements of the hostile powers there is mentioned only that they wish to protect freedom from autocracy.

THE CARPER: That's the same thing. In the instinct of the most unfree being of humanity lives the yearning to protect the freedom of the spirit from the dictatorship of money, and to protect human dignity from the autocracy of commerce. Militarism provides the means for such dictatorship, instead of being employed within the state as a natural tool against such dictatorship. Ever since lethal weapons became industrial products, they have been turned against mankind, and the professional soldier has long ceased to have any idea as to what strivings he serves as tool. Russia, too, fights against autocracy. Out of a final cultural instinct she defends herself against the force most perilous to spirit and human dignity. And it is fundamentally submissive Christian thought which succumbs most easily to that same force when it comes to the signing of the most wretched pacts imaginable.

THE OPTIMIST: But can the heterogeneous nations drummed together by this war have just such a common yearning? Russian autocracy and Western democracy?

THE CARPER: These very antitheses demonstrate the deeper community which extends beyond political goals. And the fact that the contrasts are transcended proves that Germany's wretched politics, her impotence in the face of elementary diplomatic rules, was the expression of a developmental necessity.

THE OPTIMIST: But this mixture of allies is much too motley.

THE CARPER: This mixture proves the authenticity of the hate.

THE OPTIMIST: But that hate makes use of the falsest arguments.

THE CARPER: Hate always does that, but false arguments give the best proof of the truth of instincts.

THE OPTIMIST: The Germans would then have to draw their cultural refreshment from the realm of lies?

THE CARPER: Yes, indeed, but victory would make that appear quite unnecessary. The Germans could not then be cured of their most serious truths. For all that, it is questionable if the "lies of foreign lands," assuming that they too are not *made in Germany,* do not contain more life juice than the truth of a Wolff* bureau. In the case of the former, natural lies can be distinguished from the truth of reason; here truth is uttered as printed, everything originating on paper. If lying is in Romance lands an intoxication, it is here a science and consequently dangerous to the organism. Those over there are virtuosos of the lie, they themselves not believing what they say, but still wanting to hear lies uttered because lies say more clearly what they experience: their truth. Those over here utter no lie in excess of those required for the purpose in question; they are engineers of the lie, and by lies they ensure the existence of the falsehoods they have made of war and life.

THE OPTIMIST: The reproach that Germany's conduct in the war is barbaric is simply absurd.

THE CARPER: Let us accept, along with God, that Germany's war conduct is no more barbaric than that of others, except for a few measures adopted as reprisals, which happen to involve civilian populations by chance, and except for examples like that of the "Lusitania," which go by the common name of "incidents." However, when others say that Germany's war conduct is barbaric, they actually feel, and quite rightly, it is Germany's conduct in peace that is barbaric. And that must indeed be so, for Germany's conduct in peace was for generations predicated on Germany's preparing to conduct war.

THE OPTIMIST: But the Germans are, after all, the nation of poets and thinkers. Doesn't German culture contradict the materialism you ascribe to them?

THE CARPER: German culture is not substance but beautify-your-home material with which the nation of judges and hangmen ornaments its emptiness.

---

* German news bureau.

THE OPTIMIST: The nation of judges and hangmen? Is that what you call the Germans? The nation of Goethe and Schopenhauer?

THE CARPER: Since it is cultured, it can call itself by that description, but at the risk of being hailed into court on the basis of the most popular section of the penal code, namely, for gross misconduct.

THE OPTIMIST: Why then?

THE CARPER: Because Goethe and Schopenhauer could hold against the present state of the German nation all that they held against their German contemporaries, and with more justification and more acuteness than Le Matin.* Nowadays they would be lucky to make it across the border as undesirable natives. The prosperous state in which his nation found itself during the war of liberation left Goethe with nothing but a feeling of emptiness, and German colloquial speech as well as journalese could thank the Lord if it occupied today the plateau upon which Schopenhauer found it to be so wretched. No nation lives more remote from its language, hence the source of its life, than the Germans. What Neapolitan beggar is not closer to his language than a German professor to his! Yes, but cultured is this nation like no other, and because its doctors invariably—that is, if they do not take refuge in the quarters reserved for the press—busy themselves with gas bombs, this nation makes its generals equivalent to doctors. What would have been Schopenhauer's reaction to a philosophical faculty which bestows its highest honor on an organizer of mechanical death? Cultured they are, that British jealousy cannot take away from them, and they know what's what. Their language serves exactly the purpose of saying what's what. This nation writes today the most antiquated jargon of world clerkdom and—barring Iphigenia's being accidentally saved by Esperanto—classic after classic is handed over to the relentless barbarity of literary pirates; at a time when no human being can guess at or experience the word, compensation is derived from luxury editions, bibliophilism, and similar aesthetic lecheries, which are as much the authentic stigmas of barbarity as the bombardment of a cathedral.

THE OPTIMIST: But the cathedrals of Reims were military observation posts!

THE CARPER: Of no interest to me. Mankind, itself, is a military observation post—I wish cathedrals would open fire on it.

THE OPTIMIST: But that about the German language I cannot wholly understand. You are someone who is literally engaged to the German language, and in your writings against Heineism have acknowledged the superiority of German to the Romance languages. Now you are evidently of another mind.

THE CARPER: Only a German could now find my thinking changed. I think exactly as I do because I am engaged to the German tongue. And I am also faithful to her. And I know this war will confirm that

---

* Radical French newspaper.

and confirm also that a victory, from which God preserve us, would be the most complete betrayal of the spirit.

THE OPTIMIST: But you do consider the German language to be more profound?

THE CARPER: But profoundly below her the German speaker.

THE OPTIMIST: And the other languages, in your view, far below German?

THE CARPER: But the other speakers higher.

THE OPTIMIST: Are you then in a position to set up a meaningful connection between language and war?

THE CARPER: Perhaps this: that the language which has most petrified into a repository of catchwords will tend to find itself blameless of the very things that turn others into objects of reproaches.

THE OPTIMIST: And that is supposed to be a quality of the German language?

THE OPTIMIST: By and large. That language is today the kind of ready-made merchandise upon whose quick turnover the life substance of present-day speakers depends, and the soul of that language is that of an upright Philistine who has no time to spare for the commission of a wickedness because his life revolves purely about his business, and who may be left with a deficit even after investing his very life.

THE OPTIMIST: Aren't these far-fetched thoughts?

THE CARPER: They're fetched from what is furthest—from the language.

THE OPTIMIST: And the others are not out for business?

THE CARPER: But their life does not wholly revolve around it.

THE OPTIMIST: The English are turning war into business and they have always had mercenaries do their fighting.

THE CARPER: For the very reason that the English are not idealists—they are not prepared to risk their lives for business.

THE OPTIMIST: Mercenary (*Söldner*) derives directly from pay (*Sold*) —there's your language for you!

THE CARPER: A clear case. But soldier (*Soldat*) even more directly. The difference is certainly that the soldier receives less pay and more honor when he goes to his death for the Fatherland.

THE OPTIMIST: But our soldiers do fight for the Fatherland.

THE CARPER: Yes, that they do, indeed, and, fortunately, out of enthusiasm, for otherwise it would be out of compulsion. The English are no idealists. On the contrary, when they wish to engage in business, they do not call the business "Fatherland"—they are not even supposed to have in their language a word for such activity: they leave their ideals alone when their export trade is in danger.

THE OPTIMIST: They are traders.

THE CARPER: We are heroes.

THE OPTIMIST: Yes, but then again you say that the English, together with all the others, are fighting for an idea?

THE CARPER: I maintain that they are in a position to do that on the basis of the most materialistic pretexts, whereas we exploit the most idealistic pretexts for business.

THE OPTIMIST: Do you consider it an ideal to stand in the way of German business?

THE CARPER: Certainly, exactly that which we take to be the jealousy of competition. In truth, it is knowing who will benefit from an expansion of the cultural establishment and who will not. There are nations who cannot eat too much because they have bad cultural digestion. Their neighbors realize this in no time, more distressingly, in fact, than they themselves do. World trade would isolate the German spirit—of which German culture has known nothing for a long time. But to remain in spiritual connection with the world, you do not need an expansion of export trade. That kind of thing suits the English without doing any damage to the impoverished soul we attribute to them. They can treat themselves to the luxury of ornaments as well as necessities without any danger, and they can tolerate bustle as easily as they do their monarchy. In the German being—through which the world is supposed to recover—all heterogeneous elements are immediately merged into a wretched interrelationship. The British have culture because they know how to separate the little inner life they have from problems of consumption. They do not wish to be compelled by some filth-competitor to work more than six hours, and so the rest of the day belongs to those occupations for which God has created the Britisher: God or sport, whereby being busy with God would deserve to be called an inward concern even if such concern were mere hypocrisy—because it would nonetheless be a mode of thought leading one far away from daily labor. And that is the principal point. In contrast, the German labors twenty-four hours a day and discharges within his work those obligations—spiritual, emotional, artistic—which he would be bound to neglect through a division of his time; he employs the substance of those obligations equally as ornament, merchandising trade-mark, and window dressing. He is intent upon omitting nothing. And this mixing up of inner realities with necessities of life, this making of the means for living life's whole purpose and the simultaneous utilization of life's aim for the sake of life's expedients, e.g., "Art in the service of the merchant," is the accursed element in which German genius flourishes and withers. This and nothing else, the execrable spirit of eternal connection-making, turning things upside down and starting all over again, is the problem of the world war. We are traders and heroes working for a firm.

THE OPTIMIST: Everyone knows that the problem of the world war is that Germany wishes to have a place in the sun.

THE CARPER: That is well known, but one cannot be sure that if such a place were captured, the sun might not sink from sight altogether. To which the *Norddeutsche Allgemeine* would no doubt reply that we would then do our fighting in the shadows. To be sure, up to the victorious end and even beyond.

THE OPTIMIST: You are a carper.

THE CARPER: That I am, although I gladly acknowledge that you are an optimist.

THE OPTIMIST: Prior to this did you not sing a song of praise to German organization and favor it at least in comparison with the wild disorder to be found in the Romance lands?

THE CARPER: Prior to this and even now. German organization—assuming it withstands this unfettered war—is a talent, and like every talent, time- and world-bound. It is practical, second-rate, and serves the personality availing itself of it better than a scatter-brained environment, in which even the second-rate type of person has personality. But how much a nation must have divested itself of personality to reach the capacity for ordering the course of outward life so smoothly! My acknowledgment was never a compliment, and in deciding between values of humanity—for which there was no call before the war—the needs of the nervous individual become irrelevant. In an evil life and especially in the chaos to which this evil life has been condemned on our native grounds, such an individual could well yearn for order; in such a critical situation he could well employ technology as a pontoon bridge in order to come to himself; he could well not mind being surrounded by humanity consisting only of chauffeurs, whom he could cheerfully deprive of their right to vote. What we are concerned with now is the personality of nations.

THE OPTIMIST: And who will triumph?

THE CARPER: As carper, I am obligated to see the dark side and to fear that the victor will be the one who has preserved the least degree of individuality, namely, the German. Within the spiritual boundaries of European Christianity I see things taking such a course in darker hours. This to be followed by spiritual starvation.

THE OPTIMIST: This is the result of the world war?

THE CARPER: Of the European war, and in prelude to the decision which the true world war against a Europe united in spirit must bring. The rebellion of the Slavic-Romance lands, supported by auxiliary nations, will remain an episode, till all of Europe has had enough German morality, stink bombs, and universal military training to profit from the instruction of Asian mores. Such are my fears, on occasion. However, in the main I am optimistic, but not the way you are. Then I hope with confidence that matters will terminate happily and realize that all this victory stuff is wanton waste of time and blood for the postponement of unavoidable defeat.

THE OPTIMIST: Be careful!

THE CARPER: I only say this to you and publicly. You will not repeat it, and the executioner does not understand my style. I would gladly be clearer. But I let the Prussians go all out for glory and stick to my own ideas.

THE OPTIMIST: But by virtue of what you conceal you are guilty of a contradiction.

THE CARPER: It is no contradiction that I fear we shall triumph and hope we shall be defeated.

THE OPTIMIST: And there is no contradiction between your praise and censure of Germanic essence?

THE CARPER: No, there is no contradiction between praise for a civilization which makes outer life frictionless, replaces street filth with asphalt, supplying those voracious for fantasy with phantoms instead of with a worthless sense of reality, and the censure of a culture which has evaporated for this very frictionlessness, promptness, and skill. It is not contradiction but tautology. In a generally misshapen world, I would feel most happy where order reigned and society was sufficiently emptied to surround me with mute actors, in a world where one person looked like the next, so that my memory would not be burdened with a variety of physiognomies. But it is not my wish that this be the condition of mankind, I am far from setting my comfort above a nation's need for happiness, and I consider it wrong when happiness is reduced to a batallion of Aschinger* rolls on a string.

THE OPTIMIST: Enlighten me then on the contradiction implied by your view that the military type is relatively the finest of civil life.

THE CARPER: That is no more a contradiction than the other. Among all the mediocre types on view in the chaos of a world at peace, the military type is the most useful. Duty is the limit of infinite insignificance. Discipline, fulfillment of obligations for their own sake, is the decorum of banality. Thus the perspective of a moneyed bourgeoisie. Even jobbers, forced for once to serve instead of ordering come home looking less disturbing and with less fat.

THE OPTIMIST: That would seem, indeed, to be praise of war.

THE CARPER: No, just fatigue. Indeed! Any plusses are canceled out by death.

THE OPTIMIST: That is true. But when jobbers die, then it must suit you fine.

THE CARPER: The jobbers do not die. And, above all, such calisthenics are more than made up for by death. The heroism of the unqualified is the most gruesome prospect of this war. Some day it will prove to be the background upon which a lowness—multiplied and unchanged—will throw itself into more favorably picturesque relief.

---

* A German restaurant chain.

THE OPTIMIST: But there is real dying taking place. Do take notice of the daily newspaper heading "Hero's Death."

THE CARPER: Certainly, it was under the same heading that the awarding of the title "Councilor of Commerce" was formerly announced. But this sad accident of a grenade splinter will also procure for surviving commercial interests—for whom the others died—nothing less than an aureole.

THE OPTIMIST: Are you referring to those who remained at home?

THE CARPER: Yes, these will get their compensation for the force to which the others were sacrificed, for the force in the service of a foreign idea which necessitated their dying—all of which goes by the name of universal military training.

THE OPTIMIST: The returning fighters will know how to treat such wantonness.

THE CARPER: The returning fighters will break into the hinterlands and there the war will first get started. Whatever successes they were denied they will make it their business to snatch up, and what constitutes the life substance of war—murder, plunder, and desecration—will be child's play in comparison with the peace which will now break out. May the god of battle preserve us from the offensive now looming! A dreadful burst of activity, liberated from trenches, guided no more by any command, will seize at arms and gratification in every sphere of life, and more death and disease will invade the world than the war itself exacted. May heaven protect children from the sabers that will prove a domestic tool of chastisement, as well as from such toys as souvenir grenades!

THE OPTIMIST: It is certainly dangerous to let children play with grenades.

THE CARPER: And adults who do the same thing are not even careful to avoid playing with grenades! I have seen a cross built with one.

THE OPTIMIST: These are attendant phenomena. Otherwise this war did not always have in you such a confirmed scorner.

THE CARPER: Otherwise I, also, did not always have in you such a confirmed misinterpreter. Otherwise war was a tournament engaged in by a minority and every example was potent. Now war is a mechanical risk for everyone and you remain an optimist.

THE OPTIMIST: The development of weapons certainly cannot lag behind the technological advancements of modern times.

THE CARPER: No, but it is the imagination of modern times that has lagged behind the technological advancements of mankind.

THE OPTIMIST: Yes, but is war conducted with imagination?

THE CARPER: No, for if the latter were still with us, the former would no more be conducted.

THE OPTIMIST: Why not?

THE CARPER: For then the linguistic leftovers from a worn-out ideal would have no opportunity to keep brains in fog; for then one would be able to picture in the imagination the most unimaginable abominations and be able to know in advance how quickly the road from colorful figures of speech and from all the flags of enthusiasm winds up in the misery of gray fields; because the prospect of dying at the Ruhr for the Fatherland or of having one's feet frozen off would fail to mobilize any more pathos; because one would at least pull out with the certainty of acquiring lice for the Fatherland, and because one would realize that man has invented the machine in order to be overpowered by it, and because one would not overtrump the folly of having invented the machine with the more malign folly of letting oneself be killed by it; because man would feel that he must defend himself against an enemy of whom he sees nothing but billowing smoke and suspect that representing himself with a munitions factory provides no adequate protection against the offerings of a hostile munitions factory. If one possessed imagination, one would realize that it is a crime to expose life to accident, sin to debase death to accident, that it is folly to build armored vessels to outwit destroyers, to produce mortars when in defense against them trenches are dug in which the only ones lost are those who stick their heads out first, that it is folly to chase mankind in flight from their weapons into rat holes and to let men enjoy a future peace only beneath the earth. If instead of newspapers, we had imagination, technology would not be a means of aggravating life and science would not be concerned with its destruction. Ach, the hero's death hovers in a gas cloud and we unbind our experience in reports! "Forty thousand Russian corpses perish entangled in barbed wire" made up one special edition, which was later read aloud during intermission by a soubrette for the benefit of humanity's dregs so that a call would go out for the librettist who turned the watchwords "I gave gold for iron" into an operetta. This self-devouring quantity retains feeling only for that which befalls oneself and one's immediate physical neighbor, only for what one can directly grasp and touch. Is it not discernible that in all this business, which for lack of any heroes makes each man his own hero, everyone sneaks away with his own separate destiny? Never did greater developments witness less community feeling. Never was the dominant style of the world a more gigantic pettiness. Reality has the dimensions of a mere report trying to catch up with it in gasping clarity. The reporting messenger, who conveys action and imagination at the same time, has placed himself before action and rendered it inconceivable. And his representation operates so malignly that I would like to take hold of all these pitiable figures who are now assaulting our ears with their eternally inescapable cry "special edition" as the responsible instigators of this catastrophe. And is not the messenger also the culprit? The printed word has made it possible for a hollow mankind to commit atrocities which it can no more imagine, and the dreadful curse of multiplication has been made a property of the word—which must give birth to a continuously generated evil. All that is happening is happening only for those who are describing it and for those who are not experiencing it. A spy being led to the gallows must take quite a walk so that those in movie houses have their need for diversion gratified, and he must stare again and again at the camera to make sure those in movie houses are happy with his facial expression. Let me not pursue this train of thought to the gallows of mankind—nonetheless I must, because I am mankind's dying spy, and I am anguished that this unique proliferation of happenings confronts in the spirits of men the same vacuum it does in machinery!

THE OPTIMIST: It is inevitable that great matters be accompanied by filthy attendant phenomena. It is quite possible that on the night of August 1, 1914, the world underwent no change. Also, it does seem to me that imagination does not belong among those traits which are manifested in war. But if I understand you correctly, you wish to deny altogether that a modern war affords any scope to human qualities.

THE CARPER: You understand me correctly; it leaves no scope because war's actuality subsists on the negation of human qualities. There are none of the latter.

THE OPTIMIST: What is there then?

THE CARPER: What you have are quantities which reduce themselves in a reciprocally uniform fashion, inasmuch as they are attempting to demonstrate that they are no match for transformed mechanical energies; that mortars can even take care of multitudes. That proof of this should have been undertaken was made possible and necessitated only by that failure of the imagination resulting from mankind's conversion into mechanical energies.

THE OPTIMIST: If the quantities are bound to diminish each other uniformly, when will the whole thing end?

THE CARPER: When the tails of two lions will prove superfluous. Or if this exception is not realized: when the larger quantity achieves an advantage. I dread having to wish for that. But I dread even more having to fear that the more fundamental quantity may achieve an advantage.

THE OPTIMIST: Which one would that be?

THE CARPER: Quite certainly, the smaller one. The larger one could well exhaust itself through a residue of preserved humanity. But the smaller quantity carries on its fight fervently, believing in a God who wanted these developments.

THE OPTIMIST: We could use a Bismarck. He would wind things up a bit earlier.

THE CARPER: There can be none.

THE OPTIMIST: Why not?

THE CARPER: When the world has reached the point where books are balanced with bombs, no such figure can arise.

THE OPTIMIST: How then are we to defend ourselves against the infernal plan to starve us out?

THE CARPER: The infernal plan to starve us out is part of a war which revolves around the highest goods of a nation, namely, wage-earning and feeding oneself, and that plan is a far more moral expedient than recourse to flame throwers, mines, and gases. The means of war are simply drawn from the fabric of the war itself. If markets are turning into battlefields and vice versa, it is the desire of a mishmash culture which builds temples with paraffin candles and has placed art at the service of the merchant. But industry can get no artists to work for it and no cripples to deliver. A false principle of life carries on as a false principle of death-making—once again the means diverge from the end. If two cooperative societies were to get in each other's hair, then the most moral party would be the one that allowed hired police to establish order rather than letting consumers do the job themselves, and if that same society were to content itself with driving away customers, or even merchandise, then it would be acting in the most moral fashion. All this apart from the fact that the blockade is only a warning to the Central Powers, to turn them away from their inferiors through the termination of an absurd war. If the bookkeeper has not yet restrained the knight, then he should do so now, for it is a matter of recognizing clearly that one is concerned here not with a tournament but with cotton.

THE OPTIMIST: This war deals with—

THE CARPER: Indeed, this is a dealer's war! But the difference is this: One side means export and says ideals, the others say export and just this honesty taken by itself, this very separation, makes the ideal possible, even if it were not otherwise present.

THE OPTIMIST: Don't tell me the others are concerned with an ideal!

THE CARPER: Certainly not, they only want to take it away from us and by that very act to win it back for us, in that they wish to cure German humanity from the anticultural disposition to treat ideals as window dressing for manufactured goods. For the German, ideals first come into play when other goods have been loaded by shipping agents. They believe that it won't do to lay out a subway without God and art. That is the cancer. In a Berlin paper establishment I saw a roll of toilet paper on whose sheets the sense and humor of the prevailing situation were elucidated by printed quotations from Shakespeare. Shakespeare is nonetheless a hostile author. But even Schiller and Goethe were forced upon that roll, which included the entire classical culture of the Germans. Never before did I have so much the impression that this is the nation of poets and thinkers.

THE OPTIMIST: Good; in the war waged by the others you discern the operation of an instinct for culture, and in the war waged by the Germans, interests of economic expansion. But would not economic well-being directly make of German spiritual life—

THE CARPER: No, it would not, but rather the opposite. The total absence of this spiritual life was a precondition for these endeavors. The self-starvation of the spirit, which promised the success of those endeavors, could be grasped by no imagination, even if such were still around.

THE OPTIMIST: But aren't you yourself convinced of the necessity for the war as such when you refer to a war of quantities? Because you will grant that it will put the population problem into order for a time.

THE CARPER: That it will do thoroughly. Anxieties about overpopulation will be permitted to give place to anxieties about depopulation. This could be accomplished much more painlessly by legalized abortion.

THE OPTIMIST: Prevailing moral conceptions would never agree to that!

THE CARPER: I never imagined so, since the prevailing moral conception agrees only that fathers who did not manage to get killed by accident creep through the world as jobless cripples, and that mothers have children so that they can be torn apart by bombers.

THE OPTIMIST: You're not going to assert that such things are done deliberately?

THE CARPER: No, worse: accidentally! It's nobody's fault that it happens, but it happens on purpose. With regret and nonetheless. In this area an enrichment of conscious experience is afforded those who sow murder from their air, and those entrusted with carrying it through—they aim for arsenals and munition works and hit instead bedrooms and schools for little girls. Repetition should teach them that such are the consequences of those attacks which are later remembered in glorifying announcements as successful bombing missions.

THE OPTIMIST: All in all, these are permissible means of war, and once air mastery is achieved—

THE CARPER: —the human scoundrel will immediately exploit the opportunity to make the earth just as unsafe. Read the description of the rise of a balloon in Jean Paul's *Kampanertal.* Those five pages could not be written today because the guests in the air retain no reverence for the nearby sky, but as air burglars they employ the secure distance from the earth in order to assault it. Man takes part in no progress without avenging himself therefor. That which should prove of help to life is immediately directed against it. That which should alleviate is used to aggravate. The ascent of the balloon was in the nature of devotion, the ascent of an airplane a danger for those who do not go along.

THE OPTIMIST: But a danger as well for the bomb-dropping flyer.

THE CARPER: Of course, but not the danger of being killed by those whom he will kill, and he gets away more easily from the machine guns lying in wait than the defenseless. More easily than in a fight

between two equally armed murderers, a fight which is at least honest
to the extent that the desecration of the elements in which such a fight
takes place allows of such a valuation. May the "daring" manipulate
as they wish, at all times the bomber signifies the arming of cowardice,
every bit as nefarious as the U-boat, which is malice incarnate armed
to the teeth, the kind of malicious trickery that permits a dwarf to
triumph over an armed giant. But infants killed by flyers are not armed,
and even if they were, they could hardly get at the flyer as surely
as the latter at them. The greatest disgrace of the war is that the one
discovery which brought man closer to the stars has served only to
preserve earthly wretchedness in the air, as if the earth did not afford
enough scope for it.

THE OPTIMIST: And the infants who are being subjected to starvation?

THE CARPER: The governments of the Central Powers have the option
to spare their infants this fate by curing their adults' addiction to primers.
But even if we assume that hostile rulers are as guilty for the blockade
as ours, the bombing of hostile infants in reprisal—that is a thought
pattern which does German ideology much honor, a spiritual foxhole
in which I—by the God of Germany—do not wish to reside!

THE OPTIMIST: You wish to pick holes in the way the Germans conduct
their war without considering that the others employ the same means.

THE CARPER: I've well considered it, and I'm not disposed to exempt
from the shame of mankind those French airplanes which serve approximately the same kind of heroic villainy. Besides priority, it seems to
me the difference lies in temperament—on the one side, what is horrible
is done both with knowledge and ignorance, the other side, however,
is not content with dropping bombs but sends along jokes and even
Christmas greetings in such wrappings. Here again we have the terribly
shocking mixture of objects of utility—namely, the bomb—with the inner
life—namely, the joke—and even of the joke with holiness itself—that
mixture which is absolutely the greatest abomination, the most extreme
promiscuity whereby a life impoverished by rules refreshes itself—an
organic compensation for discipline, drill, and morality. It is the humor
of the executioner, the freedom of a moral code, that has turned love
into a section of the penal code.

THE OPTIMIST: Compensation for discipline? But you always welcomed
that as a restraint upon unruliness?

THE CARPER: But not as a lever for power! Better chaos than order
at the price of humanity! Militarism as a form of physical exercise
and militarism as a condition of the spirit—there is a world of difference
here. It is the nature of militarism to be a tool. When, without beginning
to realize it, militarism becomes the tool of those powers which oppose
its very character, when, in short, militarism starts posing as an end
in itself toward force-threatened mankind, then an irreconcilable enmity
obtains between militarism and the spirit. Its core of honor has been

perverted to childish sport through association with cowardly techniques, and in the framework of universal compulsion its self-chosen duties have degenerated to lies. It remains nothing but subterfuge and compensation for a slavery which displays its wretched power behind machines. So much have the means become ends in themselves that in peace we are able to think only in military terms, and war is only a means for arriving at new weapons. This war is in honor of the arms industry. We do not want more exports and therefore more cannons, we want more cannons for their own sake: and that is why they must explode. Our life and thought are dedicated to the interests of heavy industry; that is a terrible burden. We live under the cannon. And since such forces have allied themselves with God, we are lost. That is the situation.

THE OPTIMIST: But such a state of things could be viewed also from the perspective of a Nietzchean ideal, and that would give us an essentially different picture.

THE CARPER: Yes, one could certainly do that and come to experience Nietzsche's surprise that after Sedan *The Will to Power* did not manifest itself as a triumph of the spirit but in the form of more and more factory smokestacks. Nietzsche was a thinker who had imagined things otherwise. Namely, the spiritual upswing of 1870. In that of 1914 he might never have believed from the very start just as he might not have allowed himself to be dumbfounded by the victory of his own thoughts. And he might well have exposed as a liar the conqueror who sets out on the path to war with *The Will to Power* in his knapsack, along with other implements of culture.

THE OPTIMIST: If this war brings with it no cultural blessing, then it brings none to all nations participating. Unless you are determined on principle to acknowledge cultural possibilities only in those areas where guerrilla fighters murder sleeping soldiers.

THE CARPER: Certainly not in those areas where a Wolff bureau exists to assert that. But it is certainly a unique example of mankind's current state that flyers who hurl bombs upon infants are employing war means sanctioned by international law, while guerrilla fighters who commit murder in order to avenge other murders are not permitted to do so because they have no license, because they do not do their murdering under orders but rather in madness, in short, from the only motive which offers any extenuation of murder; they are unauthorized murderers because they cannot identify themselves as members of an *Ergänzungsbezirkskommando, Kader, Ersatzkörper* or whatever else the disgrace is called. Do not let me pass judgment upon the moral difference between a flyer who kills a sleeping child and a civilian who kills a sleeping soldier. Let the choice be put to you—in terms of danger only and not responsibility—between attacking a sleeping soldier and an infant who is awake.

THE OPTIMIST: There you may well be right, but if you are looking for traits of humanity on the other side, you'll have to search with a magnifying glass.

THE CARPER: To be sure, if I do my looking in our newspapers.

THE OPTIMIST: Contemplate the heading: "How the Russians made themselves at home in Galicia."

THE CARPER: I could not gather from that whether it was Polish peasant or *Honveds* who plundered the castles of Galicia. There would probably be many a tale more of Russian noble deeds under that title if the compulsion to lie were shaken off.

THE OPTIMIST: You don't mean the report about the rape?

THE CARPER: Whether *Honveds** and *Deutschmeister** are the type to plead hat in hand for a glass of water from the women of their own land, not to speak of those in hostile territory, I leave to your optimism, whose imperturbable basis seems to be the reportage of our war headquarters.

THE OPTIMIST: Don't you find that with us even the enemy receives justice?

THE CARPER: Yes, at times one is content with the humor of idiotic picture post cards.

THE OPTIMIST: No, at times he does receive justice.

THE CARPER: If he receives justice, it is of the biting kind. So one could mention as a curiosity—for the intelligentsia of Central Europe will let no truth about the most slandered nation of Europe get out—that the Russians did no shooting on Christmas Eve but left wishes for blessedness and peace in the trenches for their enemies.

THE OPTIMIST: Surely the Austrians reciprocated?

THE CARPER: Certainly, for example, Dr. Fischl, who drew up official documents for the Advocate's Bureau until August 1, had a letter on active service drawn up in which was stated: "Tomorrow the Russians celebrate Christmas—we shall use the occasion to give them a right proper tickling."

THE OPTIMIST: That was a joke.

THE CARPER: Quite right, that was a joke.

THE OPTIMIST: One is not permitted to generalize.

THE CARPER: I do so. You can build on my injustices. If militarism served at home to combat the hegemony of garbage, I would be a patriot. If it declared fit for service those who are not worth anything and if it conducted war in order to tread off the human filth from hostile powers, I would be a militarist! But this militarism sacrifices genuine

* Austro-Hungarian elite regiments.

worth and endows scum with glory, and makes of that same scum
the victor over its own might. Only this prospect can explain why heaps
of humanity tolerate an insult to nature such as universal military training. The garbage knows that it itself is the idea for which it fights,
and with this certainty it fights even for the Fatherland, which is, first
of all and last of all, a foreign idea to it, even if every variety of
primer ideology is used to drum that idea into it. Otherwise, would
they not come to realize that the compulsion to die for an idea foreign
to them constitutes serfdom a thousand times more oppressive than the
most reactionary substance of accursed tsarism? Would people who have
never enjoyed the privileges of the military profession allow themselves
to be forced to share its dangers? To let oneself be torn away from
one's own occupation, livelihood, and family in order to be marched
off to barracks and thereafter to die for the preservation of Bucowina?
Naturally, an explanation of what motivates such behavior is afforded
by the fact that those refusing to die for Bucowina would be shot dead
to start with. But all of this still could not arise if the quantity did
not know that it, apparent victim of autocratic appetites, is bound eventually to prove triumphant over the victor himself. You see, I too am
an optimist. I cannot come to the conclusion that mankind is such a
hopeless canaille as to surrender itself for the sake of a foreign will
to a time of need and death and filth.

THE OPTIMIST: The heightened state that the call of the Fatherland
gives rise to is, however, still a better explanation for what prevails
than force or advantage.

THE CARPER: The Fatherland? Very likely, this call carries among stage
managers the most powerful suggestiveness. But the intoxication into
which one has been lulled by general defenselessness would fail to affect
the more awake intelligentsia if there was not simultaneously the feeling
that a victory is bound to enthrone them as masters of life.

THE OPTIMIST: But not while we have war.

THE CARPER: Here they simply economize on what they allow within
the realm of the conceivable: in this area they have the ability to relax.
They don't have to rack their brains since the enemy provides them
with what they have not enough imagination to picture. For the war
is transforming life into a nursery, in which it is always the other fellow
who started the fighting, in which one glories in the crimes for which
one reproaches others, and in which brawling takes on the form of
playing soldier. When a war is on, the soldier-playing of children is
held in low esteem. It is a much too premature preparation for the childish
stupidity of adults.

THE OPTIMIST: The soldier-playing of children is actually the product
of fresh impulses. Do you know the game "Let's play world war"?

THE CARPER: That is exactly the reverse side of seriousness: Our game
is "Nursery." It is to be wished of this mankind that its infants commence
to starve one another out or to cover each other with bombs—or at
least to drive off their reconnoitering wet nurses.

THE OPTIMIST: To go by your ideas, even before the world war mankind was slated for extinction. But thank God, man is prepared—

THE CARPER: You mean—armed.

THE OPTIMIST: Mankind develops from generation to generation. You mentioned five pages by Jean Paul which could not be written today. I am of the opinion, however, that the invention of Count Zeppelin has in no way made it impossible for Germany to bring forth poets. Even today there are poets who are not to be despised.

THE CARPER: I despise, nonetheless.

THE OPTIMIST: In fact, it is during this war that German poetry has received invigorating impulses.

THE CARPER: It should have received a slap in the face.

THE OPTIMIST: You're trying to be hard rather than truthful. Whatever you may think about the war, the creations of our poets have profited from the breath of fire with which this great time has swept across the commonplace.

THE CARPER: Between the breath of fire and the banal a common ground was quickly established: the catchwords which our conformity-prone poets quickly appropriated. They are more ready to go into mechanical action than even their dumbfounded clientele desired. The poets of Germany! You are a practiced optimist, but your optimism would degenerate to ridicule if you wished to prove the greatness of the time with such creativity. I still draw a moral distinction between poor philistines, who are forced to leave the office for trenches, and those miserable scrawlers who pursue a far more dreadful activity at home, namely, editorials or rhymes in which they work up to a despicable efficacy a wholly unoriginal gesture which was false to start with and who do the same with a breath of fire from the mouth of universality. In these creations I have not found a line from which I did not avert a pained expression during peacetime, which did not make me want to retch rather than respond with feeling. The only worthy line I've come across is in the Kaiser's manifesto, which must have been the work of a sensitive stylist presumably immersed in the events of our time: "I have thought everything over maturely." The time still to come will show even better than the time we have already gone through that an even more mature consideration would have prevented the unspeakable horrors in question. But as the line stands, alone, it functions like a poem, and perhaps especially so when placed in the context of certain thoughts. Take a look here—this pillar will have its effect upon you.

THE OPTIMIST: Where?

THE CARPER:—Ach, what a pity, just that part of the manifesto with the line I mentioned is covered by the face of the Gersthof Wolf. You see, there is the real Tyrtaeus of this war! And now the whole thing is a poem.

THE OPTIMIST: I am acquainted with your exaggerated perspectives. You allow for no accidents. And nonetheless the Gersthof Wolf, never very dear to me—

THE CARPER: Really?

THE OPTIMIST:—and nonetheless what we're dealing with here is simply an advertising poster like any other—for that matter, an old one finished just before the war. It's a matter of some display space having once been rented—possibly the nightclub is still open for business—I really don't know—such things can change overnight—it's all superficial—but I am convinced—

THE CARPER: It goes without saying that you have been convinced.

THE OPTIMIST:—indeed, that the people of Vienna, who overnight were truly transformed into an earnest nation and who, as the press has rightly stated, "are equally distant from arrogance and weakness in their grasp of the seriousness of the situation"—I am convinced that in a year from now they will be in no mood for the things you object to, whether the war be over by that time or not. About that I am, indeed, convinced!

THE CARPER: Let me say that I nurse no such convictions and it makes no difference to me whether things will be one way or another and whether one reacts with approval or censure to a mob going into action. In opposition to you, I would rather approve.

THE OPTIMIST: Then I do not understand you.

THE CARPER: You see, I am convinced only that it matters little how one reacts. But I say: In a year the Gersthof Wolf—which is not an operetta hall but a symbol—will, to suit the requirements of this time of greatness, grow even larger, and on every street corner the Wolf will cover the line "I have thought everything over maturely," and the Gersthof Wolf will cover as well anything that may have space nearby, and the truthful perspective of a false life will be fully established. An in over a year—when a million people will have been buried—the survivors will look the Gersthof Wolf in the eye, and in that countenance will be a bloody look like a world rent asunder. One will read therein that the time is difficult and that for tonight a double concert is scheduled!

THE OPTIMIST: It cuts into my heart to hear you speak so—that is really a deliberate attempt to see as small a time which must appear great even to those who are shortsighted. If this time is done with anything, it is your peculiar perspectives.

THE CARPER: God grant it!

THE OPTIMIST: May He give you greater thoughts. Perhaps they'll be enlarged by your going with me to hear Mozart's *Requiem*—the net proceeds will be donated to war relief—

THE CARPER: No, that poster is enough for me—there right next to the Gersthof Wolf! But what kind of singular drawing do we have there? A church window? If I am not betrayed by my nearsightedness—a mortar! Is it possible? Yes, who could say he succeeded in getting those two worlds into the same boat? Mozart and mortars! What a concert arrangement! Who makes such happy connections? No, one must not weep over that. Only tell me whether in the culture of the Senegalese, whom our enemies have called on for help against us, such a betrayal of God would be possible! You see, that is the world against us.

THE OPTIMIST (*after a pause*): I think you are right. But God knows, only you can see this. Us it eludes, and therefore the future is viewed in a rosy light. You see it, and therefore it exists. Your eye summons it up and thus can see it.

THE CARPER: Because it is nearsighted. It perceives the contours and imagination does the rest. And my ear hears noises that others do not hear, and the music of the spheres that others do not hear I find disturbed by these noises. Think about this and if you still arrive at no resolution, then call on me. I am happy to converse with you. You are a provider of cues for my monologue. I would like to appear with you in front of an audience. Now I can only tell the world that I am silent and, if possible, what it is I am silent about.

THE OPTIMIST: Approximately what?

THE CARPER: Approximately that this war, if it does not kill those who are good, will very likely leave those who are good upon a moral island, those same ones who were good without a war. But that this war will transform the whole surrounding world into vast hinterlands of deceit, decrepitude, and inhuman betrayal of God, in that the evil of this war will continue to propagate itself, growing fat behind a façade of idealism and nourishing itself upon human sacrifice! That in this war, the war of today, culture is not renewing itself but can save itself from the hangman only by self-slaughter. That the war was more than sin: that it was lies, daily lies, flowing like blood from printer's ink, one lie feeding upon the other, gushing in every conceivable direction, a delta to the great waters of madness. That this war will from now on be nothing but an outbreak of peace and that it cannot be ended by peace but by a cosmic war against this mad-dog planet! That unheard-of human victims had to perish, and not for the lamentable reasons that a foreign will drove them to slaughter, but because they, tragically, had to atone for an unknown guilt. That for one person who is tortured by the unprecedented injustice which an evil world continues to inflict upon itself—that for that person only, a single last moral duty remains: to sleep unfeelingly through this anxious time till he is redeemed by the word or by God's impatience.

THE OPTIMIST: You are an optimist. You believe and hope that the world is coming to an end.

THE CARPER: No, the world is simply passing away like an anxious dream, and when I die, everything is done with. Do sleep well! (*He exits.*)

selected bibliography

Baal, A Man's A Man, and the Elephant Calf. Edited by Eric Bentley. New York: Grove Press, 1964.

Baumann, Gerhart. *Georg Büchner, Die dramatische Ausdruckswelt.* Göttingen: Vandenhoeck and Ruprecht, 1961.

Baxandall, Lee. "Georg Büchner's *Danton's Death,*" *Tulane Drama Review,* VI, No. 3 (March, 1962), pp. 136–49.

Becker, Hellmuth. *Napoleon oder die hundert Tage.* Leipzig: K. F. Koehler, 1921.

Beckley, Richard. "Adaptation as a Feature of Brecht's Dramatic Technique," *German Life and Letters,* XV, No. 1 (1961–1962), 274–84.

Bentley, Eric. "Bertolt Brecht's First Play," *Kenyon Review,* XXVI, No. 1 (Winter, 1964), 83–92.

———— (ed.). *The Modern Theatre.* VI. New York: Anchor Books, 1960.

————. *The Playwright as Thinker.* New York: The World Publishing Co., 1955.

Bergmann, Alfred (ed.). *Christian Dietrich Grabbe, Ein Brevier.* Munich: Verlag Kurt Desch, 1955.

Bin Gorion, Emanuel. *Der Fackel Reiter.* Berlin: Morgenland, 1932.

Boesch, Bruno (ed.). *Deutsche Literaturgeschichte in Grundzügen.* Bern: A Francke Ag. Verlag, 1946.

Böttcher, Kurt, and Krohn, Paul Günter. *Sturm und Drang.* Berlin: Volk and Wissen Volkseigener Verlag, 1958.

Brecht, Bertolt. "An Expression of Faith in Wedekind," *Tulane Drama Review,* VI, No. 1 (Autumn, 1961), pp. 26–27.

————. *Schriften zum Theater.* 7 vols. Frankfurt-am-Main: Suhrkamp Verlag, 1963–1964.

————. *Stücke.* 12 vols. Berlin: Suhrkamp Verlag, 1959–1962.

————. *Versuche.* 15. Berlin: Suhrkamp Verlag, 1957.

Bruford, W. H. *Theatre, Drama and Audience in Goethe's Germany.* London: Routledge and Paul, 1950.

Brustein, Robert. *The Theatre of Revolt.* Boston: Little, Brown and Company, 1965.

Büchner, Georg. *Werke und Briefe.* Edited by Fritz Bergemann. Wiesbaden: Insel-Verlag, 1958.

Büttner, Ludwig. *Georg Büchner, Revolutionär und Pessimist.* Nürnberg: Verlag Hans Carl, 1948.

Clark, Barrett H. *European Theories of the Drama.* Revised ed. by H. Popkin. New York: Crown Publishers, 1947.

Crumbach, Franz Hubert. *Die Struktur des Epischen Treaters: Dramaturgie der Kontraste.* Braunschweig: Waisenhaus, 1960.

Dehnow, Fritz. *Frank Wedekind.* Leipzig: Reisland, 1922.

Diebold, Bernhard. *Anarchie im Drama: Kritik und Darstellung der moderne Dramatik.* Frankfurt: Frankfurter Verlags-Anstalt, 1922.

Diekmann, Ernst. *Christian Dietrich Grabbe: Der Wesengehalt seiner Dichtung.* Meyersche Hofbuchhandlung: Max Staercke Verlag, 1936.

Dietrich, Margret. *Das moderne Drama.* Stuttgart: Kröner Verlag, 1961.

Dunlop, Goeffrey. *The Plays of Georg Büchner.* New York: Irving Ravin, 1952.

Duwe, Willi. "Die dramatische Form Wedekinds in ihrem Verhältnis zur Ausdruckskunst." Unpublished Ph.D. dissertation, Friedrich-Wilhelm University, Bonn, 1936.

Eloesser, Arthur. *Die deutsche Literatur von der Romantik bis zur Gegenwart.* Berlin: Bruno Cassirer, 1931.

Emrich, Wilhelm. "Die Lulu-Tragödie," *Das deutsche Drama vom Barock bis zur Gegenwart.* Edited by Benno von Wiese. II. 2nd ed. Düsseldorf: A. Bagel Verlag, 1962.

Esslin, Martin. *Brecht The Man and his Work.* New York: Anchor Books, 1961.

Faesi, Robert. "Ein Vorläufer: Frank Wedekind," *Expressionismus Gestalten einer literarischen Bewegung.* Edited by Hermann Friedmann and Otto Mann. Heidelberg: W. Rothe, 1956.

Fechter, Paul. *Frank Wedekind, Der Mensch und das Werk.* Jena: Lichtenstein, 1920.

Fink, G. L. "Volkslied und Verseinlage in den Dramen Büchners," *Deutsches Vierteljahrschrift,* XXXV, No. 4 (1961), 558–93.

Fischer, Heinz. "Acedia und Landschaft in den Dramen Georg Büchners." Unpublished dissertation, Ludwig-Maxmillian University, Munich, 1958.

Friedrich, Werner P. *History of German Literature.* New York: Barnes and Noble, 1959.

Garland, H. B. *Storm and Stress.* London: George G. Harrap and Co., 1952.

Gassner, John. "Varieties of Epic Theatre in the Modern Drama," *Comparative Literature Studies* (Special Advance Number, 1963), pp. 25–41.

Georg Büchner, Complete Plays and Prose. Translated by Carl Richard Müeller. New York: Hall and Wang, 1963.

Gombrich, Ernst. *Art and Illusion.* New York: Pantheon Books, 1960.

Gorelik, Mordecai. *New Theatres for Old.* 8th ed. Binghamton: Samuel French, 1952.

Grabbes Werke. Edited by Albin Franz and Paul Zaunert. 3 vols. Leipzig: Bibliographisches Institut, 1910.

Grabert, W. *Geschichte der deutschen Literatur.* Munich: Bayerischer Schulbach Verlag, 1957.

Gray, Ronald. *Brecht.* New York: Grove Press, 1961.

Grimm, Reinhold. *Bertolt Brecht: Die Struktur seines Werkes.* Nürnberg: H. Carl, 1959.

Grossvogel, David I., *Four Playwrights and a Postscript. Brecht. Ionesco. Beckett. Genet.* Ithaca, N.Y.: Cornell University Press, 1962.

Gundolf, Friedrich. *Frank Wedekind.* Munich: Georg Müller Verlag, 1954.

————. *Shakespeare und der deutsche Geist.* Berlin: Georg Müller Verlag, 1920.

Guthke, Karl S. *Geschichte und Poetik der deutschen Tragikomödie.* Göttingen: Vanderhoeck and Ruprecht, 1961.

Haas, Willy. *Bert Brecht.* Berlin: Colloquium Verlag, 1958.

Hamburger, Michael. *Reason and Energy.* New York: Grove Press, 1957.

Hauser, Arnold. *The Social History of Art.* New York: A. A. Knopf, 1952.

Hess, Richard, A. "Über die Technik in Grabbes Dramen 'Die Hohenstaufen' und 'Napoleon.'" Unpublished dissertation, Ludwigsuniversität at Giessen, 1922.

Heidemann, Christel. "Satirische und Polemische Formen in der Publizistik von Karl Kraus." Unpublished dissertation, University of Berlin, 1958.

Heller, Erich. *The Disinherited Mind.* Philadelphia: Dufour and Saifer, 1952.

Henel, Heinrich. "Szenisches und paroramisches Theater: Gedanken zum modernen deutschen Drama," *Die Neue Rundschau,* 1963, pp. 235–49.

Hillekamps, C. H. "Ch. D. Grabbes Briefe als biographische *Quelle.*" Unpublished dissertation, Westphalian Wilhelms University, Münster, 1929.

Hinck, Walter. *Die Dramaturgie des späten Brecht.* Göttingen: Vandenhoeck and Ruprecht, 1962.

Hochhuth, Rolf. *Der Stellvertreter.* Hamburg: Rowohlt, 1963.

Höllerer, Walter. "Dantons Tod," *Das deutsche Drama vom Barock bis zur Gegenwart.* Edited by Benno von Wiese. II. 2nd ed. Düsseldorf: A. Bagel Verlag, 1962.

———. "Die Soldaten," *Das deutsche Drama vom Barock bis zur Gegenwart.* Edited by Benno von Wiese. I. 2nd ed. Düsseldorf: A. Bagel Verlag, 1958.

———. *Zwischen Klassik und Moderne: Lachen und Weinen in der Dichtung einer Übergangszeit.* Stuttgart: Ernst Klett Verlag, 1958.

Huber-Bindschedler, Berta. "Die Motivierung in den Dramen von J. M. R. Lenz." Unpublished dissertation, University of Zurich, 1922.

Hultberg, Helge. *Die Ästhetischen Anschauungen Bertolt Brechts.* Copenhagen: Munksgaard, 1962.

Ihering, Herbert. *Bertolt Brecht.* Berlin: Rembrandt-Verlag, 1959.

Jaeggi, Willy, and Oesch, Hans. *Das Ärgernis Brecht.* Basel: Basler Verlagsanstalt, 1961.

Jahn, Gunther. "Uebermensch Mensch und Zeit in den Dramen Christian Dietrich Grabbes." Unpublished dissertation, University of Göttingen, 1950.

Johann, Ernst. *Büchner in Selbstzeugnissen und Bilddokumenten.* Hamburg: Rowohlt, 1958.

Johst, Hanns. *Der Einsame: Ein Menschenuntergang.* Munich: Delphin Verlag, 1917.

Kaiser, Ursula. "Die Mechanisierung des Lebens im Dichterischen Werk Georg Büchners." Unpublished dissertation, J. W. Goethe University, Frankfurt, 1952.

Kapp, Julius. *Frank Wedekind: Seine Eigenart und seine Werke.* Berlin: Barsdorf, 1909.

Kaufmann, Friedrich Wilhelm. "Die Realistische Tendenz in Grabbes Dramen," *Smith College Studies in Modern Languages,* XII, No. 4 (July, 1931), 1–47.

Kesting, Marianne. *Bertolt Brecht.* Hamburg: Rowohlt, 1959.

————. *Das Epische Theater.* Stuttgart: W. Kohlhammer Verlag, 1959.

Kindermann, Heinz. *J. M. R. Lenz und die deutsche Romantik.* Vienna: Wilhelm Braumüller, 1925.

Klotz, Volker. *Bertolt Brecht: Versuch über das Werk.* Bad Homburg: Hermann Gentner Verlag, 1961.

Knight, A. H. J. *George Büchner.* Oxford: Basil Blackwell, 1951.

Krapp, Helmut. *Der Dialog bei George Büchner.* Darmstadt: Hermann Gentner Verlag, 1958.

Kraus, Karl. *Auswahl aus dem Werk.* Edited by Heinrich Fisher. Munich: Kösel Verlag, 1957.

————. *Die chinesische Mauer.* Leipzig: K. Wolff, 1914.

————. *Die letzten Tage der Menschheit.* Munich: Kösel Verlag, 1957.

————. *Heine und die Folgen.* Munich: A. Langen, 1910.

————. *Sittlichkeit und Kriminalität.* Leipzig: L. Rosner, 1908.

Kutscher, Artur. *Frank Wedekind: Sein Leben und seine Werke.* I–III. Munich: Müller, 1922–1931.

Landsberg, Hans. *Georg Büchners Drama 'Dantons Tod.'* Berlin: E. Eberling, 1900.

Lenz, Jakob Michael Reinhold. *Gesammelte Schriften.* Edited by Franz Blei. Munich: Georg Müller Verlag, 1909.

Liegler, Leopold. *Karl Kraus und sein Werk.* Vienna: Richard Lanyi, 1920.

Lindenberger, Herbert. *Georg Büchner.* Carbondale: Southern Illinois University Press, 1964.

Lipmann, Heinz. *Georg Büchner und die Romantik.* Munich: Max Hueber, 1923.

Lüthy, Herbert. "Of Poor Bert Brecht," *Encounter,* VII, No. 1 (July, 1956), 33–53.

Lukacs, Georg. *Dutsche Realisten des 19. Jahrhunderts.* Bern: A. Francke Ag. Verlag, 1951.

Mander, John. "Brecht is Best," *The New Statesman.* LXIII, No. 1621 (April 6, 1962), 502.

Mann, Otto. *B. B. Mass oder Mythos.* Heidelberg: Wolfgang Rothe Verlag, 1958.

————. *Geschichte des deutschen Dramas.* Stuttgart: Alfred Kröner Verlag, 1960.

Marcuse, Ludwig. *Die Welt der Tragödie.* Leipzig: Franz Schneider Verlag, 1923.

Marlowe, Christopher. *Edward II.* San Francisco: Chandler Publishing Co., 1961.

Martens, Wolfgang. "Ideologie und Verzweiflung: Religiöse Motive in Büchner's Revolutionsdrama," *Euphorion,* LIV (1960), 83–108.

————. "Zur Karikatur in der Dichtung Büchners (Woyzecks Hauptmann)," *Germanisch-Romanische Monatsschrift,* XXXIX (1958), 64–71.

Martini, Fritz. "Napoleon oder die hundert Tage," *Das deutsche Drama vom Barock bis zur Gegenwart.* Edited by Benno von Wiese. II. 2nd ed. Düsseldorf: A. Bagel Verlag, 1962.

May, Kurt, "Woyzeck," *Das deutsche Drama vom Barock bis zur Gegenwart.* Edited by Benno von Wiese. II. 2nd ed. Düsseldorf: A. Bagel Verlag, 1962.

Mayer, Hans. *Bertolt Brecht und die Tradition.* Stuttgart: Neske, 1961.

————. *Deutsche Literatur und Weltliteratur.* Berlin: Rütten and Loening, 1957.

————. *Georg Büchner und seine Zeit.* Wiesbaden: Limes-Verlag, 1946.

Mautner, Franz H. "Die letzten Tage der Menschheit," *Das deutsche drama vom Barock bis zur Gegenwart.* Edited by Benno von Wiese. II. 2nd ed. Düsseldorf: A. Bagel, 1962.

Melchinger, Siegfried. *Theater der Gegenwart.* Frankfurt: Fischer Bücherei, 1956.

Milkereit, Gertrud. "Die Idee der Freiheit im Werke von Frank Wedekind." Unpublished Ph.D. dissertation, University of Cologne, 1957.

Mittenzwei, Werner. *Bertolt Brecht Von der 'Massnahme' zu 'Leben des Galilei.'* Berlin: Aufbau Verlag, 1962.

Nieten, Otto. *Christian Dietrich Grabbe, Sein Leben und Seine Werke.* Dortmund: Fr. Wilh. Ruhfus, 1908.

Pascal, Roy. *The German Sturm und Drang.* Manchester: Manchester University Press, 1959.

————. *Shakespeare in Germany.* Cambridge: The University Press, 1937.

Peacock, Ronald. *The Poet in the Theatre.* New York: Hill and Wang, 1960.

Rollett, Edwin. *Karl Kraus.* Vienna: Verlag Carl Fromme, 1934.

Rosanow, M. N. *Jakob M. R. Lenz, Der Dichter der Sturm-und-Drang Periode.* Translated by C. von Gütschow. Leipzig: Schulze Verlag, 1909.

Runge, Edith Amelie. *Primitivism and Related Ideas in Sturm und Drang Literature.* Baltimore: The Johns Hopkins Press, 1946.

Rychner, Max. *Karl Kraus.* Vienna: Richard Lanyi, 1924.

Schlegel, August Wilhelm von. *Über dramatische Kunst und Literatur.* Vol. 3, 2nd ed. Heidelberg: Mohr und Winter, 1817.

Schneider, Ferdinand Josef. *Christian Dietrich Grabbe: Persönlichkeit und Werk.* Munich: E. H. Beck'sche Verlag, 1934.

Schumacher, Ernst. *Die Dramatischen Versuche Bertolt Brechts 1918–1933.* Berlin: Rütten and Loening, 1955.

Schweizer, Ernst. "Das Groteske und das Drama Frank Wedekinds." Unpublished Ph.D. dissertation, University of Tübingen, 1929.

Seven Plays by Bertolt Brecht. Edited by Eric Bentley. New York: Grove Press, 1961.

Sokel, Walter H. (ed.) *An Anthology of German Expressionist Drama.* New York: Anchor Books, 1963.

————. "Brecht's Split Characters and his Sense of the Tragic," *Brecht: A Collection of Critical Essays,* Edited by Peter Demetz. Englewood Cliffs, N.J., 1962.

Steiner, George. *The Death of Tragedy.* New York: Hill and Wang, 1961.

Strudthoff, Ingeborg. *Die Rezeption Georg Büchners durch das deutsche Theater.* Berlin: Colloquium Verlag, 1957.

Szondi, Peter. "Dantons Tod," *Die Neue Rundschau,* 1960, pp. 652–57.

————. *Theorie des modernen Dramas.* Frankfurt-am-Main: Suhrkamp, 1963.

Trilling, Lionel (ed.). *The Selected Letters of John Keats.* New York: Farrar, Straus and Young, 1951.

Viertel, Berthold. *Karl Kraus.* Dresden: Rudolf Kämmerer Verlag, 1921.

Viëtor, Karl. *Georg Büchners Politik. Dichtung. Wissenschaft.* Bern: A. Francke Ag. Verlag, 1949.

Vogeley, Heinrich. *Georg Büchner und Shakespeare.* Unpublished dissertation, Philipps-Universität, Marburg, 1934.

Wedekind, Frank. *Five Tragedies of Sex.* Translated by Frances Fawcett and Stephen Spender. New York: Theatre Arts Books, 1952.

————. *Gesammelte Werke.* I–IX. Munich: G. Müller, 1924.

————. *Prosa, Dramen, Verse.* Munich: Albert Langen, Georg Müller, 1960.

Weideli, Walter. *The Art of Bertolt Brecht.* New York: New York University Press, 1963.

Westra, Pier. "Georg Büchner dans ses rapports avec ses contemporains." Unpublished dissertation, Univeristy of Paris, 1946.

Willett, John. *Brecht on Theatre.* New York: Hill and Wang, 1964.

————. *The Theatre of Bertolt Brecht.* New York: New Directions, 1959.

Zweig, Arnold. *Lessing, Kleist, Büchner.* Berlin: J. M. Spaeth Verlag, 1925.

index

270

designer : Gerard Valerio

typesetter : Maple Press

typefaces : Garamond, American Text

printer : Maple Press

paper : 60 lb. Mohawk Tosca Book

binder : Maple Press

cover material : Columbia Spindrift Quality #5

Woodcuts by Jerry Dadds